P9-DNO-721

William Shakespeare

The Tragedy of Othello
The Moor of Venice

With New and Updated
Critical Essays
and a Revised Bibliography

Edited by Alvin Kernan

THE SIGNET CLASSICS SHAKESPEARE
General Editor: Sylvan Barnet

SIGNET CLASSICS

SIGNET CLASSICS
Published by New American Library, a division of
Penguin Group (USA) Inc., 375 Hudson Street,
New York, New York 10014, USA
Penguin Group (Canada), 90 Eglinton Avenue East, Suite 700, Toronto,
Ontario M4P 2Y3, Canada (a division of Pearson Penguin Canada Inc.)
Penguin Books Ltd., 80 Strand, London WC2R 0RL, England
Penguin Ireland, 25 St. Stephen's Green, Dublin 2,
Ireland (a division of Penguin Books Ltd.)
Penguin Group (Australia), 250 Camberwell Road, Camberwell, Victoria 3124,
Australia (a division of Pearson Australia Group Pty. Ltd.)
Penguin Books India Pvt. Ltd., 11 Community Centre, Panchsheel Park,
New Delhi - 110 017, India
Penguin Group (NZ), cnr Airborne and Rosedale Roads, Albany,
Auckland 1310, New Zealand (a division of Pearson New Zealand Ltd.)
Penguin Books (South Africa) (Pty.) Ltd., 24 Sturdee Avenue,
Rosebank, Johannesburg 2196, South Africa

Penguin Books Ltd., Registered Offices:
80 Strand, London WC2R 0RL, England

Published by Signet Classics, an imprint of New American Library, a division of
Penguin Group (USA) Inc. The Signet Classics edition of *Othello* was first published in 1963, and an updated edition was published in 1986.

First Signet Classics Printing (Second Revised Edition), April 1998
30 29 28 27 26 25 24

Copyright © Alvin Kernan, 1963, 1986
Copyright © Sylvan Barnet, 1963, 1986, 1998
All rights reserved

 REGISTERED TRADEMARK—MARCA REGISTRADA

Library of Congress Catalog Card Number: 97-69694

Printed in the United States of America

Without limiting the rights under copyright reserved above, no part of this publication may be reproduced, stored in or introduced into a retrieval system, or
transmitted, in any form, or by any means (electronic, mechanical, photocopying,
recording, or otherwise), without the prior written permission of both the copyright owner and the above publisher of this book.

If you purchased this book without a cover you should be aware that this book
is stolen property. It was reported as "unsold and destroyed" to the publisher
and neither the author nor the publisher has received any payment for this
"stripped book."

The scanning, uploading, and distribution of this book via the Internet or via any
other means without the permission of the publisher is illegal and punishable by
law. Please purchase only authorized electronic editions, and do not participate
in or encourage electronic piracy of copyrighted materials. Your support of the
author's rights is appreciated.

Contents

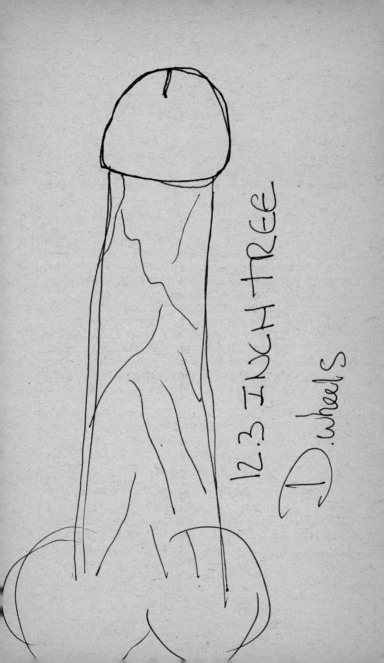

12.3 INCH TREE

D.wheels

Shakespeare: An Overview

Biographical Sketch

Between the record of his baptism in Stratford on 26 April 1564 and the record of his burial in Stratford on 25 April 1616, some forty official documents name Shakespeare, and many others name his parents, his children, and his grandchildren. Further, there are at least fifty literary references to him in the works of his contemporaries. More facts are known about William Shakespeare than about any other playwright of the period except Ben Jonson. The facts should, however, be distinguished from the legends. The latter, inevitably more engaging and better known, tell us that the Stratford boy killed a calf in high style, poached deer and rabbits, and was forced to flee to London, where he held horses outside a playhouse. These traditions are only traditions; they may be true, but no evidence supports them, and it is well to stick to the facts.

Mary Arden, the dramatist's mother, was the daughter of a substantial landowner; about 1557 she married John Shakespeare, a tanner, glove-maker, and trader in wool, grain, and other farm commodities. In 1557 John Shakespeare was a member of the council (the governing body of Stratford), in 1558 a constable of the borough, in 1561 one of the two town chamberlains, in 1565 an alderman (entitling him to the appellation of "Mr."), in 1568 high bailiff—the town's highest political office, equivalent to mayor. After 1577, for an unknown reason he drops out of local politics. What *is* known is that he had to mortgage his wife's property, and that he was involved in serious litigation.

The birthday of William Shakespeare, the third child and the eldest son of this locally prominent man, is unrecorded, but the Stratford parish register records that the infant was baptized on 26 April 1564. (It is quite possible that he was born on 23 April, but this date has probably been assigned by tradition because it is the date on which, fifty-two years later, he died, and perhaps because it is the feast day of St. George, patron saint of England.) The attendance records of the Stratford grammar school of the period are not extant, but it is reasonable to assume that the son of a prominent local official attended the free school—it had been established for the purpose of educating males precisely of his class—and received substantial training in Latin. The masters of the school from Shakespeare's seventh to fifteenth years held Oxford degrees; the Elizabethan curriculum excluded mathematics and the natural sciences but taught a good deal of Latin rhetoric, logic, and literature, including plays by Plautus, Terence, and Seneca.

On 27 November 1582 a marriage license was issued for the marriage of Shakespeare and Anne Hathaway, eight years his senior. The couple had a daughter, Susanna, in May 1583. Perhaps the marriage was necessary, but perhaps the couple had earlier engaged, in the presence of witnesses, in a formal "troth plight" which would render their children legitimate even if no further ceremony were performed. In February 1585, Anne Hathaway bore Shakespeare twins, Hamnet and Judith.

That Shakespeare was born is excellent; that he married and had children is pleasant; but that we know nothing about his departure from Stratford to London or about the beginning of his theatrical career is lamentable and must be admitted. We would gladly sacrifice details about his children's baptism for details about his earliest days in the theater. Perhaps the poaching episode is true (but it is first reported almost a century after Shakespeare's death), or perhaps he left Stratford to be a schoolmaster, as another tradition holds; perhaps he was moved (like Petruchio in *The Taming of the Shrew*) by

> Such wind as scatters young men through the world,
> To seek their fortunes farther than at home
> Where small experience grows.   (1.2.49–51)

In 1592, thanks to the cantankerousness of Robert Greene, we have our first reference, a snarling one, to Shakespeare as an actor and playwright. Greene, a graduate of St. John's College, Cambridge, had become a playwright and a pamphleteer in London, and in one of his pamphlets he warns three university-educated playwrights against an actor who has presumed to turn playwright:

> There is an upstart crow, beautified with our feathers, that with his *tiger's heart wrapped in a player's hide* supposes he is as well able to bombast out a blank verse as the best of you, and being an absolute Johannes-factotum [i.e., jack-of-all-trades] is in his own conceit the only Shake-scene in a country.

The reference to the player, as well as the allusion to Aesop's crow (who strutted in borrowed plumage, as an actor struts in fine words not his own), makes it clear that by this date Shakespeare had both acted and written. That Shakespeare is meant is indicated not only by *Shake-scene* but also by the parody of a line from one of Shakespeare's plays, *3 Henry VI*: "O, tiger's heart wrapped in a woman's hide" (1.4.137). If in 1592 Shakespeare was prominent enough to be attacked by an envious dramatist, he probably had served an apprenticeship in the theater for at least a few years.

In any case, although there are no extant references to Shakespeare between the record of the baptism of his twins in 1585 and Greene's hostile comment about "Shake-scene" in 1592, it is evident that during some of these "dark years" or "lost years" Shakespeare had acted and written. There are a number of subsequent references to him as an actor. Documents indicate that in 1598 he is a "principal comedian," in 1603 a "principal tragedian," in 1608 he is one of the "men players." (We do not have, however, any solid information about which roles he may have played; later traditions say he played Adam in *As You Like It* and the ghost in *Hamlet*, but nothing supports the assertions. Probably his role as dramatist came to supersede his role as actor.) The profession of actor was not for a gentleman, and it occasionally drew the scorn of university men like Greene who resented writing speeches for persons less educated than themselves, but it was respectable enough; players, if prosperous, were in effect members of the bourgeoisie, and there is nothing to suggest that Stratford considered William Shakespeare less than a solid citizen. When, in 1596, the Shakespeares were granted a coat of arms—i.e., the right to be considered gentlemen—the grant was made to Shakespeare's father, but probably William Shakespeare had arranged the matter on his own behalf. In subsequent transactions he is occasionally styled a gentleman.

Although in 1593 and 1594 Shakespeare published two narrative poems dedicated to the Earl of Southampton, *Venus and Adonis* and *The Rape of Lucrece*, and may well have written most or all of his sonnets in the middle nineties, Shakespeare's literary activity seems to have been almost entirely devoted to the theater. (It may be significant that the two narrative poems were written in years when the plague closed the theaters for several months.) In 1594 he was a charter member of a theatrical company called the Chamberlain's Men, which in 1603 became the royal company, the King's Men, making Shakespeare the king's playwright. Until he retired to Stratford (about 1611, apparently), he was with this remarkably stable company. From 1599 the company acted primarily at the Globe theater, in which Shakespeare held a one-tenth interest. Other Elizabethan dramatists are known to have acted, but no other is known also to have been entitled to a share of the profits.

Shakespeare's first eight published plays did not have his name on them, but this is not remarkable; the most popular play of the period, Thomas Kyd's *The Spanish Tragedy*, went through many editions without naming Kyd, and Kyd's authorship is known only because a book on the profession of acting happens to quote (and attribute to Kyd) some lines on the interest of Roman emperors in the drama. What is remarkable is that after 1598 Shakespeare's name commonly appears on printed plays—some of which are not his. Presumably his name was a drawing card, and publishers used it to attract potential buyers. Another indication of his popularity comes from Francis Meres, author of *Palladis Tamia: Wit's Treasury* (1598). In this anthology of snippets accompanied by an essay on literature, many playwrights are mentioned, but Shakespeare's name occurs more often than any other, and Shakespeare is the only play-wright whose plays are listed.

From his acting, his play writing, and his share in a playhouse, Shakespeare seems to have made considerable money. He put it to work, making substantial investments in Stratford real estate. As early as 1597 he bought New Place, the second-largest house in Stratford. His family moved in soon afterward, and the house remained in the family until a granddaughter died in 1670. When Shakespeare made his will in 1616, less than a month before he died, he sought to leave his property intact to his descendants. Of small bequests to relatives and to friends (including three actors, Richard Burbage, John Heminges, and Henry Condell), that to his wife of the second-best bed has provoked the most comment. It has sometimes been taken as a sign of an unhappy marriage (other supposed signs are the apparently hasty marriage, his wife's seniority of eight years, and his residence in London without his family). Perhaps the second-best bed was the bed the couple had slept in, the best bed being reserved for visitors. In any case, had Shakespeare not excepted it, the bed would have gone (with the rest of his household possessions) to his daughter and her husband.

On 25 April 1616 Shakespeare was buried within the chancel of the church at Stratford. An unattractive monument to his memory, placed on a wall near the grave, says that he died on 23 April. Over the grave itself are the lines, perhaps by Shakespeare, that (more than his literary fame) have kept his bones undisturbed in the crowded burial ground where old bones were often dislodged to make way for new:

> Good friend, for Jesus' sake forbear
> To dig the dust enclosed here.
> Blessed be the man that spares these stones
> And cursed be he that moves my bones.

A Note on the Anti-Stratfordians, Especially Baconians and Oxfordians

Not until 1769—more than a hundred and fifty years after Shakespeare's death—is there any record of anyone expressing doubt about Shakespeare's authorship of the plays and poems. In 1769, however, Herbert Lawrence nominated Francis Bacon (1561–1626) in *The Life and Adventures of Common Sense*. Since then, at least two dozen other nominees have been offered, including Christopher Marlowe, Sir Walter Raleigh, Queen Elizabeth I, and Edward de Vere, 17th earl of Oxford. The impulse behind all anti-Stratfordian movements is the scarcely concealed snobbish opinion that "the man from Stratford" simply could not have written the plays because he was a country fellow without a university education and without access to high society. Anyone, the argument goes, who used so many legal terms, medical terms, nautical terms, and so forth, and who showed some familiarity with classical writing, must have attended a university, and anyone who knew so much about courtly elegance and courtly deceit must himself have moved among courtiers. The plays do indeed reveal an author whose interests were exceptionally broad, but specialists in any given field—law, medicine, arms and armor, and so on—soon find that the plays do not reveal deep knowledge in specialized matters; indeed, the playwright often gets technical details wrong.

The claim on behalf of Bacon, forgotten almost as soon as it was put forth in 1769, was independently reasserted by Joseph C. Hart in 1848. In 1856 it was reaffirmed by W. H. Smith in a book, and also by Delia Bacon in an article; in 1857 Delia Bacon published a book, arguing that Francis Bacon had directed a group of intellectuals who wrote the plays.

Francis Bacon's claim has largely faded, perhaps because it was advanced with such evident craziness by Ignatius Donnelly, who in *The Great Cryptogram* (1888) claimed to break a code in the plays that proved Bacon had written not only the plays attributed to Shakespeare but also other Renaissance works, for instance the plays of Christopher Marlowe and the essays of Montaigne.

Consider the last two lines of the Epilogue in *The Tempest*:

As you from crimes would pardoned be,
Let your indulgence set me free.

What was Shakespeare—sorry, Francis Bacon, Baron Verulam—*really* saying in these two lines? According to Baconians, the lines are an anagram reading, "Tempest of Francis Bacon, Lord Verulam; do ye ne'er divulge me, ye words." Ingenious, and it is a pity that in the quotation the letter *a* appears only twice in the cryptogram, whereas in the deciphered message it appears three times. Oh, no problem; just alter "Verulam" to "Verul'm" and it works out very nicely.

Most people understand that with sufficient ingenuity one can torture any text and find in it what one wishes. For instance: Did Shakespeare have a hand in the King James Version of the Bible? It was nearing completion in 1610, when Shakespeare was forty-six years old. If you look at the 46th Psalm and count forward for forty-six words, you will find the word *shake*. Now if you go to the end of the psalm and count backward forty-six words, you will find the word *spear*. Clear evidence, according to some, that Shakespeare slyly left his mark in the book.

Bacon's candidacy has largely been replaced in the twentieth century by the candidacy of Edward de Vere (1550–1604), 17th earl of Oxford. The basic ideas behind the Oxford theory, advanced at greatest length by Dorothy and Charlton Ogburn in *This Star of England* (1952, rev. 1955), a book of 1297 pages, and by Charlton Ogburn in *The Mysterious William Shakespeare* (1984), a book of 892 pages, are these: (1) The man from Stratford could not possibly have had the mental equipment and the experience to have written the plays—only a courtier could have written them; (2) Oxford had the requisite background (social position, education, years at Queen Elizabeth's court); (3) Oxford did not wish his authorship to be known for two basic reasons: writing for the public theater was a vulgar pursuit, and the plays show so much courtly and royal disreputable behavior that they would have compromised Oxford's position at court. Oxfordians offer countless details to support the claim. For example, Hamlet's phrase "that ever I was born to set it right" (1.5.89) barely conceals "E. Ver, I was born to set it right," an unambiguous announcement of de Vere's authorship, according to *This Star of England* (p. 654). A second example: Consider Ben

Jonson's poem entitled "To the Memory of My Beloved Master William Shakespeare," prefixed to the first collected edition of Shakespeare's plays in 1623. According to Oxfordians, when Jonson in this poem speaks of the author of the plays as the "swan of Avon," he is alluding not to William Shakespeare, who was born and died in Stratford-on-Avon and who throughout his adult life owned property there; rather, he is alluding to Oxford, who, the Ogburns say, used "William Shakespeare" as his pen name, and whose manor at Bilton was on the Avon River. Oxfordians do not offer any evidence that Oxford took a pen name, and they do not mention that Oxford had sold the manor in 1581, forty-two years before Jonson wrote his poem. Surely a reference to the Shakespeare who was born in Stratford, who had returned to Stratford, and who had died there only seven years before Jonson wrote the poem is more plausible. And exactly why Jonson, who elsewhere also spoke of Shakespeare as a playwright, and why Heminges and Condell, who had acted with Shakespeare for about twenty years, should speak of Shakespeare as the author in their dedication in the 1623 volume of collected plays is never adequately explained by Oxfordians. Either Jonson, Heminges and Condell, and numerous others were in on the conspiracy, or they were all duped—equally unlikely alternatives. Another difficulty in the Oxford theory is that Oxford died in 1604, and some of the plays are clearly indebted to works and events later than 1604. Among the Oxfordian responses are: At his death Oxford left some plays, and in later years these were touched up by hacks, who added the material that points to later dates. *The Tempest*, almost universally regarded as one of Shakespeare's greatest plays and pretty clearly dated to 1611, does indeed date from a period after the death of Oxford, but it is a crude piece of work that should not be included in the canon of works by Oxford.

The anti-Stratfordians, in addition to assuming that the author must have been a man of rank and a university man, usually assume two conspiracies: (1) a conspiracy in Elizabethan and Jacobean times, in which a surprisingly large number of persons connected with the theater knew that the actor Shakespeare did not write the plays attributed to him but for some reason or other pretended that he did; (2) a conspiracy of today's Stratfordians, the professors who teach Shakespeare in the colleges and universities, who are said to have a vested interest in preserving Shakespeare as the author of the plays they teach. In fact, (1) it is inconceivable that the secret of Shakespeare's non-authorship could have been preserved by all of the people who supposedly were in on the conspiracy, and (2) academic fame awaits any scholar today who can disprove Shakespeare's authorship.

The Stratfordian case is convincing not only because hundreds or even thousands of anti-Stratford arguments—of the sort that say "ever I was born" has the secret double meaning "E. Ver, I was born"—add up to nothing at all but also because irrefutable evidence connects the man from Stratford with the London theater and with the authorship of particular plays. The anti-Stratfordians do not seem to understand that it is not enough to dismiss the Stratford case by saying that a fellow from the provinces simply couldn't have written the plays. Nor do they understand that it is not enough to dismiss all of the evidence connecting Shakespeare with the plays by asserting that it is perjured.

The Shakespeare Canon

We return to William Shakespeare. Thirty-seven plays as well as some nondramatic poems are generally held to constitute the Shakespeare canon, the body of authentic works. The exact dates of composition of most of the works are highly uncertain, but evidence of a starting point and/or of a final limiting point often provides a framework for informed guessing. For example, *Richard II* cannot be earlier than 1595, the publication date of some material to which it is indebted; *The Merchant of Venice* cannot be later than 1598, the year Francis Meres mentioned it. Sometimes arguments for a date hang on an alleged topical allusion, such as the lines about the unseasonable weather in *A Midsummer Night's Dream*, 2.1.81–117, but such an allusion, if indeed it is an allusion to an event in the real world, can be variously interpreted, and in any case there is always the possibility that a topical allusion was inserted years later, to bring the play up to date. (The issue of alterations in a text between the time that Shakespeare drafted it and the time that it was printed—alterations due to censorship or playhouse practice or Shakespeare's own second thoughts—will be discussed in "The Play Text as a Collaboration" later in this overview.) Dates are often attributed on the basis of style, and although conjectures about style usually rest on other conjectures (such as Shakespeare's development as a playwright, or the appropriateness of lines to character), sooner or later one must rely on one's literary sense. There is no documentary proof, for example, that *Othello* is not as early as *Romeo and Juliet*, but one feels that *Othello* is a later, more mature work, and because the first record of its performance is 1604, one is glad enough to set its composition at that date and not push it back into Shakespeare's early years. (*Romeo and Juliet* was first published in 1597, but evidence suggests that it was written a little earlier.) The following chronology, then, is indebted not only to facts but also to informed guesswork and sensitivity. The dates, necessarily imprecise for some works, indicate something like a scholarly consensus concerning the time of original composition. Some plays show evidence of later revision.

Plays. The first collected edition of Shakespeare, published in 1623, included thirty-six plays. These are all accepted as Shakespeare's, though for one of them, *Henry VIII*, he is thought to have had a collaborator. A thirty-seventh play, *Pericles*, published in 1609 and attributed to Shakespeare on the title page, is also widely accepted as being partly by Shakespeare even though it is not included in the 1623 volume. Still another play not in the 1623 volume, *The Two Noble Kinsmen*, was first published in 1634, with a title page attributing it to John Fletcher and Shakespeare. Probably most students of the subject now believe that Shakespeare did indeed have a hand in it. Of the remaining plays attributed at one time or another to Shakespeare, only one, *Edward III*, anonymously published in 1596, is now regarded by some scholars as a serious candidate. The prevailing opinion, however, is that this rather simple-minded play is not Shakespeare's; at most he may have revised some passages, chiefly scenes with the Countess of

Salisbury. We include *The Two Noble Kinsmen* but do not include *Edward III* in the following list.

1588–94	*The Comedy of Errors*
1588–94	*Love's Labor's Lost*
1589–91	*2 Henry VI*
1590–91	*3 Henry VI*
1589–92	*1 Henry VI*
1592–93	*Richard III*
1589–94	*Titus Andronicus*
1593–94	*The Taming of the Shrew*
1592–94	*The Two Gentlemen of Verona*
1594–96	*Romeo and Juliet*
1595	*Richard II*
1595–96	*A Midsummer Night's Dream*
1596–97	*King John*
1594–96	*The Merchant of Venice*
1596–97	*1 Henry IV*
1597	*The Merry Wives of Windsor*
1597–98	*2 Henry IV*
1598–99	*Much Ado About Nothing*
1598–99	*Henry V*
1599	*Julius Caesar*
1599–1600	*As You Like It*
1599–1600	*Twelfth Night*
1600–1601	*Hamlet*
1601–1602	*Troilus and Cressida*
1602–1604	*All's Well That Ends Well*
1603–1604	*Othello*
1604	*Measure for Measure*
1605–1606	*King Lear*
1605–1606	*Macbeth*
1606–1607	*Antony and Cleopatra*
1605–1608	*Timon of Athens*
1607–1608	*Coriolanus*
1607–1608	*Pericles*
1609–10	*Cymbeline*
1610–11	*The Winter's Tale*
1611	*The Tempest*

| 1612–13 | *Henry VIII* |
| 1613 | *The Two Noble Kinsmen* |

Poems. In 1989 Donald W. Foster published a book in which he argued that "A Funeral Elegy for Master William Peter," published in 1612, ascribed only to the initials W.S., *may* be by Shakespeare. Foster later published an article in a scholarly journal, *PMLA* 111 (1996), in which he asserted the claim more positively. The evidence begins with the initials, and includes the fact that the publisher and the printer of the elegy had published Shakespeare's *Sonnets* in 1609. But such facts add up to rather little, especially because no one has found any connection between Shakespeare and William Peter (an Oxford graduate about whom little is known, who was murdered at the age of twenty-nine). The argument is based chiefly on statistical examinations of word patterns, which are said to correlate with Shakespeare's known work. Despite such correlations, however, many readers feel that the poem does not sound like Shakespeare. True, Shakespeare has a great range of styles, but one quality that unites his work is that it is imaginative and interesting. Many readers find neither of these qualities in "A Funeral Elegy."

1592–93	*Venus and Adonis*
1593–94	*The Rape of Lucrece*
1593–1600	*Sonnets*
1600–1601	*The Phoenix and the Turtle*

Shakespeare's English

1. Spelling and Pronunciation. From the philologist's point of view, Shakespeare's English is modern English. It requires footnotes, but the inexperienced reader can comprehend substantial passages with very little help, whereas for the same reader Chaucer's Middle English is a foreign language. By the beginning of the fifteenth century the chief grammatical changes in English had taken place, and the final unaccented -*e* of Middle English had been lost (though it survives even today in spelling, as in *name*); during the fifteenth century the dialect of London, the commercial and political center, gradually displaced the provincial dialects, at least in writing; by the end of the century, printing had helped to regularize and stabilize the language, especially spelling. Elizabethan spelling may seem erratic to us (there were dozens of spellings of *Shakespeare*, and a simple word like *been* was also spelled *beene* and *bin*), but it had much in common with our spelling. Elizabethan spelling was conservative in that for the most part it reflected an older pronunciation (Middle English) rather than the sound of the language as it was then spoken, just as our spelling continues to reflect medieval pronunciation—most obviously in the now silent but formerly pronounced letters in a word such as *knight*. Elizabethan pronunciation, though not identical with ours, was much closer to ours than to that of the Middle Ages. Incidentally, though no one can be certain about what Elizabethan English sounded like, specialists tend to believe it was rather like the speech of a modern stage Irishman (*time* apparently was pronounced *toime*, *old* pronounced *awld*, *day* pronounced *die*, and *join* pronounced *jine*) and not at all like the Oxford speech that most of us think it was.

An awareness of the difference between our pronunciation and Shakespeare's is crucial in three areas—in accent, or number of syllables (many metrically regular lines may look irregular to us); in rhymes (which may not look like rhymes); and in puns (which may not look like puns). Examples will be useful. Some words that were at least on occasion stressed differently from today are *aspèct*, *còmplete*, *fòrlorn*, *revènue*, and *sepùlcher*. Words that sometimes had an additional syllable are *emp[e]ress*, *Hen[e]ry*, *mon[e]th*, and *villain* (three syllables, *vil-lay-in*). An additional syllable is often found in possessives, like *moon*'s (pronounced *moones*) and in words ending in *-tion* or *-sion*. Words that had one less syllable than they now have are *needle* (pronounced *neel*) and *violet* (pronounced *vilet*). Among rhymes now lost are *one* with *loan*, *love* with *prove*, *beast* with *jest*, *eat* with *great*. (In reading, trust your sense of metrics and your ear, more than your eye.) An example of a pun that has become obliterated by a change in pronunciation is Falstaff's reply to Prince Hal's "Come, tell us your reason" in *1 Henry IV*: "Give you a reason on compulsion? If reasons were as plentiful as blackberries, I would give no man a reason upon compulsion, I" (2.4.237–40). The *ea* in *reason* was pronounced rather like a long *a*, like the *ai* in *raisin*, hence the comparison with blackberries.

Puns are not merely attempts to be funny; like metaphors they often involve bringing into a meaningful relationship areas of experience normally seen as remote. In *2 Henry IV,* when Feeble is conscripted, he stoically says, "I care not. A man can die but once. We owe God a death" (3.2.242–43), punning on *debt,* which was the way *death* was pronounced. Here an enormously significant fact of life is put into simple commercial imagery, suggesting its commonplace quality. Shakespeare used the same pun earlier in *1 Henry IV,* when Prince Hal says to Falstaff, "Why, thou owest God a death," and Falstaff replies, " 'Tis not due yet: I would be loath to pay him before his day. What need I be so forward with him that calls not on me?" (5.1.126–29).

Sometimes the puns reveal a delightful playfulness; sometimes they reveal aggressiveness, as when, replying to Claudius's "But now, my cousin Hamlet, and my son," Hamlet says, "A little more than kin, and less than kind!" (1.2.64–65). These are Hamlet's first words in the play, and we already hear him warring verbally against Claudius. Hamlet's "less than kind" probably means (1) Hamlet is not of Claudius's family or nature, *kind* having the sense it still has in our word *mankind*; (2) Hamlet is not kindly (affectionately) disposed toward Claudius; (3) Claudius is not naturally (but rather unnaturally, in a legal sense incestuously) Hamlet's father. The puns evidently were not put in as sops to the groundlings; they are an important way of communicating a complex meaning.

2. Vocabulary. A conspicuous difficulty in reading Shakespeare is rooted in the fact that some of his words are no longer in common use—for example, words concerned with armor, astrology, clothing, coinage, hawking, horsemanship, law, medicine, sailing, and war. Shakespeare had a large vocabulary—something near thirty thousand words—but it was not so much a vocabulary of big words as a vocabulary drawn from a wide range of life, and it is partly his ability to call upon a great body of concrete language that gives his plays the sense of being in close contact with life. When the right word did not already exist, he made it up. Among words thought to be his coinages are *accommodation, all-knowing, amazement, bare-faced, countless, dexterously, dislocate, dwindle, fancy-free, frugal, indistinguishable, lackluster, laughable, overawe, premeditated, sea change, star-crossed.* Among those that have not survived are the verb *convive*, meaning to feast together, and *smilet*, a little smile.

Less overtly troublesome than the technical words but more treacherous are the words that seem readily intelligible to us but whose Elizabethan meanings differ from their modern ones. When Horatio describes the Ghost as an "erring spirit," he is saying not that the ghost has sinned or made an error but that it is wandering. Here is a short list of some of the most common words in Shakespeare's plays that often (but not always) have a meaning other than their most usual modern meaning:

'a	he
abuse	deceive
accident	occurrence
advertise	inform
an, and	if
annoy	harm
appeal	accuse
artificial	skillful
brave	fine, splendid
censure	opinion
cheer	(1) face (2) frame of mind
chorus	a single person who comments on the events
closet	small private room
competitor	partner
conceit	idea, imagination
cousin	kinsman
cunning	skillful
disaster	evil astrological influence
doom	judgment
entertain	receive into service

envy	malice
event	outcome
excrement	outgrowth (of hair)
fact	evil deed
fancy	(1) love (2) imagination
fell	cruel
fellow	(1) companion (2) low person (often an insulting term if addressed to someone of approximately equal rank)
fond	foolish
free	(1) innocent (2) generous
glass	mirror
hap, haply	chance, by chance
head	army
humor	(1) mood (2) bodily fluid thought to control one's psychology
imp	child
intelligence	news
kind	natural, acting according to nature
let	hinder
lewd	base
mere(ly)	utter(ly)
modern	commonplace
natural	a fool, an idiot
naughty	(1) wicked (2) worthless
next	nearest
nice	(1) trivial (2) fussy
noise	music
policy	(1) prudence (2) stratagem
presently	immediately
prevent	anticipate
proper	handsome
prove	test
quick	alive
sad	serious
saw	proverb
secure	without care, incautious
silly	innocent

sensible	capable of being perceived by the senses
shrewd	sharp
so	provided that
starve	die
still	always
success	that which follows
tall	brave
tell	count
tonight	last night
wanton	playful, careless
watch	keep awake
will	lust
wink	close both eyes
wit	mind, intelligence

All glosses, of course, are mere approximations; sometimes one of Shakespeare's words may hover between an older meaning and a modern one, and as we have seen, his words often have multiple meanings.

3. Grammar. A few matters of grammar may be surveyed, though it should be noted at the outset that Shakespeare sometimes made up his own grammar. As E.A. Abbott says in *A Shakespearian Grammar,* "Almost any part of speech can be used as any other part of speech": a noun as a verb ("he childed as I fathered"); a verb as a noun ("She hath made compare"); or an adverb as an adjective ("a seldom pleasure"). There are hundreds, perhaps thousands, of such instances in the plays, many of which at first glance would not seem at all irregular and would trouble only a pedant. Here are a few broad matters.

Nouns: The Elizabethans thought the *-s* genitive ending for nouns (as in *man's*) derived from *his*; thus the line " 'gainst the count his galleys I did some service," for "the count's galleys."

Adjectives: By Shakespeare's time adjectives had lost the endings that once indicated gender, number, and case. About the only difference between Shakespeare's adjectives and ours is the use of the now redundant *more* or *most* with the comparative ("some more fitter place") or superlative

("This was the most unkindest cut of all"). Like double
comparatives and double superlatives, double negatives
were acceptable; Mercutio "will not budge for no man's
pleasure."

Pronouns: The greatest change was in pronouns. In
Middle English *thou, thy,* and *thee* were used among famil-
iars and in speaking to children and inferiors; *ye, your,* and
you were used in speaking to superiors (servants to masters,
nobles to the king) or to equals with whom the speaker was
not familiar. Increasingly the "polite" forms were used in all
direct address, regardless of rank, and the accusative *you*
displaced the nominative *ye.* Shakespeare sometimes uses
ye instead of *you,* but even in Shakespeare's day *ye* was
archaic, and it occurs mostly in rhetorical appeals.

Thou, thy, and *thee* were not completely displaced, however, and Shakespeare occasionally makes significant use of
them, sometimes to connote familiarity or intimacy and
sometimes to connote contempt. In *Twelfth Night* Sir Toby
advises Sir Andrew to insult Cesario by addressing him as
thou: "If thou thou'st him some thrice, it shall not be amiss"
(3.2.46–47). In *Othello* when Brabantio is addressing an
unidentified voice in the dark he says, "What are you?"
(1.1.91), but when the voice identifies itself as the foolish
suitor Roderigo, Brabantio uses the contemptuous form,
saying, "I have charged thee not to haunt about my doors"
(93). He uses this form for a while, but later in the scene,
when he comes to regard Roderigo as an ally, he shifts back
to the polite *you,* beginning in line 163, "What said she to
you?" and on to the end of the scene. For reasons not yet sat-
isfactorily explained, Elizabethans used *thou* in addresses to
God—"O God, thy arm was here," the king says in *Henry V*
(4.8.108)—and to supernatural characters such as ghosts
and witches. A subtle variation occurs in *Hamlet.* When
Hamlet first talks with the Ghost in 1.5, he uses *thou,* but
when he sees the Ghost in his mother's room, in 3.4, he uses
you, presumably because he is now convinced that the Ghost
is not a counterfeit but is his father.

Perhaps the most unusual use of pronouns, from our point
of view, is the neuter singular. In place of our *its, his* was
often used, as in "How far that little candle throws *his*

beams." But the use of a masculine pronoun for a neuter noun came to seem unnatural, and so *it* was used for the possessive as well as the nominative: "The hedge-sparrow fed the cuckoo so long / That it had it head bit off by it young." In the late sixteenth century the possessive form *its* developed, apparently by analogy with the *-s* ending used to indicate a genitive noun, as in *book*'s, but *its* was not yet common usage in Shakespeare's day. He seems to have used *its* only ten times, mostly in his later plays. Other usages, such as "you have seen Cassio and she together" or the substitution of *who* for *whom,* cause little problem even when noticed.

Verbs, Adverbs, and Prepositions: Verbs cause almost no difficulty: The third person singular present form commonly ends in *-s,* as in modern English (e.g., "He blesses"), but sometimes in *-eth* (Portia explains to Shylock that mercy "blesseth him that gives and him that takes"). Broadly speaking, the *-eth* ending was old-fashioned or dignified or "literary" rather than colloquial, except for the words *doth, hath,* and *saith.* The *-eth* ending (regularly used in the King James Bible, 1611) is very rare in Shakespeare's dramatic prose, though not surprisingly it occurs twice in the rather formal prose summary of the narrative poem *Lucrece.* Sometimes a plural subject, especially if it has collective force, takes a verb ending in *-s,* as in "My old bones aches." Some of our strong or irregular preterites (such as *broke*) have a different form in Shakespeare (*brake*); some verbs that now have a weak or regular preterite (such as *helped*) in Shakespeare have a strong or irregular preterite (*holp*). Some adverbs that today end in *-ly* were not inflected: "grievous sick," "wondrous strange." Finally, prepositions often are not the ones we expect: "We are such stuff as dreams are made on," "I have a king here to my flatterer."

Again, none of the differences (except meanings that have substantially changed or been lost) will cause much difficulty. But it must be confessed that for some elliptical passages there is no widespread agreement on meaning. Wise editors resist saying more than they know, and when they are uncertain they add a question mark to their gloss.

Shakespeare's Theater

In Shakespeare's infancy, Elizabethan actors performed wherever they could—in great halls, at court, in the courtyards of inns. These venues implied not only different audiences but also different playing conditions. The innyards must have made rather unsatisfactory theaters: on some days they were unavailable because carters bringing goods to London used them as depots; when available, they had to be rented from the innkeeper. In 1567, presumably to avoid such difficulties, and also to avoid regulation by the Common Council of London, which was not well disposed toward theatricals, one John Brayne, brother-in-law of the carpenter turned actor James Burbage, built the Red Lion in an eastern suburb of London. We know nothing about its shape or its capacity; we can say only that it may have been the first building in Europe constructed for the purpose of giving plays since the end of antiquity, a thousand years earlier. Even after the building of the Red Lion theatrical activity continued in London in makeshift circumstances, in marketplaces and inns, and always uneasily. In 1574 the Common Council required that plays and playing places in London be licensed because

> sundry great disorders and inconveniences have been found to ensue to this city by the inordinate haunting of great multitudes of people, specially youth, to plays, interludes, and shows, namely occasion of frays and quarrels, evil practices of incontinency in great inns having chambers and secret places adjoining to their open stages and galleries.

The Common Council ordered that innkeepers who wished licenses to hold performance put up a bond and make contributions to the poor.

The requirement that plays and innyard theaters be licensed, along with the other drawbacks of playing at inns and presumably along with the success of the Red Lion, led James Burbage to rent a plot of land northeast of the city walls, on property outside the jurisdiction of the city. Here he built England's second playhouse, called simply the Theatre. About all that is known of its construction is that it was wood. It soon had imitators, the most famous being the Globe (1599), essentially an amphitheater built across the Thames (again outside the city's jurisdiction), constructed with timbers of the Theatre, which had been dismantled when Burbage's lease ran out.

Admission to the theater was one penny, which allowed spectators to stand at the sides and front of the stage that jutted into the yard. An additional penny bought a seat in a covered part of the theater, and a third penny bought a more comfortable seat and a better location. It is notoriously diffi- cult to translate prices into today's money, since some things that are inexpensive today would have been expensive in the past and vice versa—a pipeful of tobacco (imported, of course) cost a lot of money, about three pennies, and an orange (also imported) cost two or three times what a chicken cost—but perhaps we can get some idea of the low cost of the penny admission when we realize that a penny could also buy a pot of ale. An unskilled laborer made about five or sixpence a day, an artisan about twelve pence a day, and the hired actors (as opposed to the sharers in the com- pany, such as Shakespeare) made about ten pence a perfor- mance. A printed play cost five or sixpence. Of course a visit to the theater (like a visit to a baseball game today) usually cost more than the admission since the spectator probably would also buy food and drink. Still, the low entrance fee meant that the theater was available to all except the very poorest people, rather as movies and most athletic events are today. Evidence indicates that the audience ranged from apprentices who somehow managed to scrape together the minimum entrance fee and to escape from their masters for a few hours, to prosperous members of the middle class and aristocrats who paid the additional fee for admission to the galleries. The exact proportion of men to women cannot be determined, but women of all classes certainly were present. Theaters were open every afternoon but Sundays for much of the year, except in times of plague, when they were closed because of fear of infection. By the way, no evidence sug- gests the presence of toilet facilities. Presumably the patrons relieved themselves by making a quick trip to the fields sur- rounding the playhouses.

There are four important sources of information about the

structure of Elizabethan public playhouses—drawings, a contract, recent excavations, and stage directions in the plays. Of drawings, only the so-called de Witt drawing (c. 1596) of the Swan—really his friend Aernout van Buchell's copy of Johannes de Witt's drawing—is of much significance. The drawing, the only extant representation of the interior of an Elizabethan theater, shows an amphitheater of three tiers, with a stage jutting from a wall into the yard or

Johannes de Witt, a Continental visitor to London, made a drawing of the Swan theater in about the year 1596. The original drawing is lost; this is Aernout van Buchell's copy of it.

center of the building. The tiers are roofed, and part of the stage is covered by a roof that projects from the rear and is supported at its front on two posts, but the groundlings, who paid a penny to stand in front of the stage or at its sides, were exposed to the sky. (Performances in such a playhouse were held only in the daytime; artificial illumination was not used.) At the rear of the stage are two massive doors; above the stage is a gallery.

The second major source of information, the contract for the Fortune (built in 1600), specifies that although the Globe (built in 1599) is to be the model, the Fortune is to be square, eighty feet outside and fifty-five inside. The stage is to be forty-three feet broad, and is to extend into the middle of the yard, i.e., it is twenty-seven and a half feet deep.

The third source of information, the 1989 excavations of the Rose (built in 1587), indicate that the Rose was fourteen-sided, about seventy-two feet in diameter with an inner yard almost fifty feet in diameter. The stage at the Rose was about sixteen feet deep, thirty-seven feet wide at the rear, and twenty-seven feet wide downstage. The relatively small dimensions and the tapering stage, in contrast to the rectangular stage in the Swan drawing, surprised theater historians and have made them more cautious in generalizing about the Elizabethan theater. Excavations at the Globe have not yielded much information, though some historians believe that the fragmentary evidence suggests a larger theater, perhaps one hundred feet in diameter.

From the fourth chief source, stage directions in the plays, one learns that entrance to the stage was by the doors at the rear (*"Enter one citizen at one door, and another at the other"*). A curtain hanging across the doorway—or a curtain hanging between the two doorways—could provide a place where a character could conceal himself, as Polonius does, when he wishes to overhear the conversation between Hamlet and Gertrude. Similarly, withdrawing a curtain from the doorway could "discover" (reveal) a character or two. Such discovery scenes are very rare in Elizabethan drama, but a good example occurs in *The Tempest* (5.1.171), where a stage direction tells us, *"Here Prospero discovers Ferdinand and Miranda playing at chess."* There was also some sort of playing space "aloft" or "above" to represent, for instance, the top of a city's walls or a room above the street. Doubtless each theater had its own peculiarities, but perhaps we can talk about a "typical" Elizabethan theater if we realize that no theater need exactly fit the description, just as no mother is the average mother with 2.7 children.

This hypothetical theater is wooden, round, or polygonal (in *Henry V* Shakespeare calls it a "wooden *O*") capable of holding some eight hundred spectators who stood in the yard around the projecting elevated stage—these spectators were the "groundlings"—and some fifteen hundred additional spectators who sat in the three roofed galleries. The stage, protected by a "shadow" or "heavens" or roof, is entered from two doors; behind the doors is the "tiring house" (attiring house, i.e., dressing room), and above the stage is some sort of gallery that may sometimes hold spectators but can be used (for example) as the bedroom from which Romeo—according to a stage direction in one text—"goeth down." Some evidence suggests that a throne can be lowered onto the platform stage, perhaps from the "shadow"; certainly characters can descend from the stage through a trap or traps into the cellar or "hell." Sometimes this space beneath the stage accommodates a sound-effects man or musician (in *Antony and Cleopatra* "*music of the hautboys* [oboes] *is under the stage*") or an actor (in *Hamlet* the "*Ghost cries under the stage*"). Most characters simply walk on and off through the doors, but because there is no curtain in front of the platform, corpses will have to be carried off (Hamlet obligingly clears the stage of Polonius's corpse, when he says, "I'll lug the guts into the neighbor room"). Other characters may have fallen at the rear, where a curtain on a doorway could be drawn to conceal them.

Such may have been the "public theater," so called because its inexpensive admission made it available to a wide range of the populace. Another kind of theater has been called the "private theater" because its much greater admission charge (sixpence versus the penny for general admission at the public theater) limited its audience to the wealthy or the prodigal. The private theater was basically a large room, entirely roofed and therefore artificially illuminated, with a stage at one end. The theaters thus were distinct in two ways: One was essentially an amphitheater that catered to the general public; the other was a hall that catered to the wealthy. In 1576 a hall theater was established in Blackfriars, a Dominican priory in London that had been suppressed in 1538 and confiscated by the Crown and thus was not under the city's jurisdiction. All the actors in this Blackfriars theater were boys about eight to thirteen years old (in the public theaters similar boys played female parts; a boy Lady Macbeth played to a man Macbeth). Near the end of this section on Shakespeare's theater we will talk at some length about possible implications in this convention of using boys to play female roles, but for the moment we should say that it doubtless accounts for the relative lack of female roles in Elizabethan drama. Thus, in *A Midsummer Night's Dream*, out of twenty-one named roles, only four are female; in *Hamlet*, out of twenty-four, only two (Gertrude and Ophelia) are female. Many of Shakespeare's characters have fathers but no mothers—for instance, King Lear's daughters. We need not bring in Freud to explain the disparity; a dramatic company had only a few boys in it.

To return to the private theaters, in some of which all of the performers were children—the "eyrie of . . . little eyases" (nest of unfledged hawks—2.2.347–48) which Rosencrantz mentions when he and Guildenstern talk with Hamlet. The theater in Blackfriars had a precarious existence, and ceased operations in 1584. In 1596 James Burbage, who had already made theatrical history by building the Theatre, began to construct a second Blackfriars theater. He died in 1597, and for several years this second Blackfriars theater was used by a troupe of boys, but in 1608 two of Burbage's sons and five other actors (including Shakespeare) became joint operators of the theater, using it in the winter when the open-air Globe was unsuitable. Perhaps such a smaller theater, roofed, artificially illuminated, and with a tradition of a wealthy audience, exerted an influence in Shakespeare's late plays.

Performances in the private theaters may well have had intermissions during which music was played, but in the public theaters the action was probably uninterrupted, flowing from scene to scene almost without a break. Actors would enter, speak, exit, and others would immediately enter and establish (if necessary) the new locale by a few properties and by words and gestures. To indicate that the scene took place at night, a player or two would carry a torch. Here are some samples of Shakespeare establishing the scene:

This is Illyria, lady.   (*Twelfth Night,* 1.2.2)

Well, this is the Forest of Arden.   (*As You Like It,* 2.4.14)

This castle has a pleasant seat; the air
Nimbly and sweetly recommends itself
Unto our gentle senses.   (*Macbeth,* 1.6.1–3)

The west yet glimmers with some streaks of day.
                                                          (*Macbeth,* 3.3.5)

Sometimes a speech will go far beyond evoking the minimal setting of place and time, and will, so to speak, evoke the social world in which the characters move. For instance, early in the first scene of *The Merchant of Venice* Salerio suggests an explanation for Antonio's melancholy. (In the following passage, *pageants* are decorated wagons, floats, and *cursy* is the verb "to curtsy," or "to bow.")

Your mind is tossing on the ocean,
There where your argosies with portly sail—
Like signiors and rich burghers on the flood,
Or as it were the pageants of the sea—
Do overpeer the petty traffickers
That cursy to them, do them reverence,
As they fly by them with their woven wings.   (1.1.8–14)

Late in the nineteenth century, when Henry Irving produced the play with elaborate illusionistic sets, the first scene showed a ship moored in the harbor, with fruit vendors and dock laborers, in an effort to evoke the bustling and exotic life of Venice. But Shakespeare's words give us this exotic, rich world of commerce in his highly descriptive language when Salerio speaks of "argosies with portly sail" that fly with "woven wings"; equally important, through Salerio Shakespeare conveys a sense of the orderly, hierarchical society in which the lesser ships, "the petty traffickers," curtsy and thereby "do . . . reverence" to their superiors, the merchant prince's ships, which are "Like signiors and rich burghers."

On the other hand, it is a mistake to think that except for verbal pictures the Elizabethan stage was bare. Although Shakespeare's Chorus in *Henry V* calls the stage an "unworthy scaffold" (Prologue 1.10) and urges the spectators to "eke out our performance with your mind" (Prologue 3.35), there was considerable spectacle. The last act of *Macbeth,* for instance, has five stage directions calling for *"drum and colors,"* and another sort of appeal to the eye is indicated by the stage direction *"Enter Macduff, with Macbeth's head."* Some scenery and properties may have been substantial; doubtless a throne was used, but the pillars supporting the roof would have served for the trees on which Orlando pins his poems in *As You Like It*.

Having talked about the public theater—"this wooden *O*"—at some length, we should mention again that Shakespeare's plays were performed also in other locales. Alvin Kernan, in *Shakespeare, the King's Playwright: Theater in the Stuart Court 1603–1613* (1995) points out that "several of [Shakespeare's] plays contain brief theatrical performances, set always in a court or some noble house. When Shakespeare portrayed a theater, he did not, except for the choruses in *Henry V*, imagine a public theater" (p. 195). (Examples include episodes in *The Taming of the Shrew*, *A Midsummer Night's Dream*, *Hamlet*, and *The Tempest*.)

A Note on the Use of Boy Actors in Female Roles

Until fairly recently, scholars were content to mention that the convention existed; they sometimes also mentioned that it continued the medieval practice of using males in female roles, and that other theaters, notably in ancient Greece and in China and Japan, also used males in female roles. (In classical Noh drama in Japan, males still play the female roles.) Prudery may have been at the root of the academic failure to talk much about the use of boy actors, or maybe there really is not much more to say than that it was a convention of a male-centered culture (Stephen Green-

xxxiv SHAKESPEARE: AN OVERVIEW

blatt's view, in *Shakespearean Negotiations* [1988]). Further, the very nature of a convention is that it is not thought about: Hamlet is a Dane and Julius Caesar is a Roman, but in Shakespeare's plays they speak English, and we in the audience never give this odd fact a thought. Similarly, a character may speak in the presence of others and we understand, again without thinking about it, that he or she is not heard by the figures on the stage (the aside); a character alone on the stage may speak (the soliloquy), and we do not take the character to be unhinged; in a realistic (box) set, the fourth wall, which allows us to see what is going on, is miraculously missing. The no-nonsense view, then, is that the boy actor was an accepted convention, accepted unthinkingly—just as today we know that Kenneth Branagh is not Hamlet, Al Pacino is not Richard II, and Denzel Washington is not the Prince of Aragon. In this view, the audience takes the performer for the role, and that is that; such is the argument we now make for race-free casting, in which African-Americans and Asians can play roles of persons who lived in medieval Denmark and ancient Rome. But gender perhaps is different, at least today. It is a matter of abundant academic study: The Elizabethan theater is now sometimes called a transvestite theater, and we hear much about cross-dressing.

Shakespeare himself in a very few passages calls attention to the use of boys in female roles. At the end of *As You Like It* the boy who played Rosalind addresses the audience, and says, "O men, . . . if I were a woman, I would kiss as many of you as had beards that pleased me." But this is in the Epilogue; the plot is over, and the actor is stepping out of the play and into the audience's everyday world. A second reference to the practice of boys playing female roles occurs in *Antony and Cleopatra*, when Cleopatra imagines that she and Antony will be the subject of crude plays, her role being performed by a boy:

> The quick comedians
> Extemporally will stage us, and present
> Our Alexandrian revels: Antony
> Shall be brought drunken forth, and I shall see
> Some squeaking Cleopatra boy my greatness.   (5.2.216–20)

In a few other passages, Shakespeare is more indirect. For instance, in *Twelfth Night* Viola, played of course by a boy, disguises herself as a young man and seeks service in the house of a lord. She enlists the help of a Captain, and (by way of explaining away her voice and her beardlessness) says,

> I'll serve this duke
> Thou shalt present me as an eunuch to him.   (1.2.55–56)

In *Hamlet*, when the players arrive in 2.2, Hamlet jokes with the boy who plays a female role. The boy has grown since Hamlet last saw him: "By'r Lady, your ladyship is nearer to heaven than when I saw you last by the altitude of a chopine" (a lady's thick-soled shoe). He goes on: "Pray God your voice . . . be not cracked" (434–38).

Exactly how sexual, how erotic, this material was and is, is now much disputed. Again, the use of boys may have been unnoticed, or rather not thought about—an unexamined convention—by most or all spectators most of the time, perhaps *all* of the time, except when Shakespeare calls the convention to the attention of the audience, as in the passages just quoted. Still, an occasional bit seems to invite erotic thoughts. The clearest example is the name that Rosalind takes in *As You Like It*, Ganymede—the beautiful youth whom Zeus abducted. Did boys dressed to play female roles carry homoerotic appeal for straight men (Lisa Jardine's view, in *Still Harping on Daughters* [1983]), or for gay men, or for some or all women in the audience? Further, when the boy actor played a woman who (for the purposes of the plot) disguised herself as a male, as Rosalind, Viola, and Portia do—so we get a boy playing a woman playing a man—what sort of appeal was generated, and for what sort of spectator?

Some scholars have argued that the convention empowered women by letting female characters display a freedom unavailable in Renaissance patriarchal society; the convention, it is said, undermined rigid gender distinctions. In this view, the convention (along with plots in which female characters for a while disguised themselves as young men) allowed Shakespeare to say what some modern gender critics say: Gender is a constructed role rather than a bio-logical given, something we make, rather than a fixed binary opposition of male and female (see Juliet Dusinberre, in *Shakespeare and the Nature of Women* [1975]). On the other hand, some scholars have maintained that the male disguise assumed by some female characters serves only to reaffirm traditional social distinctions since female characters who don male garb (notably Portia in *The Merchant of Venice* and Rosalind in *As You Like It*) return to their female garb and at least implicitly (these critics say) reaffirm the status quo. (For this last view, see Clara Claiborne Park, in an essay in *The Woman's Part*, ed. Carolyn Ruth Swift Lenz et al. [1980].) Perhaps no one answer is right for all plays; in *As You Like It* cross-dressing empowers Rosalind, but in *Twelfth Night* cross-dressing comically traps Viola.

Shakespeare's Dramatic Language: Costumes, Gestures and Silences; Prose and Poetry

Because Shakespeare was a dramatist, not merely a poet, he worked not only with language but also with costume, sound effects, gestures, and even silences. We have already discussed some kinds of spectacle in the preceding section, and now we will begin with other aspects of visual language; a theater, after all, is literally a "place for seeing." Consider the opening stage direction in *The Tempest*, the first play in the first published collection of Shakespeare's plays: *"A tempestuous noise of thunder and Lightning heard: Enter a Ship-master, and a Boteswain."*

Costumes: What did that shipmaster and that boatswain wear? Doubtless they wore something that identified them as men of the sea. Not much is known about the costumes that Elizabethan actors wore, but at least three points are clear: (1) many of the costumes were splendid versions of contemporary Elizabethan dress; (2) some attempts were made to approximate the dress of certain occupations and of antique or exotic characters such as Romans, Turks, and Jews; (3) some costumes indicated that the wearer was supernatural. Evidence for elaborate Elizabethan clothing can be found in the plays themselves and in contemporary comments about the "sumptuous" players who wore the discarded clothing of noblemen, as well as in account books that itemize such things as "a scarlet cloak with two broad gold laces, with gold buttons down the sides."

The attempts at approximation of the dress of certain occupations and nationalities also can be documented from the plays themselves, and it derives additional confirmation from a drawing of the first scene of Shakespeare's *Titus Andronicus*—the only extant Elizabethan picture of an identifiable episode in a play. (See pp. xxxviii–xxxix.) The drawing, probably done in 1594 or 1595, shows Queen Tamora pleading for mercy. She wears a somewhat medieval-looking robe and a crown; Titus wears a toga and a wreath, but two soldiers behind him wear costumes fairly close to Elizabethan dress. We do not know, however, if the drawing represents an actual stage production in the public theater, or perhaps a private production, or maybe only a reader's visualization of an episode. Further, there is some conflicting evidence: In *Julius Caesar* a reference is made to Caesar's doublet (a close-fitting jacket), which, if taken literally, suggests that even the protagonist did not wear Roman clothing; and certainly the lesser characters, who are said to wear hats, did not wear Roman garb.

It should be mentioned, too, that even ordinary clothing can be symbolic: Hamlet's "inky cloak," for example, sets him apart from the brightly dressed members of Claudius's court and symbolizes his mourning; the fresh clothes that are put on King Lear partly symbolize his return to sanity. Consider, too, the removal of disguises near the end of some plays. For instance, Rosalind in *As You Like It* and Portia and Nerissa in *The Merchant of Venice* remove their male attire, thus again becoming fully themselves.

Gestures and Silences: Gestures are an important part of a dramatist's language. King Lear kneels before his daughter Cordelia for a benediction (4.7.57–59), an act of humility that contrasts with his earlier speeches banishing her and that contrasts also with a comparable gesture, his ironic

kneeling before Regan (2.4.153–55). Northumberland's failure to kneel before King Richard II (3.3.71–72) speaks volumes. As for silences, consider a moment in *Coriolanus*: Before the protagonist yields to his mother's entreaties (5.3.182), there is this stage direction: *"Holds her by the hand, silent."* Another example of "speech in dumbness" occurs in *Macbeth*, when Macduff learns that his wife and children have been murdered. He is silent at first, as Malcolm's speech indicates: "What, man! Ne'er pull your hat upon your brows. Give sorrow words" (4.3.208–09). (For a discussion of such moments, see Philip C. McGuire's *Speechless Dialect: Shakespeare's Open Silences* [1985].)

Of course when we think of Shakespeare's work, we think primarily of his language, both the poetry and the prose.

Prose: Although two of his plays (*Richard II* and *King John*) have no prose at all, about half the others have at least one quarter of the dialogue in prose, and some have notably more: *1 Henry IV* and *2 Henry IV*, about half; *As You Like It*

and *Twelfth Night*, a little more than half; *Much Ado About Nothing*, more than three quarters; and *The Merry Wives of Windsor*, a little more than five sixths. We should remember that despite Molière's joke about M. Jourdain, who was amazed to learn that he spoke prose, most of us do not speak prose. Rather, we normally utter repetitive, shapeless, and often ungrammatical torrents; prose is something very different—a sort of literary imitation of speech at its most coherent.

Today we may think of prose as "natural" for drama; or even if we think that poetry is appropriate for high tragedy we may still think that prose is the right medium for comedy. Greek, Roman, and early English comedies, however, were written in verse. In fact, prose was not generally considered a literary medium in England until the late fifteenth century; Chaucer tells even his bawdy stories in verse. By the end of the 1580s, however, prose had established itself on the English comic stage. In tragedy, Marlowe made some use of prose, not simply in the speeches of clownish servants but even in the speech of a tragic hero, Doctor Faustus. Still, before Shakespeare, prose normally was used in the theater only for special circumstances: (1) letters and proclamations, to set them off from the poetic dialogue; (2) mad characters, to indicate that normal thinking has become disordered; and (3) low comedy, or speeches uttered by clowns even when they are not being comic. Shakespeare made use of these conventions, but he also went far beyond them. Sometimes he begins a scene in prose and then shifts into verse as the emotion is heightened; or conversely, he may shift from verse to prose when a speaker is lowering the emotional level, as when Brutus speaks in the Forum.

Shakespeare's prose usually is not prosaic. Hamlet's prose includes not only small talk with Rosencrantz and Guildenstern but also princely reflections on "What a piece of work is a man" (2.2.312). In conversation with Ophelia, he shifts from light talk in verse to a passionate prose denunciation of women (3.1.103), though the shift to prose here is perhaps also intended to suggest the possibility of madness. (Consult Brian Vickers, *The Artistry of Shakespeare's Prose* [1968].)

Poetry: Drama in rhyme in England goes back to the Middle Ages, but by Shakespeare's day rhyme no longer dominated poetic drama; a finer medium, blank verse (strictly speaking, unrhymed lines of ten syllables, with the stress on every second syllable) had been adopted. But before looking at unrhymed poetry, a few things should be said about the chief uses of rhyme in Shakespeare's plays. (1) A couplet (a pair of rhyming lines) is sometimes used to convey emotional heightening at the end of a blank verse speech; (2) characters sometimes speak a couplet as they leave the stage, suggesting closure; (3) except in the latest plays, scenes fairly often conclude with a couplet, and sometimes, as in *Richard II*, 2.1.145–46, the entrance of a new character within a scene is preceded by a couplet, which wraps up the earlier portion of that scene; (4) speeches of two characters occasionally are linked by rhyme, most notably in *Romeo and Juliet*, 1.5.95–108, where the lovers speak a sonnet between them; elsewhere a taunting reply occasionally rhymes with the previous speaker's last line; (5) speeches with sententious or gnomic remarks are sometimes in rhyme, as in the duke's speech in *Othello* (1.3.199–206); (6) speeches of sardonic mockery are sometimes in rhyme—for example, Iago's speech on women in *Othello* (2.1.146–58)—and they sometimes conclude with an emphatic couplet, as in Bolingbroke's speech on comforting words in *Richard II* (1.3.301–2); (7) some characters are associated with rhyme, such as the fairies in *A Midsummer Night's Dream*; (8) in the early plays, especially *The Comedy of Errors* and *The Taming of the Shrew*, comic scenes that in later plays would be in prose are in jingling rhymes; (9) prologues, choruses, plays-within-the-play, inscriptions, vows, epilogues, and so on are often in rhyme, and the songs in the plays are rhymed.

Neither prose nor rhyme immediately comes to mind when we first think of Shakespeare's medium: It is blank verse, unrhymed iambic pentameter. (In a mechanically exact line there are five iambic feet. An iambic foot consists of two syllables, the second accented, as in *away*; five feet make a pentameter line. Thus, a strict line of iambic pentameter contains ten syllables, the even syllables being stressed more heavily than the odd syllables. Fortunately, Shakespeare usually varies the line somewhat.) The first speech in *A Midsummer Night's Dream*, spoken by Duke Theseus to his betrothed, is an example of blank verse:

> Now, fair Hippolyta, our nuptial hour
> Draws on apace. Four happy days bring in
> Another moon; but, O, methinks, how slow
> This old moon wanes! She lingers my desires,
> Like to a stepdame, or a dowager,
> Long withering out a young man's revenue. (1.1.1–6)

As this passage shows, Shakespeare's blank verse is not mechanically unvarying. Though the predominant foot is the iamb (as in *apace* or *desires*), there are numerous variations. In the first line the stress can be placed on "fair," as the regular metrical pattern suggests, but it is likely that "Now" gets almost as much emphasis; probably in the second line "Draws" is more heavily emphasized than "on," giving us a trochee (a stressed syllable followed by an unstressed one); and in the fourth line each word in the phrase "This old moon wanes" is probably stressed fairly heavily, conveying by two spondees (two feet, each of two stresses) the oppressive tedium that Theseus feels.

In Shakespeare's early plays much of the blank verse is end-stopped (that is, it has a heavy pause at the end of each line), but he later developed the ability to write iambic pentameter verse paragraphs (rather than lines) that give the illusion of speech. His chief techniques are (1) enjambing, i.e., running the thought beyond the single line, as in the first three lines of the speech just quoted; (2) occasionally replacing an iamb with another foot; (3) varying the position of the chief pause (the caesura) within a line; (4) adding an occasional unstressed syllable at the end of a line, traditionally called a feminine ending; (5) and beginning or ending a speech with a half line.

Shakespeare's mature blank verse has much of the rhythmic flexibility of his prose; both the language, though richly figurative and sometimes dense, and the syntax seem natural. It is also often highly appropriate to a particular character. Consider, for instance, this speech from *Hamlet*, in which Claudius, King of Denmark ("the Dane"), speaks to Laertes:

> And now, Laertes, what's the news with you?
> You told us of some suit. What is't, Laertes?
> You cannot speak of reason to the Dane
> And lose your voice. What wouldst thou beg, Laertes,
> That shall not be my offer, not thy asking?   (1.2.42–46)

Notice the short sentences and the repetition of the name "Laertes," to whom the speech is addressed. Notice, too, the shift from the royal "us" in the second line to the more intimate "my" in the last line, and from "you" in the first three lines to the more intimate "thou" and "thy" in the last two lines. Claudius knows how to ingratiate himself with Laertes.

For a second example of the flexibility of Shakespeare's blank verse, consider a passage from *Macbeth*. Distressed by the doctor's inability to cure Lady Macbeth and by the imminent battle, Macbeth addresses some of his remarks to the doctor and others to the servant who is arming him. The entire speech, with its pauses, interruptions, and irresolution (in "Pull't off, I say," Macbeth orders the servant to remove the armor that the servant has been putting on him), catches Macbeth's disintegration. (In the first line, *physic* means "medicine," and in the fourth and fifth lines, *cast the water* means "analyze the urine.")

> Throw physic to the dogs, I'll none of it.
> Come, put mine armor on. Give me my staff.
> Seyton, send out.—Doctor, the thanes fly from me.—
> Come, sir, dispatch. If thou couldst, doctor, cast
> The water of my land, find her disease
> And purge it to a sound and pristine health,
> I would applaud thee to the very echo,
> That should applaud again.—Pull't off, I say.—
> What rhubarb, senna, or what purgative drug,
> Would scour these English hence? Hear'st thou of them?
>
> (5.3.47–56)

Blank verse, then, can be much more than unrhymed iambic pentameter, and even within a single play Shakespeare's blank verse often consists of several styles, depending on the speaker and on the speaker's emotion at the moment.

The Play Text as a Collaboration

Shakespeare's fellow dramatist Ben Jonson reported that the actors said of Shakespeare, "In his writing, whatsoever he penned, he never blotted out line," i.e., never crossed out material and revised his work while composing. None of Shakespeare's plays survives in manuscript (with the possible exception of a scene in *Sir Thomas More*), so we cannot fully evaluate the comment, but in a few instances the published work clearly shows that he revised his manuscript. Consider the following passage (shown here in facsimile) from the best early text of *Romeo and Juliet*, the Second Quarto (1599):

> *Ro.* Would I were sleepe and peace so sweet to rest
> The grey eyde morne smiles on the frowning night,
> Checkring the Easterne Clouds with streaks of light,
> And darknesse fleckted like a drunkard reeles,
> From forth daies pathway,made by *Tytans* wheeles.
> Hence will I to my ghostly Friers close cell,
> His helpe to craue,and my deare hap to tell.
>
> *Exit.*
>
> *Enter Frier alone with a basket.*   (night,
> *Fri.* The grey-eyed morne smiles on the frowning
> Checking the Easterne clowdes with streaks of light:
> And fleckeld darknesse like a drunkard reeles,
> From forth daies path,and *Titans* burning wheeles:
> Now ere the sun aduance his burning eie,

Romeo rather elaborately tells us that the sun at dawn is dispelling the night (morning is smiling, the eastern clouds are checked with light, and the sun's chariot—Titan's wheels—advances), and he will seek out his spiritual father, the Friar. He exits and, oddly, the Friar enters and says pretty much the same thing about the sun. Both speakers say that "the gray-eyed morn smiles on the frowning night," but there are small differences, perhaps having more to do with the business of printing the book than with the author's composition: For Romeo's "checkring," "fleckted," and "pathway," we get the Friar's "checking," "fleckeld," and "path." (Notice, by the way, the inconsistency in Elizabethan spelling: Romeo's "clouds" become the Friar's "clowdes.")

Both versions must have been in the printer's copy, and it seems safe to assume that both were in Shakespeare's manuscript. He must have written one version—let's say he first wrote Romeo's closing lines for this scene—and then he decided, no, it's better to give this lyrical passage to the Friar, as the opening of a new scene, but neglected to delete the first version. Editors must make a choice, and they may feel that the reasonable thing to do is to print the text as Shakespeare intended it. But how can we know what he intended? Almost all modern editors delete the lines from

Romeo's speech, and retain the Friar's lines. They don't do this because they know Shakespeare's intention, however. They give the lines to the Friar because the first published version (1597) of *Romeo and Juliet* gives only the Friar's version, and this text (though in many ways inferior to the 1599 text) is thought to derive from the memory of some actors, that is, it is thought to represent a performance, not just a script. Maybe during the course of rehearsals Shakespeare—an actor as well as an author—unilaterally decided that the Friar should speak the lines; if so (remember that we don't know this to be a fact) his final intention was to give the speech to the Friar. Maybe, however, the actors talked it over and settled on the Friar, with or without Shakespeare's approval. On the other hand, despite the 1597 version, one might argue (if only weakly) on behalf of giving the lines to Romeo rather than to the Friar, thus: (1) Romeo's comment on the coming of the daylight emphasizes his separation from Juliet, and (2) the figurative language seems more appropriate to Romeo than to the Friar. Having said this, in the Signet edition we have decided in this instance to draw on the evidence provided by earlier text and to give the lines to the Friar, on the grounds that since Q1 reflects a production, in the theater (at least on one occasion) the lines were spoken by the Friar.

A playwright sold a script to a theatrical company. The script thus belonged to the company, not the author, and author and company alike must have regarded this script not as a literary work but as the basis for a play that the actors would create on the stage. We speak of Shakespeare as the author of the plays, but readers should bear in mind that the texts they read, even when derived from a single text, such as the First Folio (1623), are inevitably the collaborative work not simply of Shakespeare with his company—doubtless during rehearsals the actors would suggest alterations—but also with other forces of the age. One force was governmental censorship. In 1606 parliament passed "an Act to restrain abuses of players," prohibiting the utterance of oaths and the name of God. So where the earliest text of *Othello* gives us "By heaven" (3.3.106), the first Folio gives "Alas," presumably reflecting the compliance of stage practice with the law. Similarly, the 1623 version of *King Lear* omits the oath "Fut" (probably from "By God's foot") at 1.2.142, again presumably reflecting the line as it was spoken on the stage. Editors who seek to give the reader the play that Shakespeare initially conceived—the "authentic" play conceived by the solitary Shakespeare— probably will restore the missing oaths and references to God. Other editors, who see the play as a collaborative work, a construction made not only by Shakespeare but also by actors and compositors and even government censors, may claim that what counts is the play as it was actually performed. Such editors regard the censored text as legitimate, since it is the play that was (presumably) finally put on. A performed text, they argue, has more historical reality than a text produced by an editor who has sought to get at what Shakespeare initially wrote. In this view, the text of a play is rather like the script of a film; the script is not the film, and the play text is not the performed play. Even if we want to talk about the play that Shakespeare "intended," we will find ourselves talking about a script that he handed over to a company with the intention that it be implemented by actors. The "intended" play is the one that the actors—we might almost say "society"—would help to construct.

Further, it is now widely held that a play is also the work of readers and spectators, who do not simply receive meaning, but who create it when they respond to the play. This idea is fully in accord with contemporary post-structuralist critical thinking, notably Roland Barthes's "The Death of the Author," in *Image-Music-Text* (1977) and Michel Foucault's "What Is an Author?," in *The Foucault Reader* (1984). The gist of the idea is that an author is not an isolated genius; rather, authors are subject to the politics and other social structures of their age. A dramatist especially is a worker in a collaborative project, working most obviously with actors—parts may be written for particular actors—but working also with the audience. Consider the words of Samuel Johnson, written to be spoken by the actor David Garrick at the opening of a theater in 1747:

> The stage but echoes back the public voice;
> The drama's laws, the drama's patrons give,
> For we that live to please, must please to live.

The audience—the public taste as understood by the playwright—helps to determine what the play is. Moreover, even members of the public who are not part of the playwright's immediate audience may exert an influence through censorship. We have already glanced at governmental censorship, but there are also other kinds. Take one of Shakespeare's most beloved characters, Falstaff, who appears in three of Shakespeare's plays, the two parts of *Henry IV* and *The Merry Wives of Windsor*. He appears with this name in the earliest printed version of the first of these plays, *1 Henry IV*, but we know that Shakespeare originally called him (after an historical figure) Sir John Oldcastle. Oldcastle appears in Shakespeare's source (partly reprinted in the Signet edition of *1 Henry IV*), and a trace of the name survives in Shakespeare's play, 1.2.43–44, where Prince Hal punningly addresses Falstaff as "my old lad of the castle." But for some reason—perhaps because the family of the historical Oldcastle complained—Shakespeare had to change the name. In short, the play as we have it was (at least in this detail) subject to some sort of censorship. If we think that a text should present what we take to be the author's intention, we probably will want to replace *Falstaff* with *Oldcastle*. But if we recognize that a play is a collaboration, we may welcome the change, even if it was forced on Shakespeare. Somehow *Falstaff*, with its hint of *false-staff*, i.e., inadequate prop, seems just right for this fat knight who, to our delight, entertains the young prince with untruths. We can go as far as saying that, at least so far as a play is concerned, an insistence on the author's original intention (even if we could know it) can sometimes impoverish the text.

The tiny example of Falstaff's name illustrates the point that the text we read is inevitably only a version—something in effect produced by the collaboration of the playwright with his actors, audiences, compositors, and editors—of a fluid text that Shakespeare once wrote, just as the *Hamlet* that we see on the screen starring Kenneth Branagh is not the *Hamlet* that Shakespeare saw in an open-air playhouse starring Richard Burbage. *Hamlet* itself, as we shall note in a moment, also exists in several versions. It is not surprising that there is now much talk about the *instability* of Shakespeare's texts.

Because he was not only a playwright but was also an actor and a shareholder in a theatrical company, Shakespeare probably was much involved with the translation of the play from a manuscript to a stage production. He may or may not have done some rewriting during rehearsals, and he may or may not have been happy with cuts that were made. Some plays, notably *Hamlet* and *King Lear*, are so long that it is most unlikely that the texts we read were acted in their entirety. Further, for both of these plays we have more than one early text that demands consideration. In *Hamlet*, the Second Quarto (1604) includes some two hundred lines not found in the Folio (1623). Among the passages missing from the Folio are two of Hamlet's reflective speeches, the "dram of evil" speech (1.4.13–38) and "How all occasions do inform against me" (4.4.32–66). Since the Folio has more numerous and often fuller stage directions, it certainly looks as though in the Folio we get a theatrical version of the play, a text whose cuts were probably made—this is only a hunch, of course—not because Shakespeare was changing his conception of Hamlet but because the playhouse demanded a modified play. (The problem is complicated, since the Folio not only cuts some of the Quarto but adds some material. Various explanations have been offered.)

Or take an example from *King Lear*. In the First and Second Quarto (1608, 1619), the final speech of the play is given to Albany, Lear's surviving son-in-law, but in the First Folio version (1623), the speech is given to Edgar. The Quarto version is in accord with tradition—usually the highest-ranking character in a tragedy speaks the final words. Why does the Folio give the speech to Edgar? One possible answer is this: The Folio version omits some of Albany's speeches in earlier scenes, so perhaps it was decided (by Shakespeare? by the players?) not to give the final lines to so pale a character. In fact, the discrepancies are so many between the two texts, that some scholars argue we do not simply have texts showing different theatrical productions. Rather, these scholars say, Shakespeare substantially revised the play, and we really have two versions of *King Lear* (and of *Othello* also, say some)—two different plays—not simply two texts, each of which is in some ways imperfect.

In this view, the 1608 version of *Lear* may derive from Shakespeare's manuscript, and the 1623 version may derive from his later revision. The Quartos have almost three hundred lines not in the Folio, and the Folio has about a hundred lines not in the Quartos. It used to be held that all the texts were imperfect in various ways and from various causes—some passages in the Quartos were thought to have been set from a manuscript that was not entirely legible, other passages were thought to have been set by a compositor who was new to setting plays, and still other passages were thought to have been provided by an actor who misremembered some of the lines. This traditional view held that an editor must draw on the Quartos and the Folio in order to get Shakespeare's "real" play. The new argument holds (although not without considerable strain) that we have two authentic plays, Shakespeare's early version (in the Quarto) and Shakespeare's—or his theatrical company's—revised version (in the Folio). Not only theatrical demands but also Shakespeare's own artistic sense, it is argued, called for extensive revisions. Even the titles vary: Q1 is called *True Chronicle Historie of the life and death of King Lear and his three Daughters*, whereas the Folio text is called *The Tragedie of King Lear*. To combine the two texts in order to produce what the editor thinks is the play that Shakespeare intended to write is, according to this view, to produce a text that is false to the history of the play. If the new view is correct, and we do have texts of two distinct versions of *Lear* rather than two imperfect versions of one play, it supports in a textual way the poststructuralist view that we cannot possibly have an unmediated vision of (in this case) a play by Shakespeare; we can only recognize a plurality of visions.

Editing Texts

Though eighteen of his plays were published during his lifetime, Shakespeare seems never to have supervised their publication. There is nothing unusual here; when a playwright sold a play to a theatrical company he surrendered his ownership to it. Normally a company would not publish the play, because to publish it meant to allow competitors to acquire the piece. Some plays did get published: Apparently hard-up actors sometimes pieced together a play for a publisher; sometimes a company in need of money sold a play; and sometimes a company allowed publication of a play that no longer drew audiences. That Shakespeare did not concern himself with publication is not remarkable; of his contemporaries, only Ben Jonson carefully supervised the publication of his own plays.

In 1623, seven years after Shakespeare's death, John Heminges and Henry Condell (two senior members of Shakespeare's company, who had worked with him for about twenty years) collected his plays—published and unpublished—into a large volume, of a kind called a folio. (A folio is a volume consisting of large sheets that have been folded once, each sheet thus making two leaves, or four pages. The size of the page of course depends on the size of the sheet—a folio can range in height from twelve to sixteen inches, and in width from eight to eleven; the pages in the 1623 edition of Shakespeare, commonly called the First Folio, are approximately thirteen inches tall and eight inches wide.) The eighteen plays published during Shakespeare's lifetime had been issued one play per volume in small formats called quartos. (Each sheet in a quarto has been folded twice, making four leaves, or eight pages, each page being about nine inches tall and seven inches wide, roughly the size of a large paperback.)

Heminges and Condell suggest in an address "To the great variety of readers" that the republished plays are presented in better form than in the quartos:

> Before you were abused with diverse stolen and surreptitious copies, maimed and deformed by the frauds and stealths of injurious impostors that exposed them; even those, are now offered to your view cured and perfect of their limbs, and all the rest absolute in their numbers, as he [i.e., Shakespeare] conceived them.

There is a good deal of truth to this statement, but some of the quarto versions are better than others; some are in fact preferable to the Folio text.

Whoever was assigned to prepare the texts for publication

in the first Folio seems to have taken the job seriously and yet not to have performed it with uniform care. The sources of the texts seem to have been, in general, good unpublished copies or the best published copies. The first play in the collection, *The Tempest*, is divided into acts and scenes, has unusually full stage directions and descriptions of spectacle, and concludes with a list of the characters, but the editor was not able (or willing) to present all of the succeeding texts so fully dressed. Later texts occasionally show signs of carelessness: in one scene of *Much Ado About Nothing* the names of actors, instead of characters, appear as speech prefixes, as they had in the Quarto, which the Folio reprints; proofreading throughout the Folio is spotty and apparently was done without reference to the printer's copy; the pagination of *Hamlet* jumps from 156 to 257. Further, the proofreading was done while the presses continued to print, so that each play in each volume contains a mix of corrected and uncorrected pages.

Modern editors of Shakespeare must first select their copy; no problem if the play exists only in the Folio, but a considerable problem if the relationship between a Quarto and the Folio—or an early Quarto and a later one—is unclear. In the case of *Romeo and Juliet*, the First Quarto (Q1), published in 1597, is vastly inferior to the Second (Q2), published in 1599. The basis of Q1 apparently is a version put together from memory by some actors. Not surprisingly, it garbles many passages and is much shorter than Q2. On the other hand, occasionally Q1 makes better sense than Q2. For instance, near the end of the play, when the parents have assembled and learned of the deaths of Romeo and Juliet, in Q2 the Prince says (5.3.208–9),

> Come, *Montague;* for thou art early vp
> To see thy sonne and heire, now earling downe.

The last three words of this speech surely do not make sense, and many editors turn to Q1, which instead of "now earling downe" has "more early downe." Some modern editors take only "early" from Q1, and print "now early down"; others take "more early," and print "more early down." Further, Q1 (though, again, quite clearly a garbled and abbreviated text) includes some stage directions that are not found in Q2, and today many editors who base their text on Q2 are glad to add these stage directions, because the directions help to give us a sense of what the play looked like on Shakespeare's stage. Thus, in 4.3.58, after Juliet drinks the potion, Q1 gives us this stage direction, not in Q2: *"She falls upon her bed within the curtains."*

In short, an editor's decisions do not end with the choice of a single copy text. First of all, editors must reckon with Elizabethan spelling. If they are not producing a facsimile, they probably modernize the spelling, but ought they to preserve the old forms of words that apparently were pronounced quite unlike their modern forms—*lanthorn, alablaster*? If they preserve these forms are they really preserving Shakespeare's forms or perhaps those of a compositor in the printing house? What is one to do when one finds *lanthorn* and *lantern* in adjacent lines? (The editors of this series in general, but not invariably, assume that words should be spelled in their modern form, unless, for instance, a rhyme is involved.) Elizabethan punctuation, too, presents problems. For example, in the First Folio, the only text for the play, Macbeth rejects his wife's idea that he can wash the blood from his hand (2.2.60–62):

> No: this my Hand will rather
> The multitudinous Seas incarnardine,
> Making the Greene one, Red.

Obviously an editor will remove the superfluous capitals, and will probably alter the spelling to "incarnadine," but what about the comma before "Red"? If we retain the comma, Macbeth is calling the sea "the green one." If we drop the comma, Macbeth is saying that his bloody hand will make the sea ("the Green") *uniformly* red.

An editor will sometimes have to change more than spelling and punctuation. Macbeth says to his wife (1.7.46–47):

> I dare do all that may become a man,
> Who dares no more, is none.

For two centuries editors have agreed that the second line is unsatisfactory, and have emended "no" to "do": "Who dares do more is none." But when in the same play (4.2.21–22) Ross says that fearful persons

> Floate vpon a wilde and violent Sea
> Each way, and moue,

need we emend the passage? On the assumption that the compositor misread the manuscript, some editors emend "each way, and move" to "and move each way"; others emend "move" to "none" (i.e., "Each way and none"). Other editors, however, let the passage stand as in the original. The editors of the Signet Classic Shakespeare have restrained themselves from making abundant emendations. In their minds they hear Samuel Johnson on the dangers of emendation: "I have adopted the Roman sentiment, that it is more honorable to save a citizen than to kill an enemy." Some departures (in addition to spelling, punctuation, and lineation) from the copy text have of course been made, but the original readings are listed in a note following the play, so that readers can evaluate the changes for themselves.

Following tradition, the editors of the Signet Classic Shakespeare have prefaced each play with a list of characters, and throughout the play have regularized the names of the speakers. Thus, in our text of *Romeo and Juliet*, all speeches by Juliet's mother are prefixed "Lady Capulet," although the 1599 Quarto of the play, which provides our copy text, uses at various points seven speech tags for this one character: *Capu. Wi.* (i.e., Capulet's wife), *Ca. Wi., Wi., Wife, Old La.* (i.e., Old Lady), *La.,* and *Mo.* (i.e., Mother). Similarly, in *All's Well That Ends Well*, the character whom we regularly call "Countess" is in the Folio (the copy text) variously identified as *Mother, Countess, Old Countess, Lady,* and *Old Lady*. Admittedly there is some loss in regularizing, since the various prefixes may give us a hint of the way Shakespeare (or a scribe who copied Shakespeare's manuscript) was thinking of the character in a particular scene—for instance, as a mother, or as an old lady. But too much can be made of these differing prefixes, since the social relationships implied are *not* always relevant to the given scene.

We have also added line numbers and in many cases act and scene divisions as well as indications of locale at the beginning of scenes. The Folio divided most of the plays into acts and some into scenes. Early eighteenth-century editors increased the divisions. These divisions, which provide a convenient way of referring to passages in the plays, have been retained, but when not in the text chosen as the basis for the Signet Classic text they are enclosed within square brackets, [ ], to indicate that they are editorial additions. Similarly, though no play of Shakespeare's was equipped with indications of the locale at the heads of scene divisions, locales have here been added in square brackets for the convenience of readers, who lack the information that costumes, properties, gestures, and scenery afford to spectators. Spectators can tell at a glance they are in the throne room, but without an editorial indication the reader may be puzzled for a while. It should be mentioned, incidentally, that there are a few authentic stage directions—perhaps Shakespeare's, perhaps a prompter's—that suggest locales, such as *"Enter Brutus in his orchard,"* and *"They go up into the Senate house."* It is hoped that the bracketed additions in the Signet text will provide readers with the sort of help provided by these two authentic directions, but it is equally hoped that the reader will remember that the stage was not loaded with scenery.

Shakespeare on the Stage

Each volume in the Signet Classic Shakespeare includes a brief stage (and sometimes film) history of the play. When we read about earlier productions, we are likely to find them eccentric, obviously wrongheaded—for instance, Nahum Tate's version of *King Lear*, with a happy ending, which held the stage for about a century and a half, from the late seventeenth century until the end of the first quarter of the nineteenth. We see engravings of David Garrick, the greatest actor of the eighteenth century, in eighteenth-century garb

as King Lear, and we smile, thinking how absurd the production must have been. If we are more thoughtful, we say,
with the English novelist L. P. Hartley, "The past is a foreign
country: they do things differently there." But if the eighteenth-century staging is a foreign country, what of the plays
of the late sixteenth and seventeenth centuries? A foreign
language, a foreign theater, a foreign audience.

Probably all viewers of Shakespeare's plays, beginning
with Shakespeare himself, at times have been unhappy with
the plays on the stage. Consider three comments about production that we find in the plays themselves, which suggest
Shakespeare's concerns. The Chorus in *Henry V* complains
that the heroic story cannot possibly be adequately staged:

> But pardon, gentles all,
> The flat unraisèd spirits that hath dared
> On this unworthy scaffold to bring forth
> So great an object. Can this cockpit hold
> The vasty fields of France? Or may we cram
> Within this wooden *O* the very casques
> That did affright the air at Agincourt?
>
> . . . .
>
> Piece out our imperfections with your thoughts.
>
> (Prologue 1.8–14,23)

Second, here are a few sentences (which may or may not
represent Shakespeare's own views) from Hamlet's longish
lecture to the players:

> Speak the speech, I pray you, as I pronounced it to you, trippingly
> on the tongue. But if you mouth it, as many of our players do, I had
> as lief the town crier spoke my lines. . . . O, it offends me to the
> soul to hear a robustious periwig-pated fellow tear a passion to tat-
> ters, to very rags, to split the ears of the groundlings. . . . And let
> those that play your clowns speak no more than is set down for
> them, for there be of them that will themselves laugh, to set on
> some quantity of barren spectators to laugh too, though in the
> meantime some necessary question of the play be then to be con-
> sidered. That's villainous and shows a most pitiful ambition in the
> fool that uses it. (3.2.1–47)

Finally, we can quote again from the passage cited earlier in this introduction, concerning the boy actors who played the female roles. Cleopatra imagines with horror a theatrical version of her activities with Antony:

> The quick comedians
> Extemporally will stage us, and present
> Our Alexandrian revels: Antony
> Shall be brought drunken forth, and I shall see
> Some squeaking Cleopatra boy my greatness
> I' th' posture of a whore.   (5.2.216–21)

It is impossible to know how much weight to put on such passages—perhaps Shakespeare was just being modest about his theater's abilities—but it is easy enough to think that he was unhappy with some aspects of Elizabethan production. Probably no production can fully satisfy a playwright, and for that matter, few productions can fully satisfy *us;* we regret this or that cut, this or that way of costuming the play, this or that bit of business.

One's first thought may be this: Why don't they just do "authentic" Shakespeare, "straight" Shakespeare, the play as Shakespeare wrote it? But as we read the plays—words written to be performed—it sometimes becomes clear that we do not know *how* to perform them. For instance, in *Antony and Cleopatra* Antony, the Roman general who has succumbed to Cleopatra and to Egyptian ways, says, "The nobleness of life / Is to do thus" (1.1.36–37). But what is "thus"? Does Antony at this point embrace Cleopatra? Does he embrace and kiss her? (There are, by the way, very few scenes of kissing on Shakespeare's stage, possibly because boys played the female roles.) Or does he make a sweeping gesture, indicating the Egyptian way of life?

This is not an isolated example; the plays are filled with lines that call for gestures, but we are not sure what the gestures should be. *Interpretation* is inevitable. Consider a passage in *Hamlet*. In 3.1, Polonius persuades his daughter, Ophelia, to talk to Hamlet while Polonius and Claudius eavesdrop. The two men conceal themselves, and Hamlet encounters Ophelia. At 3.1.131 Hamlet suddenly says to her, "Where's your father?" Why does Hamlet, apparently out of nowhere—they have not been talking about Polonius—ask this question? Is this an example of the "antic disposition" (fantastic behavior) that Hamlet earlier (1.5.172) had told Horatio and others—including us—he would display? That is, is the question about the whereabouts of her father a seemingly irrational one, like his earlier question (3.1.103) to Ophelia, "Ha, ha! Are you honest?" Or, on the other hand, has Hamlet (as in many productions) suddenly glimpsed Polonius's foot protruding from beneath a drapery at the rear? That is, does Hamlet ask the question because he has suddenly seen something suspicious and now is testing Ophelia? (By the way, in productions that do give Hamlet a physical cue, it is almost always Polonius rather than Claudius who provides the clue. This itself is an act of interpretation on the part of the director.) Or (a third possibility) does Hamlet get a clue from Ophelia, who inadvertently betrays the spies by nervously glancing at their place of hiding? This is the interpretation used in the BBC television version, where Ophelia glances in fear toward the hiding place just after Hamlet says "Why wouldst thou be a breeder of sinners?" (121–22). Hamlet, realizing that he is being observed, glances here and there *before* he asks "Where's your father?" The question thus is a climax to what he has been doing while speaking the preceding lines. Or (a fourth interpretation) does Hamlet suddenly, without the aid of any clue whatsoever, intuitively (insightfully, mysteriously, wonderfully) sense that someone is spying? Directors must decide, of course—and so must readers.

Recall, too, the preceding discussion of the texts of the plays, which argued that the texts—though they seem to be before us in permanent black on white—are unstable. The Signet text of *Hamlet*, which draws on the Second Quarto (1604) and the First Folio (1623) is considerably longer than any version staged in Shakespeare's time. Our version, even if spoken very briskly and played without any intermission, would take close to four hours, far beyond "the two hours' traffic of our stage" mentioned in the Prologue to *Romeo and Juliet*. (There are a few contemporary references to the duration of a play, but none mentions more than three hours.) Of Shakespeare's plays, only *The Comedy of Errors*, *Macbeth*, and *The Tempest* can be done in less than three hours without cutting. And even if we take a play that exists only in a short text, *Macbeth*, we cannot claim that we are experiencing the very play that Shakespeare conceived, partly because some of the Witches' songs almost surely are non-Shakespearean additions, and partly because we are not willing to watch the play performed without an intermission and with boys in the female roles.

Further, as the earlier discussion of costumes mentioned, the plays apparently were given chiefly in contemporary, that is, in Elizabethan dress. If today we give them in the costumes that Shakespeare probably saw, the plays seem not contemporary but curiously dated. Yet if we use our own dress, we find lines of dialogue that are at odds with what we see; we may feel that the language, so clearly not our own, is inappropriate coming out of people in today's dress. A common solution, incidentally, has been to set the plays in the nineteenth century, on the grounds that this attractively distances the plays (gives them a degree of foreignness, allowing for interesting costumes) and yet doesn't put them into a museum world of Elizabethan England.

Inevitably our productions are adaptations, *our* adaptations, and inevitably they will look dated, not in a century but in twenty years, or perhaps even in a decade. Still, we cannot escape from our own conceptions. As the director Peter Brook has said, in *The Empty Space* (1968):

It is not only the hair-styles, costumes and make-ups that look dated. All the different elements of staging—the shorthands of behavior that stand for emotions; gestures, gesticulations and tones of voice—are all fluctuating on an invisible stock exchange all the time. . . . A living theatre that thinks it can stand aloof from anything as trivial as fashion will wilt. (p. 16)

As Brook indicates, it is through today's hairstyles, costumes, makeup, gestures, gesticulations, tones of voice—this includes our *conception* of earlier hairstyles, costumes, and so forth if we stage the play in a period other than our own—that we inevitably stage the plays.

It is a truism that every age invents its own Shakespeare, just as, for instance, every age has invented its own classical world. Our view of ancient Greece, a slave-holding society in which even free Athenian women were severely circum-scribed, does not much resemble the Victorians' view of ancient Greece as a glorious democracy, just as, perhaps, our view of Victorianism itself does not much resemble theirs. We cannot claim that the Shakespeare on our stage is the true Shakespeare, but in our stage productions we find a Shakespeare that speaks to us, a Shakespeare that our ances-tors doubtless did not know but one that seems to us to be the true Shakespeare—at least for a while.

Our age is remarkable for the wide variety of kinds of staging that it uses for Shakespeare, but one development deserves special mention. This is the now common practice of race-blind or color-blind or nontraditional casting, which allows persons who are not white to play in Shakespeare. Previously blacks performing in Shakespeare were limited to a mere three roles, Othello, Aaron (in *Titus Andronicus*), and the Prince of Morocco (in *The Merchant of Venice*), and there were no roles at all for Asians. Indeed, African-Americans rarely could play even one of these three roles, since they were not welcome in white companies. Ira Aldridge (c.1806–1867), a black actor of undoubted talent, was forced to make his living by performing Shakespeare in England and in Europe, where he could play not only Othello but also—in whiteface—other tragic roles such as King Lear. Paul Robeson (1898–1976) made theatrical his-tory when he played Othello in London in 1930, and there was some talk about bringing the production to the United States, but there was more talk about whether American audiences would tolerate the sight of a black man—a real black man, not a white man in blackface—kissing and then killing a white woman. The idea was tried out in summer stock in 1942, the reviews were enthusiastic, and in the fol-lowing year Robeson opened on Broadway in a production that ran an astounding 296 performances. An occasional all-black company sometimes performed Shakespeare's plays, but otherwise blacks (and other minority members) were in effect shut out from performing Shakespeare. Only since about 1970 has it been common for nonwhites to play major roles along with whites. Thus, in a 1996–97 production of *Antony and Cleopatra*, a white Cleopatra, Vanessa Red-grave, played opposite a black Antony, David Harewood.

Multiracial casting is now especially common at the New York Shakespeare Festival, founded in 1954 by Joseph Papp, and in England, where even siblings such as Claudio and Isabella in *Measure for Measure* or Lear's three daughters may be of different races. Probably most viewers today soon stop worrying about the lack of realism, and move beyond the color of the performers' skin to the quality of the performance.

Nontraditional casting is not only a matter of color or race; it includes sex. In the past, occasionally a distinguished woman of the theater has taken on a male role—Sarah Bernhardt (1844–1923) as Hamlet is perhaps the most famous example—but such performances were widely regarded as eccentric. Although today there have been some performances involving cross-dressing (a drag *As You Like It* staged by the National Theatre in England in 1966 and in the United States in 1974 has achieved considerable fame in the annals of stage history), what is more interesting is the casting of women in roles that traditionally are male but that need not be. Thus, a 1993–94 English production of *Henry V* used a woman—*not* cross-dressed—in the role of the governor of Harfleur. According to Peter Holland, who reviewed the production in *Shakespeare Survey* 48 (1995), "having a female Governor of Harfleur feminized the city and provided a direct response to the horrendous threat of rape and murder that Henry had offered, his language and her body in direct connection and opposition" (p. 210). Ten years from now the device may not play so effectively, but today it speaks to us. Shakespeare, born in the Elizabethan Age, has been dead nearly four hundred years, yet he is, as Ben Jonson said, "not of an age but for all time." We must understand, however, that he is "for all time" precisely because each age finds in his abundance something for itself and something of itself.

And here we come back to two issues discussed earlier in this introduction—the instability of the text and, curiously, the Bacon/Oxford heresy concerning the authorship of the plays. *Of course* Shakespeare wrote the plays, and we should daily fall on our knees to thank him for them—and yet there is something to the idea that he is not their only author. Every editor, every director and actor, and every reader to some degree shapes them, too, for when we edit, direct, act, or read, we inevitably become Shakespeare's collaborator and re-create the plays. The plays, one might say, are so cunningly contrived that they guide our responses, tell us how we ought to feel, and make a mark on us, but (for better or for worse) we also make a mark on them.

—SYLVAN BARNET
Tufts University

Introduction

No play of Shakespeare's intersects with the hot issues of our time more frequently than *Othello*. Militarism, racism, gender, spousal abuse, colonialism, the occult, the pathology of the inexplicably evil person, these are all woven into the web of the play, and they are among the issues that haunt the world at the end of the twentieth century. Even our most sensational crime, the murders of Nicole Brown Simpson and Ronald Goldman, and the trial of O. J. Simpson, with significant differences, replays the Othello story to a remarkable degree, down to an almost identical cast of characters. *Othello* is almost perfect for a case history of how one might usefully connect today's headlines to Shakespeare, but to do so exclusively would run the risk of trading in some admittedly uncanny local similarities for the play's exploration of the surprising depths and unexpected turns of human motivation. It would also risk missing the symbolic arrangement of the world that Shakespeare constructed as a background for the characters and which sets the universal scene for their fates.

When Shakespeare wrote *Othello,* about 1604, his knowledge of human beings and his ability to dramatize it in language and action were at their height. The play offers, even in its minor characters, a number of unusually full and profound studies of humanity: Brabantio, the sophisticated, civilized Venetian senator, unable to comprehend that his delicate daughter could love and marry a Moor, speaking excitedly of black magic and spells to account for what his mind cannot understand; Cassio, the gentleman-soldier, polished in manners and gracious in bearing, wildly drunk and revealing a deeply rooted pride in his ramblings about senior officers being saved before their juniors; Emilia, the sensible and conventional waiting woman, making small talk about love and suddenly remarking that though she believes adultery to be wrong, still if the price were high enough she would sell—and so, she believes, would most women. The vision of human nature which the play offers is one of ancient terrors and primal drives—fear of the unknown, pride, greed, lust—underlying smooth, civilized surfaces—the noble senator, the competent and well-mannered lieutenant, the conventional gentlewoman.

The contrast between surface manner and inner nature is even more pronounced in two of the major characters. "Honest Iago" (1.3.289) conceals beneath his exterior of the plain soldier and blunt, practical man of the world a diabolism so intense as to defy rational explanation—it must be taken like lust or pride as simply a given part of human nature, an anti-life spirit which seeks the destruction of everything outside the self. Othello appears in the opening acts as the very personification of self-control, of the man with so secure a sense of his own worth that nothing can ruffle the consequent calmness of mind and manner. But the man who has roamed the wild and savage world unmoved by its terrors, who has not changed countenance when the cannon killed his brother standing beside him, this man is still capable of believing his wife a whore on the slightest of evidence and committing murders to revenge himself. In Desdemona alone do the heart and the hand go together: she is what she seems to be. Ironically, she alone is accused of pretending to be what she is not. Her very openness and honesty make her suspect in a world where few men are what they appear, and her chastity is inevitably brought into question in a world where every other major character is in some degree touched with sexual corruption.

Most criticism of *Othello* has concerned itself with exploring the depths of these characters and tracing the intricate, mysterious operations of their minds. I should like, however, to leave this work to the individual reader and to the critical essays printed at the back of this volume in order to discuss, briefly, what might be called the "gross mechanics" of the play, the larger patterns in which events and characters are arranged. These patterns are the context within which the individual characters are defined, just as the pattern of a sentence is the context which defines the exact meaning of the individual words within it.

Othello is probably the most neatly, the most formally constructed of Shakespeare's plays. Every character is, for example, balanced by another similar or contrasting character. Desdemona is balanced by her opposite, Iago; love and concern for others at one end of the scale, hatred and concern for self at the other. The true and loyal soldier Cassio balances the false and traitorous soldier Iago. These balances and contrasts throw into relief the essential qualities of the characters. Desdemona's love, for example, shows up a good deal more clearly in contrast to Iago's hate, and vice versa. The values of contrast are increased and the full range of human nature displayed by extending these simple contrasts into developing series. The essential purity of Desdemona stands in contrast to the more "practical" view of chastity held by Emilia, and her view in turn is illuminated by the workaday view of sensuality held by the courtesan Bianca, who treats love, ordinarily, as a commodity. Or, to take another example, Iago's success in fooling Othello is but the culmination of a series of such betrayals that includes the duping of Roderigo, Brabantio, and Cassio. Each duping is the explanatory image of the other, for in every case Iago's method and end are the same: he plays on and teases to life some hitherto controlled and concealed dark passion in his victim. In each case he seeks in some way the same end, the symbolic murder of Desdemona, the destruction in some form of the life principle of which she is the major embodiment.

These various contrasts and parallelisms ultimately blend into a larger, more general pattern that is the central movement of the play. We can begin to see this pattern in the "symbolic geography" of the play. Every play, or work of art, creates its own particular image of space and time, its own symbolic world. The outer limits of the world of *Othello* are defined by the Turks—the infidels, the unbelievers, the "general enemy" (1.3.48) as the play calls them—who, just over the horizon, sail back and forth trying to confuse and trick the Christians in order to invade their dominions and destroy them. Out beyond the horizon, reported but unseen, are also those "anters vast and deserts idle" (1.3.139) of which Othello speaks. Out there is a land of "rough quarries, rocks, and hills whose heads touch heaven" (140) inhabited by "cannibals that each other eat" (142) and

monstrous forms of men "whose heads grow beneath their
shoulders" (143–44). On the edges of this land is the raging
ocean with its "high seas, and howling winds" (2.1.68), its
"guttered rocks and congregated sands" (69) hidden beneath
the waters to "enclog the guiltless keel" (70).

Within the circle formed by barbarism, monstrosity, ste-
rility, and the brute power of nature lie the two Christian
strongholds of Venice and Cyprus. Renaissance Venice was
known for its wealth acquired by trade, its political cunning,
and its courtesans; but Shakespeare, while reminding us of the
tradition of the "supersubtle Venetian," makes Venice over
into a form of *The City,* the ageless image of government, of
reason, of law, and of social concord. Here, when Brabantio's
strong passions and irrational fears threaten to create riot and
injustice, his grievances are examined by a court of law,
judged by reason, and the verdict enforced by civic power.
Here, the clear mind of the Senate probes the actions of the
Turks, penetrates through their pretenses to their true purposes, makes sense of the frantic and fearful contradictory
messages which pour in from the fleet, and arranges the necessary defense. Act 1, Scene 3—the Senate scene—focuses on
the magnificent speeches of Othello and Desdemona as they
declare their love and explain it, but the lovers are surrounded,
guarded, by the assembled, ranked governors of Venice, who
control passions that otherwise would have led to a bloody
street brawl and bring justice out of what otherwise would
have been riot. The solemn presence and ordering power of the
Senate would be most powerfully realized in a stage production, where the senators would appear in their rich robes, with
all their symbols of office, seated in ranks around several
excited individuals expressing such primal passions as pride of
race, fear of dark powers, and violent love. In a play where so
much of the language is magnificent, rich, and of heroic pro-
portions, simpler statements come to seem more forceful; and
the meaning of *The City* is perhaps nowhere more completely
realized than in Brabantio's brief, secure answer to the first
fearful cries of theft and talk of copulating animals that Iago
and Roderigo send up from the darkness below his window:

> What tell'st thou me of robbing? This is Venice;
> My house is not a grange.   (1.1.102–03)

Here then are the major reference points on a map of the world of *Othello*: out at the far edge are the Turks, barbarism, disorder, and amoral destructive powers; closer and more familiar is Venice, *The City,* order, law, and reason. Cyprus, standing on the frontier between barbarism and *The City,* is not the secure fortress of civilization that Venice is. It is rather an outpost, weakly defended and far out in the raging ocean, close to the "general enemy" (1.3.48) and the immediate object of his attack. It is a "town of war yet wild" (2.3.212–13) where the "people's hearts [are] brimful of fear" (213). Here passions are more explosive and closer to the surface than in Venice, and here, instead of the ancient order and established government of *The City,* there is only one man to control violence and defend civilization—the Moor Othello, himself of savage origins and a converted Christian.

The movement of the play is from Venice to Cyprus, from *The City* to the outpost, from organized society to a condition much closer to raw nature, and from collective life to the life of the solitary individual. This movement is a characteristic pattern in Shakespeare's plays, both comedies and tragedies: in *A Midsummer Night's Dream* the lovers and players go from the civilized, daylight world of Athens to the irrational, magical wood outside Athens and the primal powers of life represented by the elves and fairies; Lear moves from his palace and secure identity to the savage world of the heath where all values and all identities come into question; and everyone in *The Tempest* is shipwrecked at some time on Prospero's magic island, where life seen from a new perspective assumes strange and fantastic shapes. At the other end of this journey there is always some kind of return to *The City,* to the palace, and to old relationships, but the nature of this return differs widely in Shakespeare's plays. In *Othello* the movement at the end of the play is back toward Venice, the Turk defeated; but Desdemona, Othello, Emilia, and Roderigo do not return. Their deaths are the price paid for the return.

This passage from Venice to Cyprus to fight the Turk and encounter the forces of barbarism is the geographical form of an action that occurs on the social and psychological levels as well. That is, there are social and mental conditions that correspond to Venice and Cyprus, and there are forces at work in society and in man that correspond to the Turks, the raging seas, and "cannibals that each other eat" (1.3.142)

The exposure to danger, the breakdown and the ultimate reestablishment of society—the parallel on the social level to the action on the geographical level—is quickly traced. We have already noted that the Venetian Senate embodies order, reason, justice, and concord, the binding forces that hold *The City* together. In Venice the ancient laws and the established customs of society work to control violent men and violent passions to ensure the safety and well-being of the individual and the group. But there are anarchic forces at work in the city, which threaten traditional social forms and relationships, and all these forces center in Iago. His discontent with his own rank and his determination to displace Cassio endanger the orderly military hierarchy in which the junior serves his senior. He endangers marriage, the traditional form for ordering male and female relationships, by his own unfounded suspicions of his wife and by his efforts to destroy Othello's marriage by fanning to life the darker, anarchic passions of Brabantio and Roderigo. He tries to subvert the operation of law and justice by first stirring up Brabantio to gather his followers and seek revenge in the streets; and then when the two warlike forces are met, Iago begins a quarrel with Roderigo in hopes of starting a brawl. The nature of the antisocial forces that Iago represents are focused in the imagery of his advice to Roderigo on how to call out to her father the news of Desdemona's marriage. Call, he says,

> with like timorous [frightening] accent and dire yell
> As when, by night and negligence, the fire
> Is spied in populous cities.   (1.1.72–74)

Fire, panic, darkness, neglect of duty—these are the natural and human forces that destroy great cities and turn their citizens to mobs.

In Venice, Iago's attempts to create civic chaos are frustrated by Othello's calm management of himself and the orderly legal proceedings of the Senate. In Cyprus, however, society is less secure—even as the island is more exposed to the Turks—and Othello alone is responsible for finding truth and maintaining order. Here Iago's poison begins to work, and he succeeds at once in manufacturing the riot that he failed to create in Venice. Seen on stage, the fight on the watch between Cassio and Montano is chaos come again: two drunken officers, charged with the defense of the town, trying to kill each other like savage animals, a bedlam of voices and shouts, broken, disordered furniture, and above all this the discordant clamor of the "dreadful" (2.3.174) alarm bell—used to signal attacks and fire. This success is but the prologue for other more serious disruptions of society and of the various human relationships that it fosters. The General is set against his officer, husband against wife, Christian against Christian, servant against master. Justice becomes a travesty of itself as Othello—using legal terms such as "It is the *cause*"—assumes the offices of accuser, judge, jury, and executioner of his wife. Manners disappear as the Moor strikes his wife publicly and treats her maid as a procuress. The brightly lighted Senate chamber is now replaced with a dark Cyprus street where Venetians cut one another down and men are murdered from behind. This anarchy finally gives way in the last scene, when Desdemona's faith is proven, to a restoration of order and an execution of justice on the two major criminals.

What we have followed so far is a movement expressed in geographical and social symbols from Venice to a Cyprus exposed to attack, from *The City* to barbarism, from Christendom to the domain of the Turks, from order to riot, from justice to wild revenge and murder, from truth to falsehood. It now remains to see just what this movement means on the level of the individual in the heart and mind of man. Of the three major characters, Desdemona, Othello, and Iago, the first and the last do not change their natures or their attitudes toward life during the course of the play. These two are polar opposites, the antitheses of each other. To speak in the most general terms, Desdemona expresses in her language and actions an innocent, unselfish love and concern for others. Othello catches her very essence when he speaks of her miraculous love, which transcended their differences in age, color, beauty, and culture:

> She loved me for the dangers I had passed,
> And I loved her that she did pity them.   (1.3.166–67)

This love in its various forms finds expression not only in her absolute commitment of herself to Othello, but in her gentleness, her kindness to others, her innocent trust in all men, her pleas for Cassio's restoration to Othello's favor; and it endures even past death at her husband's hands, for she comes back to life for a moment to answer Emilia's question, "who hath done this deed?" (5.2.122) with the unbelievable words,

> Nobody—I myself. Farewell.
> Commend me to my kind lord. O, farewell!
>
> (123–24)

Iago is her opposite in every way. Where she is open and guileless, he is never what he seems to be; where she thinks the best of everyone, he thinks the worst, usually turning to imagery of animals and physical functions to express his low opinion of human nature; where she seeks to serve and love others, he uses others to further his own dark aims and satisfy his hatred of mankind; where she is emotional and idealistic, he is icily logical and cynical. Desdemona and Iago are much more complicated than this, but perhaps enough has been said to suggest the nature of these two moral poles of the play. One is a life force that strives for order, community, growth, and light. The other is an anti-life force that seeks anarchy, death, and darkness. One is the foundation of all that men have built in the world, including *The City*; the other leads back toward ancient chaos and barbarism.

Othello, like most men, is a combination of the forces of love and hate, which are isolated in impossibly pure states in Desdemona and Iago. His psychic voyage from Venice to Cyprus is a passage of the soul and the will from the values of one of these characters to those of the other. This passage is charted by his acceptance and rejection of one or the other. He begins by refusing to have Iago as his lieutenant, choosing the more "theoretical" though less experienced Cassio. He marries Desdemona. Though he is not aware that he does so, he expresses the full meaning of this choice when he speaks of her in such suggestive terms as "my soul's joy" (2.1.182) and refers to her even as he is about to kill her, as "Promethean heat" (5.2.12), the vital fire that

gives life to the world. Similarly, he comes to know that all
that is valuable in life depends on her love, and in the magnificent speech beginning, "O now, forever / Farewell the
tranquil mind" (3.3.344–45), he details the emptiness of all
human activity if Desdemona be proved false. But Iago,
taking advantage of latent "Iagolike" feelings and thoughts
in Othello, persuades him that Desdemona is only common
clay. Othello then gives himself over to Iago at the end of
3.3, where they kneel together to plan the revenge, and
Othello says, "Now art thou my lieutenant" (475). To which
Iago responds with blood-chilling simplicity, "I am your
own forever" (476). The full meaning of this choice is
expressed, again unconsciously, by Othello when he says of
Desdemona,

> Perdition catch my soul
> But I do love thee! and when I love thee not,
> Chaos is come again.   (90–92)

The murder of Desdemona acts out the final destruction in
Othello himself of all the ordering powers of love, of trust,
of the bond between human beings.

Desdemona and Iago then represent two states of mind,
two understandings of life, and Othello's movement from
one to the other is the movement on the level of character
and psychology from Venice to Cyprus, from *The City* to
anarchy. His return to *The City* and the defeat of the Turk is
effected, at the expense of his own life, when he learns *what*
he has killed and executes himself as the only fitting judgment on his act. His willingness to speak of what he has
done—in contrast to Iago's sullen silence—is a willingness
to recognize the meaning of Desdemona's faith and chastity,
to acknowledge that innocence and love do exist, and that
therefore *The City* can stand, though his life is required to
validate the truth and justice on which it is built.

Othello offers a variety of interrelated symbols that locate
and define in historical, natural, social, moral, and human
terms those qualities of being and universal forces that are
forever at war in the universe and between which tragic man
is always in movement. On one side there are Turks, cannibals, barbarism, monstrous deformities of nature, the brute

force of the sea, riot, mobs, darkness, Iago, hatred, lust, concern for the self only, and cynicism. On the other side there are Venice, *The City,* law, senates, amity, hierarchy, Desdemona, love, concern for others, and innocent trust. As the characters of the play act and speak, they bring together, by means of parallelism and metaphor, the various forms of the different ways of life. There is, for example, a meaningful similarity in the underhanded way Iago works and the ruse by which the Turks try to fool the Venetians into thinking they are bound for Rhodes when their object is Cyprus. Or, there is again a flash of identification when we hear that the reefs and shoals that threaten ships are "ensteeped" (2.1.70), that is, hidden under the surface of the sea, as Iago is hidden under the surface of his "honesty." But Shakespeare binds the various levels of being more closely together by the use of imagery that compares things on one level of action with things on another. For example, when Iago swears that his low judgment of all female virtue "is true, or else I am a Turk" (113), logic demands, since one woman, Desdemona, *is* true and chaste, that we account him "a Turk." He is thus identified with the unbelievers, the Ottoman Turks, and that Asiatic power, which for centuries threatened Christendom, is shown to have its social and psychological equivalent in Iago's particular attitude toward life. Similarly, when Othello sees the drunken brawl on the watchtower, he exclaims,

> Are we turned Turks, and to ourselves do that
> Which heaven hath forbid the Ottomites? (2.3.169–70)

At the very time when the historical enemy has been defeated, his fleet providentially routed by the great storm, his characteristics—drunken loss of control, brawling over honor, disorder—begin to conquer the island only so recently and fortuitously saved. The conquest continues, and the defender of the island, Othello, convinced of Desdemona's guilt, compares his determination to revenge himself to "the Pontic Sea, / Whose icy current and compulsive course / Nev'r keeps retiring ebb" (3.3.450–52). The comparison tells us that in his rage and hatred he has become one with the savage seas and the brute, amoral powers of nature that are displayed in the storm scene at the beginning of Act

2. But most important is Othello's identification of himself at the end of the play as the "base Judean" who "threw a pearl away richer than all his tribe" (5.2.843–44). The more familiar Quarto reading is "base Indian" but both words point toward the barbarian who fails to recognize value and beauty when he possesses it—the primitive savage who picks up a pearl and throws it away not knowing its worth; or the Jews (Judas may be specifically meant) who denied and crucified another great figure of love, thinking they were dealing with only a troublesome rabble-rouser. A few lines further on Othello proceeds to the final and absolute identification of himself with the infidel. He speaks of a "malignant and a turbaned Turk" who "beat a Venetian and traduced the state" (849–50), and he then acknowledges that he is that Turk by stabbing himself, even as he once stabbed the other unbeliever. So he ends as both the Turk and the destroyer of the Turk, the infidel and the defender of the faith.

When Iago's schemes are at last exposed, Othello, finding it impossible for a moment to believe that a *man* could have contrived such evil, stares at Iago's feet and then says sadly, "but that's a fable" (282). What he hopes to find when he looks down are the cloven hoofs of the devil, and had they been there he would have been an actor in a morality play, tempted beyond his strength, like many a man before him, by a supernatural power outside himself. In some ways I have schematized *Othello* as just such a morality play, offering an allegorical journey between heaven and hell on a stage filled with purely symbolic figures. This is the kind of abstraction of art toward which criticism inevitably moves, and in this case the allegorical framework is very solidly there. But Othello does not see the cloven hoofs when he looks down; he sees a pair of human feet at the end of a very human body; and he is forced to realize that far from living in some simplified, "fabulous" world where evil is a metaphysical power raiding human life from without, he dwells where evil is somehow inextricably woven with good into man himself. On his stage the good angel does not return to heaven when defeated, but is murdered, and her body remains on the bed, "cold, cold" (272). He lives where good intentions, past services, psychic weaknesses, and an inability to see through evil cannot excuse an act, as they might in some simpler world where more perfect justice existed. In short, Othello is forced to recognize that he lives in a tragic world, and he pays the price for having been great enough to inhabit it.

Here is the essence of Shakespeare's art, an ability to create immediate, full, and total life as men actually live and experience it; and yet at the same time to arrange this reality so that it gives substance to and derives shape from a formal vision of all life that comprehends and reaches back from man and nature through society and history to cosmic powers that operate through all time and space. His plays are both allegorical and realistic at once; his characters both recognizable men and at the same time devils, demigods, and forces in nature. I have discussed only the more allegorical elements in *Othello,* the skeleton of ideas and formal patterns within which the characters must necessarily be understood. But it is equally true that the exact qualities of the abstract moral values and ideas, their full reality, exist only in the characters. It is necessary to know that Desdemona represents one particular human value, love or charity, in order to avoid making such mistakes as searching for some tragic flaw in her which would justify her death. But at the same time, if we would know what love and charity *are* in all their fullness, then our definition can only be the actions, the language, the emotions of the character Desdemona. She is Shakespeare's word for love. If we wish to know not just the obvious fact that men choose evil over good, but *why* they do so, then we must look both analytically and feelingly at all the evidence that the world offers for believing that Desdemona is false and at all the biases in Othello's mind that predispose him to believe such evidence. Othello's passage from Venice to Cyprus, from absolute love for Desdemona to extinguishing the light in her bedchamber, and to the execution of himself, these are Shakespeare's words for tragic man.

—ALVIN KERNAN
Princeton University

The Tragedy of

OTHELLO

The Moor of Venice

Dramatis Personae

Othello, the Moor
Brabantio, father to Desdemona
Cassio, an honorable lieutenant
Iago, a villain
Roderigo, a gulled gentleman
Duke of Venice
Senators
Montano, Governor of Cyprus
Gentlemen of Cyprus
Lodovico and Gratiano, two noble Venetians
Sailors
Clown
Desdemona, wife to Othello
Emilia, wife to Iago
Bianca, a courtesan
[Messenger, Herald, Officers, Gentlemen,
    Musicians, Attendants
        Scene: Venice and Cyprus]

The Tragedy of Othello

ACT 1

Scene 1. [*Venice. A street.*]

Enter Roderigo and Iago.

Roderigo. Tush! Never tell me? I take it much un-
    kindly
    That thou, Iago, who hast had my purse
    As if the strings were thine, shouldst know of this.

Iago. 'Sblood,°¹ but you'll not hear me! If ever I did
    dream
    Of such a matter, abhor me.

Roderigo.   Thou told'st me   5
    Thou didst hold him in thy hate.

Iago.   Despise me
    If I do not. Three great ones of the city,
    In personal suit to make me his lieutenant,
    Off-capped° to him; and, by the faith of man,
    I know my price; I am worth no worse a place.   10
    But he, as loving his own pride and purposes,
    Evades them with a bombast circumstance,°

---

¹ The degree sign (°) indicates a footnote, which is keyed to the text by the
line number. Text references are printed in **boldface** type; the annotation follows in roman type.   1.1.4 **'Sblood** by God's blood   9 **Off-capped** doffed
their caps—as a mark of respect   12 **bombast circumstance** stuffed, round-
about speech

Horribly stuffed with epithets of war;
Nonsuits° my mediators. For, "Certes," says he,
"I have already chose my officer." And what was

15   he?
Forsooth, a great arithmetician,°
One Michael Cassio, a Florentine,
(A fellow almost damned in a fair wife)°
That never set a squadron in the field,

20   Nor the division of a battle knows
More than a spinster; unless the bookish theoric,
Wherein the tonguèd° consuls can propose
As masterly as he. Mere prattle without practice
Is all his soldiership. But he, sir, had th' election;

25   And I, of whom his eyes had seen the proof
At Rhodes, at Cyprus, and on other grounds
Christian and heathen, must be belee'd and calmed
By debitor and creditor. This counter-caster,°
He, in good time, must his lieutenant be,
And I—God bless the mark!—his Moorship's an-

30   cient.°

Roderigo. By heaven, I rather would have been his
hangman.

Iago. Why, there's no remedy. 'Tis the curse of service:
Preferment goes by letter and affection,°
And not by old gradation,° where each second

35   Stood heir to th' first. Now, sir, be judge yourself,
Whether I in any just term am affined°
To love the Moor.

Roderigo.   I would not follow him then.

14 **Nonsuits** rejects   16 **arithmetician** theorist (rather than practical)   18
A ... wife (a much-disputed passage, which is probably best taken as a general sneer at Cassio as a dandy and a ladies' man. But in the story from which
Shakespeare took his plot the counterpart of Cassio is married, and it may be
that at the beginning of the play Shakespeare had decided to keep him married
but later changed his mind)   22 **tonguèd** eloquent   28 **counter-caster** i.e.,
a bookkeeper who *casts* (reckons up) figures on a *counter* (abacus)   30 **ancient** standard-bearer; an underofficer   33 **letter and affection** recommenda-
tions (from men of power) and personal preference   34 **old gradation**
seniority   36 **affined** bound

Iago. O, sir, content you.
    I follow him to serve my turn upon him.
    We cannot all be masters, nor all masters   *40*
    Cannot be truly followed. You shall mark
    Many a duteous and knee-crooking° knave
    That, doting on his own obsequious bondage,
    Wears out his time, much like his master's ass,
    For naught but provender; and when he's old,
      cashiered.   *45*
    Whip me such honest knaves! Others there are
    Who, trimmed in forms and visages of duty,
    Keep yet their hearts attending on themselves,
    And, throwing but shows of service on their lords,
    Do well thrive by them, and when they have lined
      their coats,   *50*
    Do themselves homage. These fellows have some
      soul;
    And such a one do I profess myself. For, sir,
    It is as sure as you are Roderigo,
    Were I the Moor, I would not be Iago.
    In following him, I follow but myself.   *55*
    Heaven is my judge, not I for love and duty,
    But seeming so, for my peculiar° end;
    For when my outward action doth demonstrate
    The native° act and figure of my heart
    In complement extern,° 'tis not long after   *60*
    But I will wear my heart upon my sleeve
    For daws to peck at; I am not what I am.

Roderigo. What a full fortune does the thick-lips owe°
    If he can carry't thus!

Iago.   Call up her father,
    Rouse him. Make after him, poison his delight,   *65*
    Proclaim him in the streets, incense her kinsmen,
    And though he in a fertile climate dwell,
    Plague him with flies; though that his joy be joy,

42 **knee-crooking** bowing   57 **peculiar** personal   59 **native** natural, innate
60 **complement extern** outward appearances   63 **owe** own

Yet throw such chances of vexation on't
70   As it may lose some color.

Roderigo. Here is her father's house. I'll call aloud.

Iago. Do, with like timorous° accent and dire yell
As when, by night and negligence, the fire
Is spied in populous cities.

Roderigo. What, ho, Brabantio! Signior Brabantio,
75   ho!

Iago. Awake! What, ho, Brabantio! Thieves! Thieves!
Look to your house, your daughter, and your bags!
Thieves! Thieves!

Brabantio above° [*at a window*].

Brabantio. What is the reason of this terrible sum-
mons?
80   What is the matter there?

Roderigo. Signior, is all your family within?

Iago. Are your doors locked?

Brabantio.   Why, wherefore ask you
this?

Iago. Zounds, sir, y'are robbed! For shame. Put on
your gown!
Your heart is burst, you have lost half your soul.
85   Even now, now, very now, an old black ram
Is tupping your white ewe. Arise, arise!
Awake the snorting citizens with the bell,
Or else the devil will make a grandsire of you.
Arise, I say!

Brabantio.   What, have you lost your wits?

Roderigo. Most reverend signior, do you know my
90   voice?

Brabantio. Not I. What are you?

---

72 **timorous** frightening   78 s.d. **above** (i.e., on the small upper stage above
and to the rear of the main platform stage, which resembled the projecting upper story of an Elizabethan house)

Roderigo. My name is Roderigo.

Brabantio.   The worser welcome!
  I have charged thee not to haunt about my doors.
  In honest plainness thou hast heard me say
  My daughter is not for thee; and now, in madness,   95
  Being full of supper and distemp'ring draughts,°
  Upon malicious knavery dost thou come
  To start° my quiet.

Roderigo. Sir, sir, sir——

Brabantio.   But thou must needs be sure
  My spirits and my place° have in their power   100
  To make this bitter to thee.

Roderigo.   Patience, good sir.

Brabantio. What tell'st thou me of robbing? This is Venice;
  My house is not a grange.°

Roderigo.   Most grave Brabantio,
  In simple and pure soul I come to you.

Iago. Zounds, sir, you are one of those that will not   105
  serve God if the devil bid you. Because we come
  to do you service and you think we are ruffians,
  you'll have your daughter covered with a Barbary°
  horse, you'll have your nephews° neigh to you,
  you'll have coursers for cousins,° and gennets for   110
  germans.°

Brabantio. What profane wretch art thou?

Iago. I am one, sir, that comes to tell you your daughter
  and the Moor are making the beast with two backs.

Brabantio. Thou art a villain.

Iago.   You are—a senator.   115

Brabantio. This thou shalt answer. I know thee,
  Roderigo.

96 **distemp'ring draughts** unsettling drinks 98 **start** disrupt 100 **place** rank, i.e., of senator 103 **grange** isolated house 108 **Barbary** Arabian, i.e., Moorish 109 **nephews** i.e., grandsons 110 **cousins** relations 110–11 **gennets for germans** Spanish horses for blood relatives

Roderigo. Sir, I will answer anything. But I beseech
          you,
    If't be your pleasure and most wise consent,
    As partly I find it is, that your fair daughter,
120   At this odd-even° and dull watch o' th' night,
    Transported, with no worse nor better guard
    But with a knave of common hire, a gondolier,
    To the gross clasps of a lascivious Moor—
    If this be known to you, and your allowance,
125   We then have done you bold and saucy wrongs;
    But if you know not this, my manners tell me
    We have your wrong rebuke. Do not believe
    That from the sense of all civility°
    I thus would play and trifle with your reverence.
130   Your daughter, if you have not given her leave,
    I say again, hath made a gross revolt,
    Tying her duty, beauty, wit, and fortunes
    In an extravagant° and wheeling stranger
    Of here and everywhere. Straight satisfy yourself.
135   If she be in her chamber, or your house,
    Let loose on me the justice of the state
    For thus deluding you.

Brabantio.   Strike on the tinder, ho!
    Give me a taper! Call up all my people!
    This accident° is not unlike my dream.
140   Belief of it oppresses me already.
    Light, I say! Light!   *Exit [above].*

Iago.   Farewell, for I must leave you.
    It seems not meet, nor wholesome to my place,
    To be produced—as, if I stay, I shall—
    Against the Moor. For I do know the State,
145   However this may gall him with some check,°
    Cannot with safety cast° him; for he's embarked
    With such loud reason to the Cyprus wars,

120 **odd-even** between night and morning   128 **sense of all civility** feeling
of what is proper   133 **extravagant** vagrant, wandering (Othello is not
Venetian and thus may be considered a wandering soldier of fortune)   139
accident happening   145 **check** restraint   146 **cast** dismiss

Which even now stands in act,° that for their souls
Another of his fathom° they have none
To lead their business; in which regard,　　　　　　　　*150*
Though I do hate him as I do hell-pains,
Yet, for necessity of present life,
I must show out a flag and sign of love,
Which is indeed but sign. That you shall surely find
　　him,
Lead to the Sagittary° the raisèd search;　　　　　　　*155*
And there will I be with him. So farewell.　　　*Exit.*

*Enter Brabantio [in his nightgown], with Servants
　　　　　　　and torches.*

Brabantio. It is too true an evil. Gone she is;
　　And what's to come of my despisèd time
　　Is naught but bitterness. Now, Roderigo,
　　Where didst thou see her?—O unhappy girl!—　　*160*
　　With the Moor, say'st thou?—Who would be a
　　　　father?—
　　How didst thou know 'twas she?—O, she deceives
　　　　me
　　Past thought!—What said she to you? Get moe°
　　　　tapers!
　　Raise all my kindred!—Are they married, think
　　　　you?
Roderigo. Truly I think they are.　　　　　　　　*165*
Brabantio. O heaven! How got she out? O treason of
　　　　the blood!
　　Fathers, from hence trust not your daughters' minds
　　By what you see them act.° Is there not charms
　　By which the property° of youth and maidhood
　　May be abused? Have you not read, Roderigo,　　*170*
　　Of some such thing?
Roderigo.　　　　　　　　Yes, sir, I have indeed.
Brabantio. Call up my brother.—O, would you had
　　　　had her!—

148 **stands in act** takes place　149 **fathom** ability　155 **Sagittary** (probably
the name of an inn)　163 **moe** more　168 **act** do　169 **property** true nature

Some one way, some another.—Do you know
Where we may apprehend her and the Moor?

175 *Roderigo.* I think I can discover him, if you please
To get good guard and go along with me.

Brabantio. Pray you lead on. At every house I'll call;
I may command at most.—Get weapons, ho!
And raise some special officers of might.—
180 On, good Roderigo; I will deserve your pains.°

                                                   Exeunt.

Scene 2. [*A street.*]

Enter Othello, Iago, Attendants with torches.

Iago. Though in the trade of war I have slain men,
Yet do I hold it very stuff° o' th' conscience
To do no contrived murder. I lack iniquity
Sometime to do me service. Nine or ten times
I had thought t' have yerked° him here, under the
5   ribs.

Othello. 'Tis better as it is.

Iago.   Nay, but he prated,
And spoke such scurvy and provoking terms
Against your honor, that with the little godliness
    I have
I did full hard forbear him. But I pray you, sir,
10 Are you fast married? Be assured of this,
That the magnifico° is much beloved,
And hath in his effect a voice potential
As double as the Duke's.° He will divorce you,
Or put upon you what restraint or grievance

180 **deserve your pains** be worthy of (and reward) your efforts   1.2.2 **stuff**
essence   5 **yerked** stabbed   11 **magnifico** nobleman   12–13 **hath . . . Duke's**
i.e., can be as effective as the Duke

The law, with all his might to enforce it on,   *15*
Will give him cable.°

Othello.   Let him do his spite.
My services which I have done the Signiory°
Shall out-tongue his complaints. 'Tis yet to know°—
Which when I know that boasting is an honor
I shall promulgate—I fetch my life and being   *20*
From men of royal siege;° and my demerits°
May speak unbonneted to as proud a fortune
As this that I have reached.° For know, Iago,
But that I love the gentle Desdemona,
I would not my unhousèd° free condition   *25*
Put into circumscription and confine
For the seas' worth. But look, what lights come
   yond?

Enter Cassio, with [Officers and] torches.

Iago. Those are the raisèd father and his friends.
You were best go in.

Othello.   Not I. I must be found.
My parts, my title, and my perfect soul°   *30*
Shall manifest me rightly. Is it they?

Iago. By Janus, I think no.

Othello. The servants of the Duke? And my lieutenant?
The goodness of the night upon you, friends.
What is the news?

Cassio.   The Duke does greet you, general;   *35*
And he requires your haste-posthaste appearance
Even on the instant.

Othello.   What is the matter, think you?

Cassio. Something from Cyprus, as I may divine.
It is a business of some heat. The galleys

16 **cable** range, scope 17 **Signiory** the rulers of Venice 18 **yet to know** unknown as yet 21 **siege** rank 21 **demerits** deserts 22–23 **May ... reached,** i.e., are the equal of the family I have married into 25 **unhousèd** unconfined 30 **perfect soul** clear, unflawed conscience

40   Have sent a dozen sequent° messengers
      This very night at one another's heels,
      And many of the consuls, raised and met,
      Are at the Duke's already. You have been hotly
         called for.
      When, being not at your lodging to be found,
45   The Senate hath sent about three several° quests
      To search you out.

Othello.   'Tis well I am found by you.
      I will but spend a word here in the house,
      And go with you.   [*Exit.*]

Cassio.   Ancient, what makes he here?

Iago. Faith, he tonight hath boarded a land carack.°
50   If it prove lawful prize, he's made forever.

Cassio. I do not understand.

Iago.   He's married.

Cassio.   To who?

[*Enter Othello.*]

Iago. Marry,° to— Come, captain, will you go?

Othello.   Have with you.

Cassio. Here comes another troop to seek for you.

Enter Brabantio, Roderigo, with Officers and torches.

Iago. It is Brabantio. General, be advised.
      He comes to bad intent.

55 *Othello.*   Holla! Stand there!

Roderigo. Signior, it is the Moor.

Brabantio.   Down with him, thief!
                           [*They draw swords.*]

Iago. You, Roderigo? Come, sir, I am for you.

Othello. Keep up your bright swords, for the dew will
      rust them.

---

40 **sequent** successive   45 **several** separate   49 **carack** treasure ship   52
Marry By Mary (an interjection)

Good signior, you shall more command with years
Than with your weapons.   60

Brabantio. O thou foul thief, where hast thou stowed
  my daughter?
  Damned as thou art, thou hast enchanted her!
  For I'll refer me to all things of sense,°
  If she in chains of magic were not bound,
  Whether a maid so tender, fair, and happy,   65
  So opposite to marriage that she shunned
  The wealthy, curlèd darlings of our nation,
  Would ever have, t' incur a general mock,°
  Run from her guardage to the sooty bosom
  Of such a thing as thou—to fear, not to delight. 70
  Judge me the world if 'tis not gross in sense°
  That thou hast practiced° on her with foul charms,
  Abused her delicate youth with drugs or minerals
  That weaken motion.° I'll have't disputed on;
  'Tis probable, and palpable to thinking.   75
  I therefore apprehend and do attach° thee
  For an abuser of the world, a practicer
  Of arts inhibited and out of warrant.°
  Lay hold upon him. If he do resist,
  Subdue him at his peril.

Othello.   Hold your hands,   80
  Both you of my inclining and the rest.
  Were it my cue to fight, I should have known it
  Without a prompter. Whither will you that I go
  To answer this your charge?

Brabantio.   To prison, till fit time
  Of law and course of direct session   85
  Call thee to answer.

Othello.   What if I do obey?
  How may the Duke be therewith satisfied,
  Whose messengers are here about my side

---

63 **refer ... sense** i.e., base (my argument) on all ordinary understanding of
nature 68 **general mock** public shame 71 **gross in sense** obvious 72
practiced used tricks 74 **motion** thought, i.e., reason 76 **attach** arrest
78 **inhibited ... warrant** prohibited and illegal (black magic)

Upon some present° business of the state
To bring me to him?

90   *Officer.*   'Tis true, most worthy signior.
The Duke's in council, and your noble self
I am sure is sent for.

Brabantio.   How? The Duke in council?
In this time of the night? Bring him away.
Mine's not an idle cause. The Duke himself,
95   Or any of my brothers° of the state,
Cannot but feel this wrong as 'twere their own;
For if such actions may have passage free,
Bondslaves and pagans shall our statesmen be.

                                        Exeunt.

Scene 3. [*A council chamber.*]

*Enter Duke, Senators, and Officers [set at a table,
with lights and Attendants].*

Duke. There's no composition° in this news
That gives them credit.°

First Senator.   Indeed, they are disproportioned.
My letters say a hundred and seven galleys.

Duke. And mine a hundred forty.

Second Senator.   And mine two hundred.
5   But though they jump° not on a just accompt°—
As in these cases where the aim°. reports
'Tis oft with difference—yet do they all confirm
A Turkish fleet, and bearing up to Cyprus.

Duke. Nay, it is possible enough to judgment.°
10   I do not so secure me in the error,

89 **present** immediate   95 **brothers** i.e., the other senators   1.3.1 **composition** agreement   2 **gives them credit** makes them believable   5 **jump** agree   5 **just accompt** exact counting   6 **aim** approximation   9 **to judgment** when carefully considered

But the main article I do approve
In fearful sense.°

Sailor. (*Within*) What, ho! What, ho! What, ho!

Enter Sailor.

Officer. A messenger from the galleys.
Duke.   Now? What's the business?
Sailor. The Turkish preparation makes for Rhodes.
So was I bid report here to the State   15
By Signior Angelo.
Duke. How say you by this change?
First Senator.   This cannot be
By no assay of reason. 'Tis a pageant°
To keep us in false gaze.° When we consider
Th' importancy of Cyprus to the Turk,   20
And let ourselves again but understand
That, as it more concerns the Turk than Rhodes,
So may he with more facile question° bear it,
For that it stands not in such warlike brace,°
But altogether lacks th' abilities   25
That Rhodes is dressed in. If we make thought of
   this,
We must not think the Turk is so unskillful
To leave that latest which concerns him first,
Neglecting an attempt of ease and gain
To wake and wage a danger profitless.   30
Duke. Nay, in all confidence he's not for Rhodes.
Officer. Here is more news.

Enter a Messenger.

Messenger. The Ottomites, reverend and gracious,
Steering with due course toward the isle of Rhodes,
Have there injointed them with an after° fleet.   35

10–12 **I do . . . sense** i.e., just because the numbers disagree in the reports, I do not doubt that the principal information (that the Turkish fleet is out) is fearfully true   18 **pageant** show, pretense   19 **in false gaze** looking the wrong way   23 **facile question** easy struggle   24 **warlike brace** "military posture"   35 **after** following

First Senator. Ay, so I thought. How many, as you
    guess?

Messenger. Of thirty sail; and now they do restem
    Their backward course, bearing with frank ap-
    pearance
    Their purposes toward Cyprus. Signior Montano,
40   Your trusty and most valiant servitor,
    With his free duty° recommends° you thus,
    And prays you to believe him.

Duke. 'Tis certain then for Cyprus.
    Marcus Luccicos, is not he in town?

45 *First Senator.* He's now in Florence.

Duke. Write from us to him; post-posthaste dispatch.

First Senator. Here comes Brabantio and the valiant
    Moor.

Enter Brabantio, Othello, Cassio, Iago, Roderigo,
and Officers.

Duke. Valiant Othello, we must straight° employ you
    Against the general° enemy Ottoman.
    [*To Brabantio*] I did not see you. Welcome, gentle
50   signior.
    We lacked your counsel and your help tonight.

Brabantio. So did I yours. Good your grace, pardon
    me.
    Neither my place, nor aught I heard of business,
    Hath raised me from my bed; nor doth the general
    care
55   Take hold on me; for my particular grief
    Is of so floodgate and o'erbearing nature
    That it engluts and swallows other sorrows,
    And it is still itself.

Duke.   Why, what's the matter?

Brabantio. My daughter! O, my daughter!

41 **free duty** unlimited respect 41 **recommends** informs 48 **straight** at
once 49 **general** universal

Senators.   Dead?

Brabantio.   Ay, to me.
   She is abused, stol'n from me, and corrupted   60
   By spells and medicines bought of mountebanks;
   For nature so prepost'rously to err,
   Being not deficient, blind, or lame of sense,
   Sans° witchcraft could not.

Duke. Whoe'er he be that in this foul proceeding   65
   Hath thus beguiled your daughter of herself,
   And you of her, the bloody book of law
   You shall yourself read in the bitter letter
   After your own sense; yea, though our proper° son
   Stood in your action.°

Brabantio.   Humbly I thank your Grace.   70
   Here is the man—this Moor, whom now, it seems,
   Your special mandate for the state affairs
   Hath hither brought.

All.   We are very sorry for't.

Duke. [*To Othello*] What in your own part can you
   say to this?

Brabantio. Nothing, but this is so.   75

Othello. Most potent, grave, and reverend signiors,
   My very noble and approved° good masters,
   That I have ta'en away this old man's daughter,
   It is most true; true I have married her.
   The very head and front° of my offending   80
   Hath this extent, no more. Rude am I in my speech,
   And little blessed with the soft phrase of peace,
   For since these arms of mine had seven years' pith°
   Till now some nine moons wasted,° they have used
   Their dearest° action in the tented field;   85
   And little of this great world can I speak

64 **Sans** without 69 **proper** own 70 **Stood in your action** were the accused in your suit 77 **approved** tested, proven by past performance 80
head and front extreme form (*front* = forehead) 83 **pith** strength 84
wasted past 85 **dearest** most important

More than pertains to feats of broils and battle;
And therefore little shall I grace my cause
In speaking for myself. Yet, by your gracious
   patience,
90   I will a round° unvarnished tale deliver
Of my whole course of love—what drugs, what
   charms,
What conjuration, and what mighty magic,
For such proceeding I am charged withal,
I won his daughter—

Brabantio.   A maiden never bold,
95   Of spirit so still and quiet that her motion
Blushed at herself;° and she, in spite of nature,
Of years, of country, credit, everything,
To fall in love with what she feared to look on!
It is a judgment maimed and most imperfect
100 That will confess perfection so could err
Against all rules of nature, and must be driven
To find out practices of cunning hell
Why this should be. I therefore vouch again
That with some mixtures pow'rful o'er the blood,
105 Or with some dram, conjured to this effect,
He wrought upon her.

Duke.   To vouch this is no proof,
Without more wider and more overt test
Than these thin habits° and poor likelihoods
Of modern° seeming do prefer against him.

110 *First Senator.* But, Othello, speak.
Did you by indirect and forcèd courses
Subdue and poison this young maid's affections?
Or came it by request, and such fair question°
As soul to soul affordeth?

Othello.   I do beseech you,
115 Send for the lady to the Sagittary

---

90 **round** blunt   95–96 **her motion/Blushed at herself** i.e., she was so modest that she blushed at every thought (and movement)   108 **habits** clothing   109 **modern** trivial   113 **question** discussion

And let her speak of me before her father.
If you do find me foul in her report,
The trust, the office, I do hold of you
Not only take away, but let your sentence
Even fall upon my life.

Duke.   Fetch Desdemona hither.   *120*

Othello. Ancient, conduct them; you best know the
   place.

        [*Exit Iago, with two or three Attendants.*]

And till she come, as truly as to heaven
I do confess the vices of my blood,
So justly to your grave ears I'll present
How I did thrive in this fair lady's love,   *125*
And she in mine.

Duke.   Say it, Othello.

Othello. Her father loved me; oft invited me;
   Still° questioned me the story of my life
   From year to year, the battle, sieges, fortune
   That I have passed.   *130*
   I ran it through, even from my boyish days
   To th' very moment that he bade me tell it.
   Wherein I spoke of most disastrous chances,
   Of moving accidents by flood and field,
   Of hairbreadth scapes i' th' imminent° deadly
      breach,   *135*
   Of being taken by the insolent foe
   And sold to slavery, of my redemption thence
   And portance° in my travel's history,
   Wherein of anters° vast and deserts idle,°
   Rough quarries, rocks, and hills whose heads touch
      heaven,   *140*
   It was my hint to speak. Such was my process.
   And of the Cannibals that each other eat,
   The Anthropophagi,° and men whose heads

128 **Still** regularly   135 **imminent** threatening   138 **portance** manner of
acting   139 **anters** caves   139 **idle** empty, sterile   143 **Anthropophagi**
man-eaters

Grew beneath their shoulders. These things to hear
145 Would Desdemona seriously incline;
But still the house affairs would draw her thence;
Which ever as she could with haste dispatch,
She'd come again, and with a greedy ear
Devour up my discourse. Which I observing,
150 Took once a pliant hour, and found good means
To draw from her a prayer of earnest heart
That I would all my pilgrimage dilate,°
Whereof by parcels she had something heard,
But not intentively.° I did consent,
155 And often did beguile her of her tears
When I did speak of some distressful stroke
That my youth suffered. My story being done,
She gave me for my pains a world of kisses.
She swore in faith 'twas strange, 'twas passing°
      strange;
160 'Twas pitiful, 'twas wondrous pitiful.
She wished she had not heard it; yet she wished
That heaven had made her such a man. She thanked
      me,
And bade me, if I had a friend that loved her,
I should but teach him how to tell my story,
165 And that would woo her. Upon this hint I spake.
She loved me for the dangers I had passed,
And I loved her that she did pity them.
This only is the witchcraft I have used.
Here comes the lady. Let her witness it.

Enter Desdemona, Iago, Attendants.

170 *Duke.* I think this tale would win my daughter too.
Good Brabantio, take up this mangled matter at the
      best.°
Men do their broken weapons rather use
Than their bare hands.

152 **dilate** relate in full   154 **intentively** at length and in sequence   159
passing surpassing   171 **Take . . . best** i.e., make the best of this disaster

Brabantio.   I pray you hear her speak.
　　If she confess that she was half the wooer,
　　Destruction on my head if my bad blame   175
　　Light on the man. Come hither, gentle mistress.
　　Do you perceive in all this noble company
　　Where most you owe obedience?

Desdemona.   My noble father,
　　I do perceive here a divided duty.
　　To you I am bound for life and education;   180
　　My life and education both do learn me
　　How to respect you. You are the lord of duty,
　　I am hitherto your daughter. But here's my husband,
　　And so much duty as my mother showed
　　To you, preferring you before her father,   185
　　So much I challenge° that I may profess
　　Due to the Moor my lord.

Brabantio.   God be with you. I have done.
　　Please it your Grace, on to the state affairs.
　　I had rather to adopt a child than get° it.
　　Come hither, Moor.   190
　　I here do give thee that with all my heart
　　Which, but thou hast already, with all my heart
　　I would keep from thee. For your sake,° jewel,
　　I am glad at soul I have no other child,
　　For thy escape would teach me tyranny,   195
　　To hang clogs on them. I have done, my lord.

Duke. Let me speak like yourself and lay a sentence°
　　Which, as a grise° or step, may help these lovers.
　　When remedies are past, the griefs are ended
　　By seeing the worst, which late on hopes depended.°   200
　　To mourn a mischief that is past and gone
　　Is the next° way to draw new mischief on.
　　What cannot be preserved when fortune takes,

---

186 **challenge** claim as right   189 **get** beget   193 **For your sake** because
of you   197 **lay a sentence** provide a maxim   198 **grise** step   200 **late on
hopes depended** was supported by hope (of a better outcome) until lately
202 **next** closest, surest

      Patience her injury a mock'ry makes.
      The robbed that smiles, steals something from the
205   thief;
      He robs himself that spends a bootless° grief.

  Brabantio. So let the Turk of Cyprus us beguile:
      We lose it not so long as we can smile.
      He bears the sentence well that nothing bears
210   But the free comfort which from thence he hears;
      But he bears both the sentence and the sorrow
      That to pay grief must of poor patience borrow.
      These sentences, to sugar, or to gall,
      Being strong on both sides, are equivocal.
215   But words are words. I never yet did hear
      That the bruisèd heart was piercèd° through the ear.
      I humbly beseech you, proceed to th' affairs of state.

  Duke. The Turk with a most mighty preparation makes
      for Cyprus. Othello, the fortitude° of the place is
220   best known to you; and though we have there a
      substitute° of most allowed sufficiency,° yet opin-
      ion, a more sovereign mistress of effects, throws a
      more safer voice on you.° You must therefore be
      content to slubber° the gloss of your new fortunes
225   with this more stubborn and boisterous° expedition.

  Othello. The tyrant Custom, most grave senators,
      Hath made the flinty and steel couch of war
      My thrice-driven° bed of down. I do agnize°
      A natural and prompt alacrity
230   I find in hardness and do undertake
      This present wars against the Ottomites.

206 **bootless** valueless 216 **piercèd** (some editors emend to *pieced,* i.e.,
healed." But *pierced* makes good sense: Brabantio is saying in effect that his
heart cannot be further hurt [pierced] by the indignity of the useless, conventional advice the Duke offers him. *Pierced* can also mean, however, "lanced"
in the medical sense, and would then mean "treated") 219 **fortitude** fortification 221 **substitute** viceroy 221 **most allowed sufficiency** generally
acknowledged capability 221–23 **opinion . . . you** i.e., the general opinion,
which finally controls affairs, is that you would be the best man in this situation 224 **slubber** besmear 225 **stubborn and boisterous** rough and violent 228 **thrice-driven** i.e., softest 228 **agnize** know in myself

Most humbly, therefore, bending to your state,
I crave fit disposition for my wife,
Due reference of place, and exhibition,°
With such accommodation and besort   *235*
As levels with° her breeding.

Duke.   Why, at her father's.

Brabantio. I will not have it so.

Othello.   Nor I.

Desdemona.   Nor would I there reside,
To put my father in impatient thoughts
By being in his eye. Most gracious Duke,
To my unfolding° lend your prosperous° ear,   *240*
And let me find a charter° in your voice,
T' assist my simpleness.

Duke.   What would you, Desdemona?

Desdemona. That I love the Moor to live with him,
My downright violence, and storm of fortunes,
May trumpet to the world. My heart's subdued   *245*
Even to the very quality of my lord.°
I saw Othello's visage in his mind,
And to his honors and his valiant parts
Did I my soul and fortunes consecrate.
So that, dear lords, if I be left behind,   *250*
A moth of peace, and he go to the war,
The rites° for why I love him are bereft me,
And I a heavy interim shall support
By his dear absence. Let me go with him.

Othello. Let her have your voice.°   *255*
Vouch with me, heaven, I therefore beg it not
To please the palate of my appetite,
Nor to comply with heat°—the young affects°

234 **exhibition** grant of funds   236 **levels with** is suitable to   240 **unfold-ing** explanation   240 **prosperous** favoring   241 **charter** permission 245–46 **My . . . lord** i.e., I have become one in nature and being with the man I married (therefore, I too would go to the wars like a soldier)   252 **rites** (may refer either to the marriage rites or to the rites, formalities, of war)   255 **voice** consent   258 **heat** lust   258 **affects** passions

In me defunct—and proper satisfaction;°
260 But to be free and bounteous to her mind;
And heaven defend° your good souls that you think
I will your serious and great business scant
When she is with me. No, when light-winged toys
Of feathered Cupid seel° with wanton° dullness
265 My speculative and officed instrument,°
That my disports corrupt and taint my business,
Let housewives make a skillet of my helm,
And all indign° and base adversities
Make head° against my estimation!°—

270 *Duke.* Be it as you shall privately determine,
Either for her stay or going. Th' affair cries haste,
And speed must answer it.

First Senator.   You must away tonight.

Othello. With all my heart.

Duke. At nine i' th' morning here we'll meet again
275 Othello, leave some officer behind,
And he shall our commission bring to you,
And such things else of quality and respect
As doth import you.

Othello.   So please your grace, my ancient;
A man he is of honesty and trust.
280 To his conveyance I assign my wife,
With what else needful your good grace shall think
To be sent after me.

Duke.   Let it be so.
Good night to every one. [*To Brabantio*] And, noble
signior,
If virtue no delighted° beauty lack,
285 Your son-in-law is far more fair than black.

First Senator. Adieu, brave Moor. Use Desdemona
well.

259 **proper satisfaction** i.e., consummation of the marriage 261 **defend** forbid 264 **seel** sew up 264 **wanton** lascivious 265 **speculative . . . instrument** i.e., sight (and, by extension, the mind) 268 **indign** unworthy 269 **Make head** form an army, i.e., attack 269 **estimation** reputation 284 **delighted** delightful

Brabantio. Look to her, Moor, if thou hast eyes to see:
   She has deceived her father, and may thee.

            [*Exeunt Duke, Senators, Officers, &c.*]

Othello. My life upon her faith! Honest Iago,
   My Desdemona must I leave to thee.   290
   I prithee let thy wife attend on her,
   And bring them after in the best advantage.°
   Come, Desdemona. I have but an hour
   Of love, of worldly matter, and direction
   To spend with thee. We must obey the time.   295

                  Exit [*Moor with Desdemona*].

Roderigo. Iago?

Iago. What say'st thou, noble heart?

Roderigo. What will I do, think'st thou?

Iago. Why, go to bed and sleep.

Roderigo. I will incontinently° drown myself.   300

Iago. If thou dost, I shall never love thee after. Why,
   thou silly gentleman?

Roderigo. It is silliness to live when to live is torment;
   and then have we a prescription to die when death is
   our physician.   305

Iago. O villainous! I have looked upon the world for
   four times seven years, and since I could distinguish
   betwixt a benefit and an injury, I never found man
   that knew how to love himself. Ere I would say I
   would drown myself for the love of a guinea hen,   310
   I would change my humanity with a baboon.

Roderigo. What should I do? I confess it is my shame
   to be so fond, but it is not in my virtue° to amend it.

Iago. Virtue? A fig! 'Tis in ourselves that we are thus,
   or thus. Our bodies are our gardens, to the which   315
   our wills are gardeners; so that if we will plant
   nettles or sow lettuce, set hyssop and weed up thyme,

292 **advantage** opportunity   300 **incontinently** at once   313 **virtue** strength
(Roderigo is saying that his nature controls him)

supply it with one gender of herbs or distract° it with
many—either to have it sterile with idleness or
320   manured with industry—why, the power and corri-
gible° authority of this lies in our wills. If the balance of our lives had not one scale of reason to poise
another of sensuality, the blood and baseness of
our natures would conduct us to most prepost'rous
325   conclusions.° But we have reason to cool our raging
motions, our carnal stings or unbitted° lusts,
whereof I take this that you call love to be a sect
or scion.°

    Roderigo. It cannot be.

330 *Iago.* It is merely a lust of the blood and a permission of
the will. Come, be a man! Drown thyself? Drown
cats and blind puppies! I have professed me thy
friend, and I confess me knit to thy deserving with
cables of perdurable toughness. I could never better
335   stead° thee than now. Put money in thy purse.
Follow thou the wars; defeat thy favor° with an
usurped° beard. I say, put money in thy purse.
It cannot be long that Desdemona should continue
her love to the Moor. Put money in thy purse. Nor
340   he his to her. It was a violent commencement in
her and thou shalt see an answerable° sequestra-
tion—put but money in thy purse. These Moors
are changeable in their wills—fill thy purse with
money. The food that to him now is as luscious as
345   locusts° shall be to him shortly as bitter as coloquintida.° She must change for youth; when she is
sated with his body, she will find the errors of her
choice. Therefore, put money in thy purse. If thou
wilt needs damn thyself, do it a more delicate way
350   than drowning. Make all the money thou canst. If

318 **distract** vary   320–21 **corrigible** corrective   325 **conclusions** ends
326 **unbitted** i.e., uncontrolled   327–28 **sect or scion** offshoot   335 **stead**
serve   336 **defeat thy favor** disguise your face   337 **usurped** assumed
341 **answerable** similar   345 **locusts** (a sweet fruit)   345–46 **coloquintida**
(a purgative derived from a bitter apple)

sanctimony° and a frail vow betwixt an erring°
barbarian and supersubtle Venetian be not too hard
for my wits, and all the tribe of hell, thou shalt enjoy
her. Therefore, make money. A pox of drowning
thyself, it is clean out of the way. Seek thou rather   *355*
to be hanged in compassing° thy joy than to be
drowned and go without her.

Roderigo. Wilt thou be fast to my hopes, if I depend
on the issue?

Iago. Thou art sure of me. Go, make money. I have   *360*
told thee often, and I retell thee again and again, I
hate the Moor. My cause is hearted;° thine hath no
less reason. Let us be conjunctive° in our revenge
against him. If thou canst cuckold him, thou dost
thyself a pleasure, me a sport. There are many   *365*
events in the womb of time, which will be delivered.
Traverse, go, provide thy money! We will have more
of this tomorrow. Adieu.

Roderigo. Where shall we meet i' th' morning?

Iago. At my lodging.   *370*

Roderigo. I'll be with thee betimes.

Iago. Go to, farewell. Do you hear, Roderigo?

Roderigo. I'll sell all my land.   *Exit.*

Iago. Thus do I ever make my fool my purse;
For I mine own gained knowledge° should profane   *375*
If I would time expend with such snipe
But for my sport and profit. I hate the Moor,
And it is thought abroad that 'twixt my sheets
H'as done my office. I know not if't be true,
But I, for mere suspicion in that kind,   *380*
Will do, as if for surety.° He holds me well;
The better shall my purpose work on him.

351 **sanctimony** sacred bond (of marriage) 351 **erring** wandering 356
compassing encompassing, achieving 362 **hearted** deep-seated in the heart
363 **conjunctive** joined 375 **gained knowledge** i.e., practical, worldly wisdom 381 **surety** certainty

Cassio's a proper° man. Let me see now:
To get his place, and to plume up my will°
385   In double knavery. How? How? Let's see.
After some time, to abuse Othello's ears
That he is too familiar with his wife.
He hath a person and a smooth dispose°
To be suspected—framed° to make women false.
390   The Moor is of a free and open nature
That thinks men honest that but seem to be so;
And will as tenderly be led by th' nose
As asses are.
I have't! It is engendered! Hell and night
395   Must bring this monstrous birth to the world's light.
                                        [*Exit.*]

383 **proper** handsome   384 **plume up my will** (many explanations have
been offered for this crucial line, which in Q1 reads "make up my will." The
general sense is something like "to make more proud and gratify my ego")
388 **dispose** manner   389 **framed** designed

ACT 2

Scene 1. [*Cyprus.*]

Enter Montano and two Gentlemen, [one above].°

Montano. What from the cape can you discern at sea?

First Gentleman. Nothing at all, it is a high-wrought
    flood.
  I cannot 'twixt the heaven and the main
  Descry a sail.

Montano. Methinks the wind hath spoke aloud at land;   *5*
  A fuller blast ne'er shook our battlements.
  If it hath ruffianed so upon the sea,
  What ribs of oak, when mountains melt on them,
  Can hold the mortise? What shall we hear of this?

Second Gentleman. A segregation° of the Turkish
    fleet.   *10*
  For do but stand upon the foaming shore,
  The chidden billow seems to pelt the clouds;
  The wind-shaked surge, with high and monstrous
    main,°
  Seems to cast water on the burning Bear
  And quench the guards of th' ever-fixèd pole.°   *15*

2.1. s.d. (the Folio arrangement of this scene requires that the First Gentleman
stand above—on the upper stage—and act as a lookout reporting sights which
cannot be seen by Montano standing below on the main stage)   10 **segrega-
tion** separation   13 **main** (both "ocean" and "strength")   14–15 **Seems . . .
pole** (the constellation Ursa Minor contains two stars which are the *guards,* or
companions, of the *pole,* or North Star)

I never did like molestation view
On the enchafèd flood.

Montano.   If that the Turkish fleet
Be not ensheltered and embayed, they are drowned;
It is impossible to bear it out.

Enter a [third] Gentleman.

20 *Third Gentleman.* News, lads! Our wars are done.
The desperate tempest hath so banged the Turks
That their designment halts. A noble ship of Venice
Hath seen a grievous wrack and sufferance°
On most part of their fleet.

Montano. How? Is this true?

25 *Third Gentleman.*   The ship is here put in,
A Veronesa; Michael Cassio,
Lieutenant to the warlike Moor Othello,
Is come on shore; the Moor himself at sea,
And is in full commission here for Cyprus.

30 *Montano.* I am glad on't. 'Tis a worthy governor.

Third Gentleman. But this same Cassio, though he
    speak of comfort
Touching the Turkish loss, yet he looks sadly
And prays the Moor be safe, for they were parted
With foul and violent tempest.

Montano.   Pray heavens he be;
35 For I have served him, and the man commands
Like a full soldier. Let's to the seaside, ho!
As well to see the vessel that's come in
As to throw out our eyes for brave Othello,
Even till we make the main and th' aerial blue
An indistinct regard.°

40 *Third Gentleman.*   Come, let's do so;
For every minute is expectancy
Of more arrivancie.°

23 **sufferance** damage   39–40 **the main . . . regard** i.e., the sea and sky become indistinguishable   42 **arrivancie** arrivals

Enter Cassio.

Cassio. Thanks, you the valiant of the warlike isle,
    That so approve° the Moor. O, let the heavens
    Give him defense against the elements,   45
    For I have lost him on a dangerous sea.

Montano. Is he well shipped?

Cassio. His bark is stoutly timbered, and his pilot
    Of very expert and approved allowance;°
    Therefore my hopes, not surfeited to death,°   50
    Stand in bold cure.° (*Within*) A sail, a sail, a sail!

Cassio. What noise?

First Gentleman. The town is empty; on the brow o'
    th' sea
    Stand ranks of people, and they cry, "A sail!"

Cassio. My hopes do shape him for the governor.   55

                                  [*A shot.*]

Second Gentleman. They do discharge their shot of
    courtesy:
    Our friends at least.

Cassio.   I pray you, sir, go forth
    And give us truth who 'tis that is arrived.

Second Gentleman. I shall.   *Exit.*

Montano. But, good lieutenant, is your general wived?   60

Cassio. Most fortunately. He hath achieved a maid
    That paragons° description and wild fame;°
    One that excels the quirks of blazoning pens,°
    And in th' essential vesture of creation°
    Does tire the ingener.°

---

44 **approve** ("honor" or, perhaps, "are as warlike and valiant as your governor") 49 **approved allowance** known and tested 50 **not surfeited to death** i.e., not so great as to be in danger 51 **Stand in bold cure** i.e., are likely to be restored 62 **paragons** exceeds 62 **wild fame** extravagant report 63 **quirks of blazoning pens** ingenuities of praising pens 64 **essential vesture of creation** i.e., essential human nature as given by the Creator 65 **tire the ingener** (a difficult line which probably means something like "outdo the human ability to imagine and picture")

Enter [Second] Gentleman.

65   How now? Who has put in?

Second Gentleman. 'Tis one Iago, ancient to the
    general.

Cassio. H'as had most favorable and happy speed:
    Tempests themselves, high seas, and howling winds,
    The guttered° rocks and congregated° sands,
70   Traitors ensteeped° to enclog the guiltless keel,
    As having sense° of beauty, do omit
    Their mortal° natures, letting go safely by
    The divine Desdemona.

Montano.   What is she?

Cassio. She that I spake of, our great captain's captain,
75   Left in the conduct of the bold Iago,
    Whose footing° here anticipates our thoughts
    A se'nnight's° speed. Great Jove, Othello guard,
    And swell his sail with thine own pow'rful breath,
    That he may bless this bay with his tall° ship,
80   Make love's quick pants in Desdemona's arms,
    Give renewed fire to our extinct spirits.

Enter Desdemona, Iago, Roderigo, and Emilia.

    O, behold! The riches of the ship is come on shore!
    You men of Cyprus, let her have your knees.
                                    [*Kneeling.*]
    Hail to thee, lady! and the grace of heaven,
85   Before, behind thee, and on every hand,
    Enwheel thee round.

Desdemona.   I thank you, valiant Cassio.
    What tidings can you tell of my lord?

Cassio. He is not yet arrived, nor know I aught
    But that he's well and will be shortly here.

90 *Desdemona.* O but I fear. How lost you company?

69 **guttered** jagged   69 **congregated** gathered   70 **ensteeped** submerged
71 **sense** awareness   72 **mortal** deadly   76 **footing** landing   77 **se'nnight's**
week's   79 **tall** brave

Cassio. The great contention of sea and skies
  Parted our fellowship. (*Within*) A sail, a sail!
    [*A shot.*]

                          But hark. A sail!

Second Gentleman. They give this greeting to the
    citadel;
  This likewise is a friend.

Cassio.   See for the news.   *95*

                          [*Exit Gentleman.*]
  Good ancient, you are welcome. [*To Emilia*] Wel-
    come, mistress.
  Let it not gall your patience, good Iago,
  That I extend° my manners. 'Tis my breeding°
  That gives me this bold show of courtesy. [*Kisses
    Emilia.*]

Iago. Sir, would she give you so much of her lips   *100*
  As of her tongue she oft bestows on me,
  You would have enough.

Desdemona.   Alas, she has no speech.

Iago. In faith, too much.
  I find it still when I have leave to sleep.°
  Marry, before your ladyship,° I grant,   *105*
  She puts her tongue a little in her heart
  And chides with thinking.

Emilia.   You have little cause to say so.

Iago. Come on, come on! You are pictures° out of
    door,
  Bells in your parlors, wildcats in your kitchens,
  Saints in your injuries,° devils being offended,   *110*

___

98 **extend** stretch   98 **breeding** careful training in manners (Cassio is considerably more the polished gentleman than Iago, and aware of it)   104 **still
. . . sleep** i.e., even when she allows me to sleep she continues to scold   105
before your ladyship in your presence   108 **pictures** models (of virtue)
110 **in your injuries** when you injure others

Players in your housewifery,° and housewives in
your beds.

Desdemona. O, fie upon thee, slanderer!

Iago. Nay, it is true, or else I am a Turk:
You rise to play, and go to bed to work.

Emilia. You shall not write my praise.

115 *Iago.*   No, let me not.

Desdemona. What wouldst write of me, if thou shouldst
praise me?

Iago. O gentle lady, do not put me to't,
For I am nothing if not critical.

Desdemona. Come on, assay. There's one gone to the
harbor?

Iago. Ay, madam.

120 *Desdemona.* [*Aside*] I am not merry; but I do beguile
The thing I am by seeming otherwise.—
Come, how wouldst thou praise me?

Iago. I am about it; but indeed my invention
Comes from my pate as birdlime° does from
frieze°—
125 It plucks out brains and all. But my Muse labors,
And thus she is delivered:
If she be fair° and wise: fairness and wit,
The one's for use, the other useth it.

Desdemona. Well praised. How if she be black° and
witty?

130 *Iago.* If she be black, and thereto have a wit,
She'll find a white that shall her blackness fit.

Desdemona. Worse and worse!

111 **housewifery** (this word can mean "careful, economical household management," and Iago would then be accusing women of only pretending to be
good housekeepers, while in bed they are either [1] economical of their favors,
or more likely [2] serious and dedicated workers)   124 **birdlime** a sticky
substance put on branches to catch birds   124 **frieze** rough cloth   127 **fair**
light-complexioned   129 **black** brunette

Emilia. How if fair and foolish?

Iago. She never yet was foolish that was fair,
    For even her folly helped her to an heir.   *135*

Desdemona. These are old fond° paradoxes to make
    fools laugh i' th' alehouse. What miserable praise
    hast thou for her that's foul and foolish?

Iago. There's none so foul, and foolish thereunto,
    But does foul pranks which fair and wise ones do.   *140*

Desdemona. O heavy ignorance. Thou praisest the
    worst best. But what praise couldst thou bestow on
    a deserving woman indeed—one that in the author-
    ity of her merit did justly put on the vouch of very
    malice itself?°   *145*

Iago. She that was ever fair, and never proud;
    Had tongue at will, and yet was never loud;
    Never lacked gold, and yet went never gay;
    Fled from her wish, and yet said "Now I may";
    She that being angered, her revenge being nigh,   *150*
    Bade her wrong stay, and her displeasure fly;
    She that in wisdom never was so frail
    To change the cod's head for the salmon's tail;°
    She that could think, and nev'r disclose her mind;
    See suitors following, and not look behind: *155*
    She was a wight° (if ever such wights were)—

Desdemona. To do what?

Iago. To suckle fools and chronicle small beer.°

Desdemona. O most lame and impotent conclusion.
    Do not learn of him, Emilia, though he be thy hus-   *160*
    band. How say you, Cassio? Is he not a most profane
    and liberal° counselor?

---

136 **fond** foolish   143–45 **one ... itself** i.e., a woman so honest and deserving that even malice would be forced to approve of her   153 **To ... tail** i.e.,
to exchange something valuable for something useless   156 **wight** person
158 **chronicle small beer** i.e., keep household accounts (the most trivial of
occupations in Iago's opinion)   162 **liberal** licentious

Cassio. He speaks home,° madam. You may relish
      him more in° the soldier than in the scholar. [*Takes*
      Desdemona's hand.]

165 *Iago.* [*Aside*] He takes her by the palm. Ay, well said,
      whisper! With as little a web as this will I ensnare
      as great a fly as Cassio. Ay, smile upon her, do! I
      will gyve° thee in thine own courtship.—You say
      true; 'tis so, indeed!—If such tricks as these strip
170   you out of your lieutenantry, it had been better you
      had not kissed your three fingers so oft—which now
      again you are most apt to play the sir° in. Very
      good! Well kissed! An excellent curtsy!° 'Tis so,
      indeed. Yet again your fingers to your lips? Would
175   they were clyster pipes° for your sake! [*Trumpets*
      within.] The Moor! I know his trumpet.°

Cassio. 'Tis truly so.

Desdemona. Let's meet him and receive him.

Cassio. Lo, where he comes.

      Enter Othello and Attendants.

Othello. O my fair warrior!

180 *Desdemona.*   My dear Othello.

Othello. It gives me wonder great as my content
      To see you here before me. O my soul's joy!
      If after every tempest come such calms,
      May the winds blow till they have wakened death.
185   And let the laboring bark climb hills of seas
      Olympus-high, and duck again as low
      As hell's from heaven. If it were now to die,
      'Twere now to be most happy; for I fear
      My soul hath her content so absolute
190   That not another comfort like to this
      Succeeds in unknown fate.

163 **speaks home** thrusts deeply with his speech   163–64 **relish him more
in** enjoy him more as   168 **gyve** bind   172 **the sir** the fashionable gentleman   173 **curtsy** courtesy, i.e., bow   175 **clyster pipes** enema tubes   176
his trumpet (great men had their own distinctive calls)

Desdemona.   The heavens forbid
    But that our loves and comforts should increase
    Even as our days do grow.

Othello.   Amen to that, sweet powers!
    I cannot speak enough of this content;
    It stops me here [*touches his heart*]; it is too much
        of joy.   *195*
    And this, and this, the greatest discords be
                                            [*They kiss.*]
    That e'er our hearts shall make!

Iago.   [*Aside*] O, you are well tuned now!
    But I'll set down the pegs° that make this music,
    As honest as I am.

Othello.   Come, let us to the castle.
    News, friends! Our wars are done; the Turks are
        drowned.   *200*
    How does my old acquaintance of this isle?
    Honey, you shall be well desired in Cyprus;
    I have found great love amongst them. O my sweet,
    I prattle out of fashion, and I dote
    In mine own comforts. I prithee, good Iago,   *205*
    Go to the bay and disembark my coffers.
    Bring thou the master to the citadel;
    He is a good one, and his worthiness
    Does challenge° much respect. Come, Desdemona,
    Once more well met at Cyprus.   *210*
        *Exit Othello and Desdemona [and all but Iago and
                                            Roderigo].*

Iago. [*To an Attendant*] Do thou meet me presently
    at the harbor. [*To Roderigo*] Come hither. If thou
    be'st valiant (as they say base men being in love
    have then a nobility in their natures more than is
    native to them), list me. The lieutenant tonight   *215*
    watches on the court of guard.° First, I must tell thee
    this: Desdemona is directly in love with him.

Roderigo. With him? Why, 'tis not possible.

198 **set down the pegs** loosen the strings (to produce discord)   209 **challenge** require, exact   216 **court of guard** guardhouse

Iago. Lay thy finger thus [*puts his finger to his lips*],
220 and let thy soul be instructed. Mark me with what
violence she first loved the Moor but for bragging
and telling her fantastical lies. To love him still for
prating? Let not thy discreet heart think it. Her
eye must be fed. And what delight shall she have to
225 look on the devil? When the blood is made dull with
the act of sport, there should be a game° to inflame
it and to give satiety a fresh appetite, loveliness in
favor,° sympathy in years,° manners, and beauties;
all which the Moor is defective in. Now for want of
230 these required conveniences,° her delicate tenderness will find itself abused, begin to heave the
gorge,° disrelish and abhor the Moor. Very nature
will instruct her in it and compel her to some second
choice. Now, sir, this granted—as it is a most preg-
235 nant° and unforced position—who stands so emi-
nent in the degree of this fortune as Cassio does?
A knave very voluble; no further conscionable°
than in putting on the mere form of civil and hu-
mane° seeming for the better compass of his salt°
240 and most hidden loose° affection. Why, none! Why,
none! A slipper° and subtle knave, a finder of
occasion, that has an eye can stamp and counterfeit
advantages, though true advantage never present
itself. A devilish knave. Besides, the knave is hand-
245 some, young, and hath all those requisites in him
that folly and green minds look after. A pestilent
complete knave, and the woman hath found him
already.

Roderigo. I cannot believe that in her; she's full of
250 most blessed condition.

Iago. Blessed fig's-end! The wine she drinks is made of
grapes. If she had been blessed, she would never

226 **game** sport (with the added sense of "gamey," "rank") 228 **favor**
countenance, appearance 228 **sympathy in years** sameness of age 230
conveniences advantages 231–32 **heave the gorge** vomit 234–35 **pregnant**
likely 237 **no further conscionable** having no more conscience 238–39
humane polite 239 **salt** lecherous 240 **loose** immoral 241 **slipper** slippery

have loved the Moor. Blessed pudding! Didst thou
not see her paddle with the palm of his hand? Didst
not mark that?   255

Roderigo. Yes, that I did; but that was but courtesy.

Iago. Lechery, by this hand! [*Extends his index finger.*]
An index° and obscure prologue to the history of
lust and foul thoughts. They met so near with their
lips that their breaths embraced together. Villainous 260
thoughts, Roderigo. When these mutualities so
marshal the way, hard at hand comes the master and
main exercise, th' incorporate° conclusion: Pish!
But, sir, be you ruled by me. I have brought you
from Venice. Watch you tonight; for the command, 265
I'll lay 't upon you. Cassio knows you not. I'll not be
far from you. Do you find some occasion to anger
Cassio, either by speaking too loud, or tainting°
his discipline, or from what other course you please
which the time shall more favorably minister.   270

Roderigo. Well.

Iago. Sir, he's rash and very sudden in choler,° and
haply may strike at you. Provoke him that he may;
for even out of that will I cause these of Cyprus to
mutiny, whose qualification shall come into no true 275
taste° again but by the displanting of Cassio. So
shall you have a shorter journey to your desires by
the means I shall then have to prefer them; and the
impediment most profitably removed without the
which there were no expectation of our prosperity. 280

Roderigo. I will do this if you can bring it to any
opportunity.

Iago. I warrant thee. Meet me by and by at the citadel.
I must fetch his necessaries ashore. Farewell.

Roderigo. Adieu.   *Exit.* 285

Iago. That Cassio loves her, I do well believe 't;

258 **index** pointer 263 **incorporate** carnal 268 **tainting** discrediting 272
choler anger 275–76 **qualification . . . taste** i.e., appeasement will not be
brought about (wine was "qualified" by adding water)

That she loves him, 'tis apt and of great credit.
The Moor, howbeit that I endure him not,
Is of a constant, loving, noble nature,
290   And I dare think he'll prove to Desdemona
A most dear° husband. Now I do love her too;
Not out of absolute° lust, though peradventure°
I stand accountant for as great a sin,
But partly led to diet° my revenge,
295   For that I do suspect the lusty Moor
Hath leaped into my seat; the thought whereof
Doth, like a poisonous mineral, gnaw my inwards;
And nothing can or shall content my soul
Till I am evened with him, wife for wife.
300   Or failing so, yet that I put the Moor
At least into a jealousy so strong
That judgment cannot cure. Which thing to do,
If this poor trash of Venice, whom I trace°
For his quick hunting, stand the putting on,
305   I'll have our Michael Cassio on the hip,
Abuse him to the Moor in the right garb°
(For I fear Cassio with my nightcap too),
Make the Moor thank me, love me, and reward me
For making him egregiously an ass
310   And practicing upon° his peace and quiet,
Even to madness. 'Tis here, but yet confused:
Knavery's plain face is never seen till used.   *Exit.*

---

291 **dear** expensive   292 **out of absolute** absolutely out of   292 **peradventure** perchance   294 **diet** feed   303 **trace** (most editors emend to "trash," meaning to hang weights on a dog to slow his hunting; but "trace" clearly means something like "put on the trace" or "set on the track")   306 **right garb** i.e., "proper fashion"   310 **practicing upon** scheming to destroy

Scene 2. [*A street.*]

Enter Othello's Herald, with a proclamation.

Herald. It is Othello's pleasure, our noble and valiant
 general, that upon certain tidings now arrived im-
 porting the mere perdition° of the Turkish fleet,
 every man put himself into triumph. Some to dance,
 some to make bonfires, each man to what sport and   5
 revels his addition° leads him. For, besides these
 beneficial news, it is the celebration of his nuptial.
 So much was his pleasure should be proclaimed.
 All offices° are open, and there is full liberty of
 feasting from this present hour of five till the bell   10
 have told eleven. Bless the isle of Cyprus and our
 noble general Othello!   *Exit.*

Scene 3. [*The citadel of Cyprus.*]

Enter Othello, Desdemona, Cassio, and Attendants.

Othello. Good Michael, look you to the guard tonight.
 Let's teach ourselves that honorable stop,
 Not to outsport discretion.

Cassio. Iago hath direction what to do;
 But notwithstanding, with my personal eye   5
 Will I look to't.

Othello.   Iago is most honest.
 Michael, good night. Tomorrow with your earliest
 Let me have speech with you. [*To Desdemona*]
   Come, my dear love,

2.2.3 **mere perdition** absolute destruction   6 **addition** rank   9 **offices**
kitchens and storerooms of food

The purchase made, the fruits are to ensue,
10 That profit's yet to come 'tween me and you.
Good night.
>   *Exit [Othello with Desdemona and Attendants].*

Enter Iago.

Cassio. Welcome, Iago. We must to the watch.

Iago. Not this hour, lieutenant; 'tis not yet ten o' th'
clock. Our general cast° us thus early for the love
15 of his Desdemona; who let us not therefore blame.
He hath not yet made wanton the night with her, and
she is sport for Jove.

Cassio. She's a most exquisite lady.

Iago. And, I'll warrant her, full of game.

20 *Cassio.* Indeed, she's a most fresh and delicate creature.

Iago. What an eye she has! Methinks it sounds a parley
to provocation.

Cassio. An inviting eye; and yet methinks right modest.

Iago. And when she speaks, is it not an alarum° to
25 love?

Cassio. She is indeed perfection.

Iago. Well, happiness to their sheets! Come, lieutenant,
I have a stoup° of wine, and here without are a
brace of Cyprus gallants that would fain have a
30 measure to the health of black Othello.

Cassio. Not tonight, good Iago. I have very poor and
unhappy brains for drinking; I could well wish
courtesy would invent some other custom of entertainment.

35 *Iago.* O, they are our friends. But one cup! I'll drink
for you.

Cassio. I have drunk but one cup tonight, and that was
craftily qualified° too; and behold what innovation

2.3.14 **cast** dismissed   24 **alarum** the call to action, "general quarters"   28
stoup two-quart tankard   38 **qualified** diluted

it makes here. I am unfortunate in the infirmity and
dare not task my weakness with any more.   *40*

Iago. What, man! 'Tis a night of revels, the gallants
desire it.

Cassio. Where are they?

Iago. Here, at the door. I pray you call them in.

Cassio. I'll do't, but it dislikes me.   *Exit.*   *45*

Iago. If I can fasten but one cup upon him
   With that which he hath drunk tonight already,
   He'll be as full of quarrel and offense
   As my young mistress' dog. Now, my sick fool
      Roderigo,
   Whom love hath turned almost the wrong side out,   *50*
   To Desdemona hath tonight caroused
   Potations pottle-deep;° and he's to watch.
   Three else° of Cyprus, noble swelling spirits,
   That hold their honors in a wary distance,°
   The very elements of this warlike isle,   *55*
   Have I tonight flustered with flowing cups,
   And they watch too. Now, 'mongst this flock of
      drunkards
   Am I to put our Cassio in some action
   That may offend the isle. But here they come.

Enter Cassio, Montano, and Gentlemen.

   If consequence do but approve my dream,   *60*
   My boat sails freely, both with wind and stream.

Cassio. 'Fore God, they have given me a rouse° already.

Montano. Good faith, a little one; not past a pint, as
I am a soldier.

Iago. Some wine, ho!   *65*
   [*Sings*] And let me the canakin clink, clink;
            And let me the canakin clink.

52 **pottle-deep** to the bottom of the cup   53 **else** others   54 **hold ... distance** are scrupulous in maintaining their honor   62 **rouse** drink

A soldier's a man;
O man's life's but a span,
70   Why then, let a soldier drink.
    Some wine, boys!

Cassio. 'Fore God, an excellent song!

Iago. I learned it in England, where indeed they are
    most potent in potting. Your Dane, your German,
75   and your swag-bellied° Hollander—Drink, ho!—
    are nothing to your English.

Cassio. Is your Englishman so exquisite° in his drink-
    ing?

Iago. Why, he drinks you with facility your Dane dead
80   drunk; he sweats not to overthrow your Almain; he
    gives your Hollander a vomit ere the next pottle can
    be filled.

Cassio. To the health of our general!

Montano. I am for it, lieutenant, and I'll do you justice.

85 *Iago.* O sweet England!
    [*Sings*] King Stephen was and a worthy peer;
            His breeches cost him but a crown;
            He held them sixpence all too dear,
            With that he called the tailor lown.°
90   He was a wight of high renown,
            And thou art but of low degree:
            'Tis pride that pulls the country down;
            And take thine auld cloak about thee.
    Some wine, ho!

95 *Cassio.* 'Fore God, this is a more exquisite song than
    the other.

Iago. Will you hear't again?

Cassio. No, for I hold him to be unworthy of his place
    that does those things. Well, God's above all; and
100   there be souls must be saved, and there be souls
    must not be saved.

---

75 **swag-bellied** hanging   77 **exquisite** superb   89 **lown** lout

Iago. It's true, good lieutenant.

Cassio. For mine own part—no offense to the general,
    nor any man of quality—I hope to be saved.

Iago. And so do I too, lieutenant.   *105*

Cassio. Ay, but, by your leave, not before me. The lieu-
    tenant is to ·be saved before the ancient. Let's have
    no more of this; let's to our affairs.—God forgive us
    our sins!—Gentlemen, let's look to our business.
    Do not think, gentlemen, I am drunk. This is my   *110*
    ancient; this is my right hand, and this is my left.
    I am not drunk now. I can stand well enough, and
    I speak well enough.

Gentlemen. Excellent well!

Cassio. Why, very well then. You must not think then   *115*
    that I am drunk.   *Exit.*

Montano. To th' platform, masters. Come, let's set
    the watch.

Iago. You see this fellow that is gone before.
    He's a soldier fit to stand by Caesar
    And give direction; and do but see his vice.   *120*
    'Tis to his virtue a just equinox,°
    The one as long as th' other. 'Tis pity of him.
    I fear the trust Othello puts him in,
    On some odd time of his infirmity,
    Will shake this island.

Montano.   But is he often thus?   *125*

Iago. 'Tis evermore his prologue to his sleep:
    He'll watch the horologe a double set°
    If drink rock not his cradle.

Montano.   It were well
    The general were put in mind of it.
    Perhaps he sees it not, or his good nature   *130*
    Prizes the virtue that appears in Cassio
    And looks not on his evils. Is not this true?

121 **just equinox** exact balance (of dark and light)   127 **watch . . . set** stay
awake twice around the clock

Enter Roderigo.

   Iago. [*Aside*] How now, Roderigo?
     I pray you after the lieutenant, go! [*Exit Roderigo.*]
135 *Montano.* And 'tis great pity that the noble Moor
     Should hazard such a place as his own second
     With one of an ingraft° infirmity.
     It were an honest action to say so
     To the Moor.

   Iago.   Not I, for this fair island!
140   I do love Cassio well and would do much
     To cure him of this evil.   (Help! Help! *Within.*)
                     But hark? What noise?

Enter Cassio, pursuing Roderigo.

   Cassio. Zounds, you rogue! You rascal!
   Montano. What's the matter, lieutenant?
   Cassio. A knave teach me my duty? I'll beat the knave
145   into a twiggen° bottle.
   Roderigo. Beat me?
   Cassio. Dost thou prate, rogue?   [*Strikes him.*]
   Montano. Nay, good lieutenant! I pray you, sir, hold
   your hand.
                     [*Stays him.*]
150 *Cassio.* Let me go, sir, or I'll knock you o'er the
   mazzard.°
   Montano. Come, come, you're drunk!
   Cassio. Drunk?   [*They fight.*]
   Iago. [*Aside to Roderigo*] Away, I say! Go out and
155   cry a mutiny!
                  [*Exit Roderigo.*]
     Nay, good lieutenant. God's will, gentlemen!
     Help, ho! Lieutenant. Sir. Montano.
     Help, masters! Here's a goodly watch indeed!
                  [*A bell rung.*]

137 **ingraft** ingrained   145 **twiggen** wicker-covered   151 **mazzard** head

Who's that which rings the bell? Diablo, ho!
The town will rise. God's will, lieutenant,   *160*
You'll be ashamed forever.

Enter Othello and Attendants.

Othello.   What is the matter here?

Montano. Zounds, I bleed still. I am hurt to the death.
He dies.   [*He and Cassio fight again.*]

Othello. Hold for your lives!

Iago. Hold, ho! Lieutenant. Sir. Montano. Gentlemen!   *165*
Have you forgot all place of sense and duty?
Hold! The general speaks to you. Hold, for shame!

Othello. Why, how now, ho? From whence ariseth this?
Are we turned Turks, and to ourselves do that
Which heaven hath forbid the Ottomites?°   *170*
For Christian shame put by this barbarous brawl!
He that stirs next to carve for his own rage
Holds his soul light;° he dies upon his motion.
Silence that dreadful bell! It frights the isle
From her propriety.° What is the matter, masters?   *175*
Honest Iago, that looks dead with grieving,
Speak. Who began this? On thy love, I charge thee.

Iago. I do not know. Friends all, but now, even now,
In quarter° and in terms like bride and groom
Devesting them for bed; and then, but now—   *180*
As if some planet had unwitted men—
Swords out, and tilting one at other's breasts
In opposition bloody. I cannot speak
Any beginning to this peevish odds,°
And would in action glorious I had lost   *185*
Those legs that brought me to a part of it!

Othello. How comes it, Michael, you are thus forgot?

Cassio. I pray you pardon me; I cannot speak.

Othello. Worthy Montano, you were wont to be civil;
The gravity and stillness of your youth   *190*

170 **heaven ... Ottomites** i.e., by sending the storm which dispersed the
Turks   173 **Holds his soul light** values his soul lightly   175 **propriety**
proper order   179 **In quarter** on duty   184 **odds** quarrel

The world hath noted, and your name is great
In mouths of wisest censure.° What's the matter
That you unlace° your reputation thus
And spend your rich opinion° for the name
195   Of a night-brawler? Give me answer to it.

   Montano. Worthy Othello, I am hurt to danger.
     Your officer, Iago, can inform you,
     While I spare speech, which something now offends°
       me,
     Of all that I do know; nor know I aught
200   By me that's said or done amiss this night,
     Unless self-charity be sometimes a vice,
     And to defend ourselves it be a sin
     When violence assails us.

   Othello.   Now, by heaven,
     My blood begins my safer guides to rule,
205   And passion, having my best judgment collied,°
     Assays to lead the way. If I once stir
     Or do but lift this arm, the best of you
     Shall sink in my rebuke. Give me to know
     How this foul rout began, who set it on;
210   And he that is approved in this offense,
     Though he had twinned with me, both at a birth,
     Shall lose me. What? In a town of war
     Yet wild, the people's hearts brimful of fear,
     To manage° private and domestic quarrel?
215   In night, and on the court and guard of safety?
     'Tis monstrous. Iago, who began't?

   Montano. If partially affined, or leagued in office,°
     Thou dost deliver more or less than truth,
     Thou art no soldier.

   Iago.   Touch me not so near.
220   I had rather have this tongue cut from my mouth
     Than it should do offense to Michael Cassio.

---

192 **censure** judgment   193 **unlace** undo (the term refers specifically to the
dressing of a wild boar killed in the hunt)   194 **opinion** reputation   198 **offends** harms, hurts   205 **collied** darkened   214 **manage** conduct   217 **If
. . . office** if you are partial because you are related ("affined") or the brother
officer (of Cassio)

Yet I persuade myself to speak the truth
Shall nothing wrong him. This it is, general.
Montano and myself being in speech,
There comes a fellow crying out for help,   225
And Cassio following him with determined sword
To execute upon him. Sir, this gentleman
Steps in to Cassio and entreats his pause.
Myself the crying fellow did pursue,
Lest by his clamor—as it so fell out—   230
The town might fall in fright. He, swift of foot,
Outran my purpose; and I returned then rather
For that I heard the clink and fall of swords,
And Cassio high in oath; which till tonight
I ne'er might say before. When I came back—   235
For this was brief—I found them close together
At blow and thrust, even as again they were
When you yourself did part them.
More of this matter cannot I report;
But men are men; the best sometimes forget.   240
Though Cassio did some little wrong to him,
As men in rage strike those that wish them best,
Yet surely Cassio I believe received
From him that fled some strange indignity,
Which patience could not pass.°

Othello.   I know, Iago,   245
Thy honesty and love doth mince° this matter,
Making it light to Cassio. Cassio, I love thee;
But never more be officer of mine.

Enter Desdemona, attended.

Look if my gentle love be not raised up.
I'll make thee an example.

Desdemona.   What is the matter, dear.   250

Othello. All's well, sweeting; come away to bed.
[*To Montano*] Sir, for your hurts, myself will be
    your surgeon.
Lead him off.   [*Montano led off.*]

245 **pass** allow to pass   246 **mince** cut up (i.e., tell only part of)

Iago, look with care about the town
255   And silence those whom this vile brawl distracted.
Come, Desdemona: 'tis the soldiers' life
To have their balmy slumbers waked with strife.

                Exit [with all but Iago and Cassio].

Iago. What, are you hurt, lieutenant?

Cassio. Ay, past all surgery.

260   *Iago.* Marry, God forbid!

Cassio. Reputation, reputation, reputation! O, I have
lost my reputation! I have lost the immortal part of
myself, and what remains is bestial. My reputation,
Iago, my reputation.

265   *Iago.* As I am an honest man, I had thought you had
received some bodily wound. There is more sense°
in that than in reputation. Reputation is an idle and
most false imposition,° oft got without merit and
lost without deserving. You have lost no reputation
270   at all unless you repute yourself such a loser. What,
man, there are more ways to recover the general
again. You are but now cast in his mood°—a
punishment more in policy° than in malice—even
so as one would beat his offenseless dog to affright
275   an imperious lion. Sue to him again, and he's yours.

Cassio. I will rather sue to be despised than to deceive
so good a commander with so slight, so drunken,
and so indiscreet an officer. Drunk! And speak
parrot!° And squabble! Swagger! Swear! and dis-
280   course fustian° with one's own shadow! O thou
invisible spirit of wine, if thou hast no name to be
known by, let us call thee devil!

Iago. What was he that you followed with your sword?
What had he done to you?

285   *Cassio.* I know not.

Iago. Is't possible?

266 **sense** physical feeling   268 **imposition** external thing   272 **cast in his
mood** dismissed because of his anger   273 **in policy** politically necessary
278–79 **speak parrot** gabble without sense   279–80 **discourse fustian** speak
nonsense ("fustian" was a coarse cotton cloth used for stuffing)

Cassio. I remember a mass of things, but nothing distinctly: a quarrel, but nothing wherefore. O God,
that men should put an enemy in their mouths to
steal away their brains! that we should with joy, *290*
pleasance, revel, and applause transform ourselves
into beasts!

Iago. Why, but you are now well enough. How came
you thus recovered?

Cassio. It hath pleased the devil drunkenness to give *295*
place to the devil wrath. One unperfectness shows
me another, to make me frankly despise myself.

Iago. Come, you are too severe a moraler. As the time,
the place, and the condition of this country stands,
I could heartily wish this had not befall'n; but since *300*
it is as it is, mend it for your own good.

Cassio. I will ask him for my place again: he shall tell
me I am a drunkard. Had I as many mouths as
Hydra, such an answer would stop them all. To be
now a sensible man, by and by a fool, and presently *305*
a beast! O strange! Every inordinate cup is unblest,
and the ingredient is a devil.

Iago. Come, come, good wine is a good familiar
creature if it be well used. Exclaim no more against
it. And, good lieutenant, I think you think I love *310*
you.

Cassio. I have well approved it, sir. I drunk?

Iago. You or any man living may be drunk at a time,
man. I tell you what you shall do. Our general's
wife is now the general. I may say so in this respect, *315*
for that he hath devoted and given up himself to the
contemplation, mark, and devotement of her parts°
and graces. Confess yourself freely to her; importune
her help to put you in your place again. She is of
so free, so kind, so apt, so blessed a disposition she *320*
holds it a vice in her goodness not to do more than

317 **devotement of her parts** devotion to her qualities

she is requested. This broken joint between you
and her husband entreat her to splinter;° and my
fortunes against any lay° worth naming, this crack
325   of your love shall grow stronger than it was before.

Cassio. You advise me well.

Iago. I protest, in the sincerity of love and honest
kindness.

Cassio. I think it freely; and betimes in the morning I
330   will beseech the virtuous Desdemona to undertake
for me. I am desperate of my fortunes if they check°
me.

Iago. You are in the right. Good night, lieutenant; I
must to the watch.

335 *Cassio.* Good night, honest Iago.   *Exit Cassio.*

Iago. And what's he then that says I play the villain,
When this advice is free° I give, and honest,
Probal to° thinking, and indeed the course
To win the Moor again? For 'tis most easy
340   Th' inclining° Desdemona to subdue
In any honest suit; she's framed as fruitful°
As the free elements.° And then for her
To win the Moor—were't to renounce his baptism,
All seals and symbols of redeemèd sin—
345   His soul is so enfettered to her love
That she may make, unmake, do what she list,
Even as her appetite° shall play the god
With his weak function.° How am I then a villain
To counsel Cassio to this parallel course,
350   Directly to his good? Divinity of hell!
When devils will the blackest sins put on,°
They do suggest at first with heavenly shows,°
As I do now. For whiles this honest fool
Plies Desdemona to repair his fortune,
355   And she for him pleads strongly to the Moor,

323 **splinter** splint   324 **lay** wager   331 **check** repulse   337 **free** generous
and open   338 **Probal to** provable by   340 **inclining** inclined (to be helpful)   341 **framed as fruitful** made as generous   342 **elements** i.e., basic
nature   347 **appetite** liking   348 **function** thought   351 **put on** advance,
further   352 **shows** appearances

I'll pour this pestilence into his ear:
That she repeals him° for her body's lust;
And by how much she strives to do him good,
She shall undo her credit with the Moor.
So will I turn her virtue into pitch,   360
And out of her own goodness make the net
That shall enmesh them all. How now, Roderigo?

Enter Roderigo.

Roderigo. I do follow here in the chase, not like a
hound that hunts, but one that fills up the cry.° My
money is almost spent; I have been tonight exceed-   365
ingly well cudgeled; and I think the issue will be,
I shall have so much experience for my pains; and
so, with no money at all, and a little more wit,
return again to Venice.

Iago. How poor are they that have not patience!   370
What wound did ever heal but by degrees?
Thou know'st we work by wit, and not by witch-
craft;
And wit depends on dilatory time.
Does't not go well? Cassio hath beaten thee,
And thou by that small hurt hath cashiered Cassio.   375
Though other things grow fair against the sun,
Yet fruits that blossom first will first be ripe.
Content thyself awhile. By the mass, 'tis morning!
Pleasure and action make the hours seem short.
Retire thee; go where thou art billeted.   380
Away, I say! Thou shalt know more hereafter.
Nay, get thee gone!   *Exit Roderigo.*
          Two things are to be done:
My wife must move° for Cassio to her mistress;
I'll set her on;
Myself awhile° to draw the Moor apart   385
And bring him jump° when he may Cassio find
Soliciting his wife. Ay, that's the way!
Dull not device by coldness and delay.   *Exit.*

357 **repeals him** asks for (Cassio's reinstatement) 364 **fills up the cry**
makes up one of the hunting pack, adding to the noise but not actually track-
ing 383 **move** petition 385 **awhile** at the same time 386 **jump** at the
precise moment and place

ACT 3

Scene 1. [*A street.*]

Enter Cassio [and] Musicians.

Cassio. Masters, play here. I will content your pains.°
Something that's brief; and bid "Good morrow,
general."   [*They play.*]

[*Enter Clown.°*]

Clown. Why, masters, have your instruments been in
Naples° that they speak i' th' nose thus?

5   *Musician.* How, sir, how?

Clown. Are these, I pray you, wind instruments?

Musician. Ay, marry, are they, sir.

Clown. O, thereby hangs a tale.

Musician. Whereby hangs a tale, sir?

10 *Clown.* Marry, sir, by many a wind instrument that I
know. But, masters, here's money for you; and the
general so likes your music that he desires you,
for love's sake, to make no more noise with it.

Musician. Well, sir, we will not.

15 *Clown.* If you have any music that may not be heard,
to't again. But, as they say, to hear music the
general does not greatly care.

3.1.1 **content your pains** reward your efforts   2 s.d. **Clown** fool   4
Naples (this may refer either to the Neapolitan nasal tone, or to syphilis—rife
in Naples—which breaks down the nose)

54

Musician. We have none such, sir.

Clown. Then put up your pipes in your bag, for I'll
   away. Go, vanish into air, away!   20

                              Exit Musicians.

Cassio. Dost thou hear me, mine honest friend?

Clown. No. I hear not your honest friend. I hear you.

Cassio. Prithee keep up thy quillets.° There's a poor
   piece of gold for thee. If the gentlewoman that
   attends the general's wife be stirring, tell her there's   25
   one Cassio entreats her a little favor of speech.
   Wilt thou do this?

Clown. She is stirring, sir. If she will stir hither, I shall
   seem to notify unto her.°   *Exit Clown.*

                    Enter Iago.

Cassio. In happy time, Iago.

Iago.   You have not been abed then?   30

Cassio. Why no, the day had broke before we parted.
   I have made bold, Iago, to send in to your wife;
   My suit to her is that she will to virtuous Desdemona
   Procure me some access.

Iago.   I'll send her to you presently,
   And I'll devise a mean to draw the Moor   35
   Out of the way, that your converse and business
   May be more free.

Cassio. I humbly thank you for 't.   *Exit [Iago].*
                    I never knew
   A Florentine° more kind and honest.

                    Enter Emilia.

Emilia. Good morrow, good lieutenant. I am sorry   40
   For your displeasure;° but all will sure be well.
   The general and his wife are talking of it,

23 **quillets** puns   29 **seem . . . her** (the Clown is mocking Cassio's overly
elegant manner of speaking)   39 **Florentine** i.e., Iago is as kind as if he were
from Cassio's home town, Florence   41 **displeasure** discomforting

And she speaks for you stoutly. The Moor replies
That he you hurt is of great fame in Cyprus
45   And great affinity,° and that in wholesome wisdom
He might not but refuse you. But he protests he loves
    you,
And needs no other suitor but his likings
To bring you in again.

Cassio.   Yet I beseech you,
If you think fit, or that it may be done,
50   Give me advantage of some brief discourse
With Desdemona alone.

Emilia.   Pray you come in.
I will bestow you where you shall have time
To speak your bosom° freely.

Cassio.   I am much bound to you.
                                   [Exeunt.]

Scene 2. [*The citadel.*]

Enter Othello, Iago, and Gentlemen.

Othello. These letters give, Iago, to the pilot
And by him do my duties to the Senate.
That done, I will be walking on the works;
Repair° there to me.

Iago.   Well, my good lord, I'll do't.

5   Othello. This fortification, gentlemen, shall we see't?

Gentlemen. We'll wait upon your lordship.   *Exeunt.*

45 **affinity** family   53 **bosom** inmost thoughts   3.2.4 **Repair** go

Scene 3. [*The citadel.*]

Enter Desdemona, Cassio, and Emilia.

Desdemona. Be thou assured, good Cassio, I will do
  All my abilities in thy behalf.

Emilia. Good madam, do. I warrant it grieves my husband
  As if the cause were his.

Desdemona. O, that's an honest fellow. Do not doubt,
  Cassio,   5
  But I will have my lord and you again
  As friendly as you were.

Cassio.   Bounteous madam,
  Whatever shall become of Michael Cassio,
  He's never anything but your true servant.

Desdemona. I know't; I thank you. You do love my
  lord.   10
  You have known him long, and be you well assured
  He shall in strangeness stand no farther off
  Than in a politic distance.°

Cassio.   Ay, but, lady,
  That policy may either last so long,
  Or feed upon such nice° and waterish diet,   15
  Or breed itself so out of circumstances,°
  That, I being absent, and my place supplied,°
  My general will forget my love and service.

Desdemona. Do not doubt° that; before Emilia here
  I give thee warrant of thy place. Assure thee,   20
  If I do vow a friendship, I'll perform it

3.3.12–13 **He ... distance** i.e., he shall act no more distant to you than is
necessary for political reasons   15 **nice** trivial   16 **Or ... circumstances**
i.e., or grow so on the basis of accidental happenings and political needs   17
supplied filled   19 **doubt** imagine

To the last article. My lord shall never rest;
I'll watch him tame° and talk him out of patience;
His bed shall seem a school, his board a shrift;°
25   I'll intermingle everything he does
With Cassio's suit. Therefore be merry, Cassio,
For thy solicitor shall rather die
Than give thy cause away.

Enter Othello and Iago [at a distance].

Emilia. Madam, here comes my lord.
30   *Cassio.* Madam, I'll take my leave.
Desdemona. Why, stay, and hear me speak.
Cassio. Madam, not now. I am very ill at ease,
   Unfit for mine own purposes.
Desdemona. Well, do your discretion.   *Exit Cassio.*
Iago. Ha! I like not that.
35   *Othello.*   What dost thou say?
Iago. Nothing, my lord; or if—I know not what.
Othello. Was not that Cassio parted from my wife?
Iago. Cassio, my lord? No, sure, I cannot think it
   That he would steal away so guilty-like,
   Seeing your coming.
40   *Othello.*   I do believe 'twas he.
Desdemona. [*Coming to them*] How now, my lord?
   I have been talking with a suitor here,
   A man that languishes in your displeasure.
Othello. Who is't you mean?
Desdemona. Why, your lieutenant, Cassio. Good my
45   lord,
   If I have any grace or power to move you,
   His present° reconciliation take.
   For if he be not one that truly loves you,

23 **watch him tame** (animals were tamed by being kept awake)   24 **board a shrift** table (seem) a confessional   47 **present** immediate

That errs in ignorance, and not in cunning,
I have no judgment in an honest face.   50
I prithee call him back.

Othello.   Went he hence now?

Desdemona. I' sooth so humbled
That he hath left part of his grief with me
To suffer with him. Good love, call him back.

Othello. Not now, sweet Desdemon; some other time.   55

Desdemona. But shall't be shortly?

Othello.   The sooner, sweet, for you.

Desdemona. Shall't be tonight at supper?

Othello.   No, not tonight.

Desdemona. Tomorrow dinner then?

Othello.   I shall not dine at home;
I meet the captains at the citadel.

Desdemona. Why then, tomorrow night, on Tuesday
    morn,   60
On Tuesday noon, or night, on Wednesday morn.
I prithee name the time, but let it not
Exceed three days. In faith, he's penitent;
And yet his trespass, in our common reason
(Save that, they say, the wars must make example   65
Out of her best), is not almost a fault
T' incur a private check.° When shall he come?
Tell me, Othello. I wonder in my soul
What you would ask me that I should deny
Or stand so mamm'ring° on. What? Michael Cassio,   70
That came awooing with you, and so many a time,
When I have spoke of you dispraisingly,
Hath ta'en your part—to have so much to do
To bring him in? By'r Lady, I could do much—

Othello. Prithee no more. Let him come when he will!   75
I will deny thee nothing.

66–67 **is ... check** is almost not serious enough for a private rebuke (let
alone a public disgrace)   70 **mamm'ring** hesitating

Desdemona.   Why, this is not a boon;
   'Tis as I should entreat you wear your gloves,
   Or feed on nourishing dishes, or keep you warm,
   Or sue to you to do a peculiar profit°
80 To your own person. Nay, when I have a suit
   Wherein I mean to touch your love indeed,
   It shall be full of poise° and difficult weight,
   And fearful to be granted.

Othello.   I will deny thee nothing!
   Whereon I do beseech thee grant me this,
85   To leave me but a little to myself.

Desdemona. Shall I deny you? No. Farewell, my lord.

Othello. Farewell, my Desdemona: I'll come to thee
   straight.°

Desdemona. Emilia, come. Be as your fancies teach
   you;
   Whate'er you be, I am obedient.   *Exit* [*with Emilia*].

90 *Othello.* Excellent wretch! Perdition catch my soul
   But I do love thee! And when I love thee not,
   Chaos is come again.

Iago. My noble lord——

Othello.   What dost thou say, Iago?

Iago. Did Michael Cassio, when you wooed my lady,
95   Know of your love?

Othello. He did, from first to last. Why dost thou ask?

Iago. But for a satisfaction of my thought,
   No further harm.

Othello.   Why of thy thought, Iago?

Iago. I did not think he had been acquainted with her.

100 *Othello.* O, yes, and went between us° very oft.

Iago. Indeed?

Othello. Indeed? Ay, indeed! Discern'st thou aught in
   that?

---

79 **peculiar profit** particularly personal good 82 **poise** weight 87
straight at once 100 **between us** i.e., as messenger

Is he not honest?

Iago.   Honest, my lord?

Othello.   Honest? Ay, honest.

Iago. My lord, for aught I know.

Othello. What dost thou think?

Iago.   Think, my lord?

Othello.   Think, my lord?   *105*
 By heaven, thou echoest me,
 As if there were some monster in thy thought
 Too hideous to be shown. Thou dost mean some-
   thing.
 I heard thee say even now, thou lik'st not that,
 When Cassio left my wife. What didst not like?   *110*
 And when I told thee he was of my counsel°
 Of my whole course of wooing, thou cried'st "In-
   deed?"
 And didst contract and purse thy brow together,
 As if thou then hadst shut up in thy brain
 Some horrible conceit.° If thou dost love me,   *115*
 Show me thy thought.

Iago. My lord, you know I love you.

Othello.   I think thou dost;
 And, for I know thou'rt full of love and honesty
 And weigh'st thy words before thou giv'st them
   breath,
 Therefore these stops° of thine fright me the more;   *120*
 For such things in a false disloyal knave
 Are tricks of custom;° but in a man that's just
 They're close dilations,° working from the heart
 That passion cannot rule.

Iago.   For Michael Cassio,
 I dare be sworn, I think that he is honest.   *125*

Othello. I think so too.

---

111 **of my counsel** in my confidence   115 **conceit** thought   120 **stops** interruptions   122 **of custom** customary   123 **close dilations** expressions of
hidden thoughts

Iago.   Men should be what they seem;
   Or those that be not, would they might seem none!

Othello. Certain, men should be what they seem.

Iago. Why then, I think Cassio's an honest man.

130 *Othello.* Nay, yet there's more in this?
   I prithee speak to me as to thy thinkings,
   As thou dost ruminate, and give thy worst of
      thoughts
   The worst of words.

Iago.   Good my lord, pardon me:
   Though I am bound to every act of duty,
135 I am not bound to that all slaves are free to.
   Utter my thoughts? Why, say they are vile and false,
   As where's that palace whereinto foul things
   Sometimes intrude not? Who has that breast so pure
   But some uncleanly apprehensions
140 Keep leets and law days,° and in sessions sit
   With meditations lawful?

Othello. Thou dost conspire against thy friend, Iago,
   If thou but think'st him wronged, and mak'st his ear
   A stranger to thy thoughts.

Iago.   I do beseech you—
145 Though I perchance am vicious in my guess
   (As I confess it is my nature's plague
   To spy into abuses, and of my jealousy
   Shape faults that are not), that your wisdom
   From one that so imperfectly conceits
150 Would take no notice, nor build yourself a trouble
   Out of his scattering and unsure observance.
   It were not for your quiet nor your good,
   Nor for my manhood, honesty, and wisdom,
   To let you know my thoughts.

Othello.   What dost thou mean?

155 *Iago.* Good name in man and woman, dear my lord,
   Is the immediate jewel of their souls.

140 **leets and law days** meetings of local courts

Who steals my purse steals trash; 'tis something,
   nothing;
'Twas mine, 'tis his, and has been slave to thousands;
But he that filches from me my good name
Robs me of that which not enriches him   *160*
And makes me poor indeed.

Othello. By heaven, I'll know thy thoughts!

Iago. You cannot, if my heart were in your hand;
   Nor shall not whilst 'tis in my custody.

Othello. Ha!

Iago.   O, beware, my lord, of jealousy!   *165*
   It is the green-eyed monster, which doth mock
   The meat it feeds on. That cuckold lives in bliss
   Who, certain of his fate, loves not his wronger;
   But O, what damnèd minutes tells° he o'er
   Who dotes, yet doubts—suspects, yet fondly° loves!   *170*

Othello. O misery.

Iago. Poor and content is rich, and rich enough;
   But riches fineless° is as poor as winter
   To him that ever fears he shall be poor.
   Good God the souls of all my tribe defend   *175*
   From jealousy!

Othello.   Why? Why is this?
   Think'st thou I'd make a life of jealousy,
   To follow still° the changes of the moon
   With fresh suspicions? No! To be once in doubt
   Is to be resolved. Exchange me for a goat   *180*
   When I shall turn the business of my soul
   To such exsufflicate and blown° surmises,
   Matching thy inference. 'Tis not to make me jealous
   To say my wife is fair, feeds well, loves company,
   Is free of speech, sings, plays, and dances;   *185*
   Where virtue is, these are more virtuous.
   Nor from mine own weak merits will I draw
   The smallest fear or doubt of her revolt,

169 **tells** counts   170 **fondly** foolishly   173 **fineless** infinite   178 **To follow still** to change always (as the phases of the moon)   182 **exsufflicate and blown** inflated and flyblown .

For she had eyes, and chose me. No, Iago;
190 I'll see before I doubt; when I doubt, prove;
And on the proof there is no more but this:
Away at once with love or jealousy!

Iago. I am glad of this; for now I shall have reason
To show the love and duty that I bear you
195 With franker spirit. Therefore, as I am bound,
Receive it from me. I speak not yet of proof.
Look to your wife; observe her well with Cassio;
Wear your eyes thus: not jealous nor secure.
I would not have your free and noble nature
200 Out of self-bounty° be abused. Look to't.
I know our country disposition well:
In Venice they do let heaven see the pranks
They dare not show their husbands; their best con-
     science
Is not to leave't undone, but kept unknown.°

205 *Othello.* Dost thou say so?

Iago. She did deceive her father, marrying you;
And when she seemed to shake and fear your looks,
She loved them most.

Othello.   And so she did.

Iago.   Why, go to then!
She that so young could give out such a seeming
210 To seel° her father's eyes up close as oak°—
He thought 'twas witchcraft. But I am much to
     blame.
I humbly do beseech you of your pardon
For too much loving you.

Othello.   I am bound to thee forever.

Iago. I see this hath a little dashed your spirits.

Othello. Not a jot, not a jot.

215 *Iago.*   Trust me, I fear it has.

---

200 **self-bounty** innate kindness (which attributes his own motives to others)
203–4 **their . . . unknown** i.e., their morality does not forbid adultery, but it
does forbid being found out   210 **seel** hoodwink   210 **oak** (a close-grained
wood)

I hope you will consider what is spoke
Comes from my love. But I do see y' are moved.
I am to pray you not to strain° my speech
To grosser issues, nor to larger reach°
Than to suspicion.   220

Othello. I will not.

Iago.   Should you do so, my lord,
My speech should fall into such vile success
Which my thoughts aimed not. Cassio's my worthy
    friend—
My lord, I see y' are moved.

Othello.   No, not much moved.
I do not think but Desdemona's honest.   225

Iago. Long live she so. And long live you to think so.

Othello. And yet, how nature erring from itself——

Iago. Ay, there's the point, as (to be bold with you)
Not to affect many proposèd matches
Of her own clime, complexion, and degree,°   230
Whereto we see in all things nature tends°—
Foh! one may smell in such a will most rank,
Foul disproportions, thoughts unnatural.
But, pardon me, I do not in position°
Distinctly° speak of her; though I may fear   235
Her will, recoiling to her better judgment,
May fall to match° you with her country forms,°
And happily° repent.

Othello.   Farewell, farewell!
If more thou dost perceive, let me know more.
Set on thy wife to observe. Leave me, Iago.   240

Iago. My lord, I take my leave.   [*Going.*]

218 **strain** enlarge the meaning of   219 **reach** meaning   230 **degree** social
station   231 **in ... tends** i.e., all things in nature seek out their own kind
234 **position** general argument   235 **Distinctly** specifically   237 **fall to
match** happen to compare   237 **country forms** i.e., the familiar appearances
of her countrymen   238 **happily** by chance

Othello. Why did I marry? This honest creature doubt-
    less
    Sees and knows more, much more, than he unfolds.

Iago. [*Returns.*] My lord, I would I might entreat your
    honor
245   To scan this thing no farther. Leave it to time.
    Although 'tis fit that Cassio have his place,
    For sure he fills it up with great ability,
    Yet, if you please to hold him off awhile,
    You shall by that perceive him and his means.
250   Note if your lady strain his entertainment°
    With any strong or vehement importunity;
    Much will be seen in that. In the meantime
    Let me be thought too busy in my fears
    (As worthy cause I have to fear I am)
255   And hold her free, I do beseech your honor.

Othello. Fear not my government.°

Iago.   I once more take my leave.

                                    Exit.

Othello. This fellow's of exceeding honesty,
    And knows all qualities,° with a learnèd spirit
    Of human dealings. If I do prove her haggard,°
260   Though that her jesses° were my dear heartstrings,
    I'd whistle her off and let her down the wind°
    To prey at fortune. Haply for° I am black
    And have not those soft parts° of conversation
    That chamberers° have, or for I am declined
265   Into the vale of years—yet that's not much—
    She's gone. I am abused, and my relief
    Must be to loathe her. O curse of marriage,
    That we can call these delicate creatures ours,
    And not their appetites! I had rather be a toad

---

250 **strain his entertainment** urge strongly that he be reinstated   256 **government** self-control   258 **qualities** natures, types of people   259 **haggard**
a partly trained hawk which has gone wild again   260 **jesses** straps which
held the hawk's legs to the trainer's wrist   261 **I'd . . . wind** I would release
her (like an untamable hawk) and let her fly free   262 **Haply for** it may be
because   263 **soft parts** gentle qualities and manners   264 **chamberers**
courtiers—or perhaps, accomplished seducers

And live upon the vapor of a dungeon   270
Than keep a corner in the thing I love
For others' uses. Yet 'tis the plague to great ones;
Prerogatived are they less than the base.
'Tis destiny unshunnable, like death.
Even then this forkèd° plague is fated to us   275
When we do quicken.° Look where she comes.

               Enter Desdemona and Emilia.

If she be false, heaven mocked itself!
I'll not believe't.

Desdemona.   How now, my dear Othello?
   Your dinner, and the generous islanders
   By you invited, do attend° your presence.   280

Othello. I am to blame.

Desdemona.   Why do you speak so faintly?
   And you not well?

Othello. I have a pain upon my forehead, here.°

Desdemona. Why, that's with watching; 'twill away
   again.
   Let me but bind it hard, within this hour   285
   It will be well.

Othello.   Your napkin° is too little;

      [*He pushes the handkerchief away, and it falls.*]
   Let it° alone. Come, I'll go in with you.

Desdemona. I am very sorry that you are not well.

                              Exit [*with Othello*].

Emilia. I am glad I have found this napkin;
   This was her first remembrance from the Moor.   290
   My wayward husband hath a hundred times
   Wooed me to steal it; but she so loves the token

275 **forkèd** horned (the sign of the cuckold was horns)   276 **do quicken** are
born   280 **attend** wait   283 **here** (he points to his imaginary horns)   286
napkin elaborately worked handkerchief   287 **it** (it makes a considerable
difference in the interpretation of later events whether this "it" refers to Othello's forehead or to the handkerchief; nothing in the text makes the reference
clear)

(For he conjured her she should ever keep it)
That she reserves it evermore about her
295 To kiss and talk to. I'll have the work ta'en out°
And give't Iago. What he will do with it,
Heaven knows, not I; I nothing° but to please his
fantasy.°

> *Enter Iago.*

Iago. How now? What do you here alone?

Emilia. Do not you chide; I have a thing for you.

Iago. You have a thing for me? It is a common
300   thing——

Emilia. Ha?

Iago. To have a foolish wife.

Emilia. O, is that all? What will you give me now
For that same handkerchief?

Iago.   What handkerchief?

305 *Emilia.* What handkerchief?
Why, that the Moor first gave to Desdemona,
That which so often you did bid me steal.

Iago. Hast stol'n it from her?

Emilia. No, but she let it drop by negligence,
310   And to th' advantage,° I, being here, took't up.
Look, here 't is.

Iago.   A good wench. Give it me.

Emilia. What will you do with't, that you have been
so earnest
To have me filch it?

Iago.   Why, what is that to you?

> [*Takes it.*]

Emilia. If it be not for some purpose of import,°
315   Give't me again. Poor lady, she'll run mad
When she shall lack° it.

---

295 **work ta'en out** needlework copied   297 **I nothing** I wish nothing
297 **fantasy** fancy, whim   310 **to th' advantage** being lucky   314 **import**
importance   316 **lack** miss

Iago.   Be not acknown on't.°
   I have use for it. Go, leave me.   *Exit Emilia.*
   I will in Cassio's lodging lose this napkin
   And let him find it. Trifles light as air
   Are to the jealous confirmations strong   *320*
   As proofs of Holy Writ. This may do something.
   The Moor already changes with my poison:
   Dangerous conceits are in their natures poisons,
   Which at the first are scarce found to distaste,°
   But, with a little,° act upon the blood,   *325*
   Burn like the mines of sulfur. I did say so.

Enter Othello.

   Look where he comes! Not poppy nor mandragora,°
   Nor all the drowsy syrups of the world,
   Shall ever medicine thee to that sweet sleep
   Which thou owedst° yesterday.

Othello.   Ha! ha! False to me?   *330*

Iago. Why, how now, general? No more of that.

Othello. Avaunt! be gone! Thou hast set me on the
   rack.
   I swear 'tis better to be much abused
   Than but to know't a little.

Iago.   How now, my lord?

Othello. What sense had I of her stol'n hours of lust?   *335*
   I saw't not, thought it not, it harmed not me;
   I slept the next night well, fed well, was free and
     merry;
   I found not Cassio's kisses on her lips.
   He that is robbed, not wanting° what is stol'n,
   Let him not know't, and he's not robbed at all.   *340*

Iago. I am sorry to hear this.

316 **Be not acknown on't** forget you ever saw it   324 **are scarce found to distaste** scarcely can be tasted   325 **with a little** in a short time   327 **poppy nor mandragora** (soporifics)   330 **owedst** possessed   339 **wanting** missing

Othello. I had been happy if the general camp,
 Pioners° and all, had tasted her sweet body,
 So I had nothing known. O now, forever
345 Farewell the tranquil mind! Farewell content!
 Farewell the plumèd troops, and the big wars
 That makes ambition virtue! O, farewell!
 Farewell the neighing steed and the shrill trump,
 The spirit-stirring drum, th' ear-piercing fife,
350 The royal banner, and all quality,
 Pride, pomp, and circumstance° of glorious war!
 And O you mortal engines° whose rude throats
 Th' immortal Jove's dread clamors° counterfeit,
 Farewell! Othello's occupation's gone!

355 *Iago.* Is't possible, my lord?

Othello. Villain, be sure thou prove my love a whore!
 Be sure of it; give me the ocular proof;
 Or, by the worth of mine eternal soul,
 Thou hadst been better have been born a dog
 Than answer my waked wrath!

360 *Iago.*   Is't come to this?

Othello. Make me to see't; or at the least so prove it
 That the probation° bear no hinge nor loop
 To hang a doubt on—or woe upon thy life!

Iago. My noble lord——

365 *Othello.* If thou dost slander her and torture me,
 Never pray more; abandon all remorse;
 On horror's head horrors accumulate;
 Do deeds to make heaven weep, all earth amazed;
 For nothing canst thou to damnation add
 Greater than that.

370 *Iago.* O grace! O heaven forgive me!
 Are you a man? Have you a soul or sense?
 God b' wi' you! Take mine office. O wretched fool,
 That lov'st to make thine honesty a vice!
 O monstrous world! Take note, take note, O world,

---

343 **Pioners** (the basest manual laborers in the army, who dug trenches and
mines) 351 **circumstance** pageantry 352 **mortal engines** lethal weapons,
i.e., cannon 353 **clamors** i.e., thunder 362 **probation** proof

To be direct and honest is not safe.   375
I thank you for this profit, and from hence
I'll love no friend, sith° love breeds such offense.

Othello. Nay, stay. Thou shouldst be honest.

Iago. I should be wise; for honesty's a fool
And loses that it works for.

Othello.   By the world,   380
I think my wife be honest, and think she is not;
I think that thou art just, and think thou art not.
I'll have some proof. My name, that was as fresh
As Dian's° visage, is now begrimed and black
As mine own face. If there be cords, or knives,   385
Poison, or fire, or suffocating streams,
I'll not endure it. Would I were satisfied!

Iago. I see you are eaten up with passion.
I do repent me that I put it to you.
You would be satisfied?

Othello.   Would? Nay, and I will.   390

Iago. And may; but how? How satisfied, my lord?
Would you, the supervisor,° grossly gape on?
Behold her topped?

Othello.   Death and damnation! O!

Iago. It were a tedious° difficulty, I think,
To bring them to that prospect.° Damn them then, 395
If ever mortal eyes do see them bolster°
More than their own! What then? How then?
What shall I say? Where's satisfaction?
It is impossible you should see this,
Were they as prime° as goats, as hot as monkeys, 400
As salt° as wolves in pride,° and fools as gross
As ignorance made drunk. But yet, I say,

377 **sith** since   384 **Dian's** Diana's (goddess of the moon and of chastity)
392 **supervisor** onlooker   394 **tedious** hard to arrange   395 **prospect**
sight (where they can be seen)   396 **bolster** go to bed   400–01 **prime, salt**
lustful   401 **pride** heat

If imputation and strong circumstances
Which lead directly to the door of truth
405   Will give you satisfaction, you might have't.

Othello. Give me a living reason she's disloyal.

Iago. I do not like the office.°
But sith I am entered in this cause so far,
Pricked° to't by foolish honesty and love,
410   I will go on. I lay with Cassio lately,
And being troubled with a raging tooth,
I could not sleep.
There are a kind of men so loose of soul
That in their sleeps will mutter their affairs.
415   One of this kind is Cassio.
In sleep I heard him say, "Sweet Desdemona,
Let us be wary, let us hide our loves!"
And then, sir, would he gripe° and wring my hand,
Cry "O sweet creature!" Then kiss me hard,
420   As if he plucked up kisses by the roots
That grew upon my lips; laid his leg o'er my thigh,
And sigh, and kiss, and then cry, "Cursèd fate
That gave thee to the Moor!"

Othello. O monstrous! monstrous!

Iago.   Nay, this was but his dream.

425 *Othello.* But this denoted a foregone conclusion,°
'Tis a shrewd doubt,° though it be but a dream.

Iago. And this may help to thicken other proofs
That do demonstrate° thinly.

Othello.   I'll tear her all to pieces!

Iago. Nay, yet be wise. Yet we see nothing done;
430   She may be honest yet. Tell me but this:
Have you not sometimes seen a handkerchief
Spotted with strawberries in your wife's hand?

Othello. I gave her such a one; 'twas my first gift.

---

407 **office** duty   409 **Pricked** spurred   418 **gripe** seize   425 **foregone conclusion** consummated fact   426 **shrewd doubt** penetrating guess   428 **demonstrate** show, appear

Iago. I know not that; but such a handkerchief—
   I am sure it was your wife's—did I today   *435*
   See Cassio wipe his beard with.

Othello.   If it be that——

Iago. If it be that, or any that was hers,
   It speaks against her with the other proofs.

Othello. O, that the slave had forty thousand lives!
   One is too poor, too weak for my revenge.   *440*
   Now do I see 'tis true. Look here, Iago:
   All my fond love thus do I blow to heaven.
   'Tis gone.
   Arise, black vengeance, from the hollow hell!
   Yield up, O Love, thy crown and hearted° throne   *445*
   To tyrannous hate! Swell, bosom, with thy fraught,°
   For 'tis of aspics'° tongues.

Iago.   Yet be content.°

Othello. O, blood, blood, blood!

Iago. Patience, I say. Your mind may change.

Othello. Never, Iago. Like to the Pontic Sea,°   *450*
   Whose icy current and compulsive course
   Nev'r keeps retiring ebb, but keeps due on
   To the Propontic and the Hellespont,
   Even so my bloody thoughts, with violent pace,
   Shall nev'r look back, nev'r ebb to humble love,   *455*
   Till that a capable and wide° revenge
   Swallow them up. [*He kneels.*] Now, by yond mar-
      ble heaven,
   In the due reverence of a sacred vow
   I here engage my words.

Iago.   Do not rise yet.

                         [*Iago kneels.*]
   Witness, you ever-burning lights above,   *460*

445 **hearted** seated in the heart   446 **fraught** burden   447 **aspics'** asps'
447 **content** patient, quiet   450 **Pontic Sea** the Black Sea (famous for the
strong and constant current with which it flows through the Bosporus into the
Mediterranean, where the water level is lower)   456 **capable and wide** sufficient and far-reaching

You elements that clip° us round about,
Witness that here Iago doth give up
The execution° of his wit, hands, heart
To wronged Othello's service! Let him command,
465   And to obey shall be in me remorse,°
What bloody business ever.°   [*They rise.*]

Othello.   I greet thy love,
Not with vain thanks but with acceptance boun-
     teous,°
And will upon the instant put thee to't.°
Within these three days let me hear thee say
470   That Cassio's not alive.

Iago. My friend is dead. 'Tis done at your request.
But let her live.

Othello.   Damn her, lewd minx! O, damn her!
Damn her!
Come, go with me apart. I will withdraw
To furnish me with some swift means of death
475   For the fair devil. Now art thou my lieutenant.

Iago. I am your own forever.   *Exeunt.*

Scene 4. [*A street.*]

Enter Desdemona, Emilia, and Clown.

Desdemona. Do you know, sirrah, where Lieutenant
Cassio lies?°

Clown. I dare not say he lies anywhere.

Desdemona. Why, man?

5   *Clown.* He's a soldier, and for me to say a soldier lies,
'tis stabbing.

---

461 **clip** enfold   463 **execution** workings, action   465 **remorse** pity   466
ever soever   467 **bounteous** absolute   468 **to't** i.e., to the work you have
said you are prepared to do   3.4.2 **lies** lodges

Desdemona. Go to. Where lodges he?

Clown. To tell you where he lodges is to tell you where
I lie.

Desdemona. Can anything be made of this?   10

Clown. I know not where he lodges, and for me to.
devise a lodging, and say he lies here or he lies there,
were to lie in mine own throat.°

Desdemona. Can you enquire him out, and be edified°
by report?   15

Clown. I will catechize the world for him; that is, make
questions, and by them answer.

Desdemona. Seek him, bid him come hither. Tell him
I have moved° my lord on his behalf and hope all
will be well.   20

Clown. To do this is within the compass° of man's wit,
and therefore I will attempt the doing it. *Exit Clown.*

Desdemona. Where should° I lose the handkerchief,
Emilia?

Emilia. I know not, madam.

Desdemona. Believe me, I had rather have lost my
purse   25
Full of crusadoes.° And but my noble Moor
Is true of mind, and made of no such baseness
As jealous creatures are, it were enough
To put him to ill thinking.

Emilia.   Is he not jealous?

Desdemona. Who? He? I think the sun where he was
born   30
Drew all such humors° from him.

Emilia.   Look where he comes.

13 **lie in mine own throat** (to lie in the throat is to lie absolutely and completely) 14 **edified** enlightened (Desdemona mocks the Clown's overly
elaborate diction) 19 **moved** pleaded with 21 **compass** reach 23
should might 26 **crusadoes** Portuguese gold coins 31 **humors** characteristics

Enter Othello.

Desdemona. I will not leave him now till Cassio
  Be called to him. How is't with you, my lord?

Othello. Well, my good lady. [*Aside*] O, hardness to
  dissemble!°—
  How do you, Desdemona?

35 *Desdemona.*   Well, my good lord.

Othello. Give me your hand. This hand is moist,°
  my lady.

Desdemona. It hath felt no age nor known no sorrow.

Othello. This argues° fruitfulness and liberal° heart.
  Hot, hot, and moist. This hand of yours requires
40 A sequester° from liberty; fasting and prayer;
  Much castigation; exercise devout;
  For here's a young and sweating devil here
  That commonly rebels. 'Tis a good hand,
  A frank one.

Desdemona. You may, indeed, say so;
45 For 'twas that hand that gave away my heart.

Othello. A liberal hand! The hearts of old gave hands,
  But our new heraldry° is hands, not hearts.

Desdemona. I cannot speak of this. Come now, your
  promise!

Othello. What promise, chuck?

Desdemona. I have sent to bid Cassio come speak with
50 you.

Othello. I have a salt and sorry rheum° offends me.
  Lend me thy handkerchief.

34 **hardness to dissemble** (Othello may refer here either to the difficulty he
has in maintaining his appearance of composure, or to what he believes to be
Desdemona's hardened hypocrisy)   36 **moist** (a moist, hot hand was taken as
a sign of a lustful nature)   38 **argues** suggests   38 **liberal** free, open (but
also with a suggestion of "licentious"; from here on in this scene Othello's
words bear a double meaning, seeming to be normal but accusing Desdemona
of being unfaithful)   40 **sequester** separation   47 **heraldry** heraldic sym-
bolism   51 **a salt and sorry rheum** a heavy, running head cold

Desdemona.　　　　　　　　　Here, my lord.

Othello. That which I gave you.

Desdemona.　　　　　　　　I have it not about me.

Othello. Not?

Desdemona. No, indeed, my lord.

Othello.　　　　　　　　　That's a fault.
That handkerchief　　　　　　　　　　　　　　　　　55
Did an Egyptian to my mother give.
She was a charmer,° and could almost read
The thoughts of people. She told her, while she
　kept it
'Twould make her amiable° and subdue my father
Entirely to her love; but if she lost it　　　　　　60
Or made a gift of it, my father's eye
Should hold her loathèd, and his spirits should hunt
After new fancies. She, dying, gave it me,
And bid me, when my fate would have me wived,
To give it her. I did so; and take heed on't;　　　　65
Make it a darling like your precious eye.
To lose't or give't away were such perdition
As nothing else could match.

Desdemona.　　　　　　　　　Is't possible?

Othello. 'Tis true. There's magic in the web° of it.
A sibyl that had numbered in the world　　　　　　70
The sun to course two hundred compasses,
In her prophetic fury° sewed the work;
The worms were hallowed that did breed the silk,
And it was dyed in mummy° which the skillful
Conserved of maidens' hearts.

Desdemona.　　　　　　　　　Indeed? Is't true?　　75

Othello. Most veritable. Therefore look to't well.

Desdemona. Then would to God that I had never
　seen't!

57 **charmer** magician　　59 **amiable** desirable　　69 **web** weaving　　72 **prophetic fury** seized by the spirit and able to prophesy　　74 **mummy** liquid drained from embalmed bodies

Othello. Ha! Wherefore?

Desdemona. Why do you speak so startingly and rash?

80   *Othello.* Is't lost? Is't gone? Speak, is it out o' th' way?

Desdemona. Heaven bless us!

Othello. Say you?

Desdemona. It is not lost. But what an if it were?

Othello. How?

85   *Desdemona.* I say it is not lost.

Othello. Fetch't, let me see't!

Desdemona. Why, so I can; but I will not now.
   This is a trick to put me from my suit:
   Pray you let Cassio be received again.

90   *Othello.* Fetch me the handkerchief! My mind misgives.

Desdemona. Come, come!
   You'll never meet a more sufficient° man——

Othello. The handkerchief!

Desdemona.   A man that all his time
   Hath founded his good fortunes on your love,
95   Shared dangers with you——

Othello. The handkerchief!

Desdemona. I'faith, you are to blame.

Othello. Away!   *Exit Othello.*

Emilia. Is not this man jealous?

100 *Desdemona.* I nev'r saw this before.
   Sure there's some wonder in this handkerchief;
   I am most unhappy in the loss of it.

Emilia. 'Tis not a year or two shows us a man.
   They are all but stomachs, and we all but food;
105 They eat us hungerly, and when they are full,
   They belch us.

92 **sufficient** complete, with all proper qualities

Enter Iago and Cassio.

            Look you, Cassio and my husband.

Iago. There is no other way; 'tis she must do't.
   And lo the happiness! Go and importune her.

Desdemona. How now, good Cassio? What's the news
      with you?

Cassio. Madam, my former suit. I do beseech you   *110*
   That by your virtuous means I may again
   Exist, and be a member of his love
   Whom I with all the office° of my heart
   Entirely honor. I would not be delayed.
   If my offense be of such mortal kind   *115*
   That nor my service past, nor present sorrows,
   Nor purposed merit in futurity,
   Can ransom me into his love again,
   But to know so must be my benefit.°
   So shall I clothe me in a forced content,   *120*
   And shut myself up in some other course
   To fortune's alms.

Desdemona.   Alas, thrice-gentle Cassio,
   My advocation° is not now in tune.
   My lord is not my lord; nor should I know him
   Were he in favor° as in humor altered.   *125*
   So help me every spirit sanctified
   As I have spoken for you all my best
   And stood within the blank° of his displeasure
   For my free speech. You must awhile be patient.
   What I can do I will; and more I will   *130*
   Than for myself I dare. Let that suffice you.

Iago. Is my lord angry?

Emilia.   He went hence but now,
   And certainly in strange unquietness.

Iago. Can he be angry? I have seen the cannon
   When it hath blown his ranks into the air   *135*
   And, like the devil, from his very arm

113 **office** duty   119 **benefit** good   123 **advocation** advocacy   125 **favor**
countenance   28 **blank** bull's-eye of a target

Puffed his own brother. And is he angry?
Something of moment° then. I will go meet him.
There's matter in't indeed if he be angry.

Desdemona. I prithee do so.   *Exit [Iago].*
140   Something sure of state,°
Either from Venice or some unhatched practice°
Made demonstrable here in Cyprus to him,
Hath puddled° his clear spirit; and in such cases
Men's natures wrangle with inferior things,
145   Though great ones are their object. 'Tis even so.
For let our finger ache, and it endues°
Our other, healthful members even to a sense
Of pain. Nay, we must think men are not gods,
Nor of them look for such observancy
150   As fits the bridal. Beshrew me much, Emilia,
I was, unhandsome warrior as I am,
Arraigning his unkindness with my soul;
But now I find I had suborned the witness,
And he's indicted falsely.

Emilia.   Pray heaven it be
155   State matters, as you think, and no conception
Nor no jealous toy° concerning you.

Desdemona. Alas the day! I never gave him cause.

Emilia. But jealous souls will not be answered so;
They are not ever jealous for the cause,
160   But jealous for they're jealous. It is a monster
Begot upon itself, born on itself.

Desdemona. Heaven keep the monster from Othello's
mind!

Emilia. Lady, amen.

Desdemona. I will go seek him. Cassio, walk here
about.
165   If I do find him fit,° I'll move your suit
And seek to effect it to my uttermost.

---

138 **moment** importance   140 **of state** state affairs   141 **unhatched practice** undisclosed plot   143 **puddled** muddied   146 **endues** leads   156 **toy**
trifle   165 **fit** receptive

Cassio. I humbly thank your ladyship.

Exit [*Desdemona with Emilia*].

Enter Bianca.

Bianca. Save you, friend Cassio!

Cassio.   What make you from
    home?
    How is't with you, my most fair Bianca?
    I' faith, sweet love, I was coming to your house.   *170*

Bianca. And I was going to your lodging, Cassio.
    What, keep a week away? Seven days and nights?
    Eightscore eight hours? And lovers' absent hours
    More tedious than the dial eightscore times?
    O weary reck'ning.°

Cassio.   Pardon me, Bianca.   *175*
    I have this while with leaden thoughts been pressed,
    But I shall in a more continuate° time
    Strike off this score° of absence. Sweet Bianca,
        [*Gives her Desdemona's handkerchief.*]
    Take me this work out.

Bianca.   O Cassio, whence came this?
    This is some token from a newer friend.   *180*
    To the felt absence now I feel a cause.
    Is't come to this? Well, well.

Cassio.   Go to, woman!
    Throw your vile guesses in the devil's teeth,
    From whence you have them. You are jealous now
    That this is from some mistress, some remembrance.   *185*
    No, by my faith, Bianca.

Bianca.   Why, whose is it?

Cassio. I know not neither; I found it in my chamber.
    I like the work well; ere it be demanded,°
    As like enough it will, I would have it copied.
    Take it and do't, and leave me for this time.   *190*

---

175 **reck'ning** addition   177 **continuate** uninterrupted   178 **Strike off this
score** i.e., pay this bill (the *score* being the account of drinks kept in a tavern)
188 **demanded** asked for (by the person who lost it)

Bianca. Leave you? Wherefore?

Cassio. I do attend here on the general
 And think it no addition, nor my wish,
 To have him see me womaned.

Bianca.   Why, I pray you?

Cassio. Not that I love you not.

195 *Bianca.*   But that you do not love me!
 I pray you bring° me on the way a little,
 And say if I shall see you soon at night.

Cassio. 'Tis but a little way that I can bring you,
 For I attend here; but I'll see you soon.

200 *Bianca.* 'Tis very good. I must be circumstanced.°
             Exeunt omnes.

196 **bring** accompany 200 **circumstanced** accept things as they are

ACT 4

Scene 1. [*A street.*]

Enter Othello and Iago.

Iago. Will you think so?

Othello.   Think so, Iago?

Iago.   What,
  To kiss in private?

Othello.   An unauthorized° kiss?

Iago. Or to be naked with her friend in bed
  An hour or more, not meaning any harm?

Othello. Naked in bed, Iago, and not mean harm?   *5*
  It is hypocrisy against the devil.
  They that mean virtuously, and yet do so,
  The devil their virtue tempts, and they tempt heaven.

Iago. If they do nothing, 'tis a venial slip.
  But if I give my wife a handkerchief——   *10*

Othello. What then?

Iago. Why, then 'tis hers, my lord; and being hers,
  She may, I think, bestow't on any man.

Othello. She is protectress of her honor too.
  May she give that?   *15*

Iago. Her honor is an essence that's not seen;
  They have it very oft that have it not.
  But for the handkerchief——

4.1.2 **unauthorized** illicit

83

Othello. By heaven, I would most gladly have forgot it!
20　　Thou said'st—O, it comes o'er my memory
　　As doth the raven° o'er the infected house,
　　Boding to all—he had my handkerchief.

Iago. Ay, what of that?

Othello.　　　　　　　　That's not so good now.

Iago. What if I had said I had seen him do you wrong?
25　　Or heard him say—as knaves be such abroad°
　　Who having, by their own importunate suit,
　　Or voluntary dotage° of some mistress,
　　Convincèd or supplied° them, cannot choose
　　But they must blab——

Othello.　　　　　　　　Hath he said anything?

30　*Iago.* He hath, my lord; but be you well assured,
　　No more than he'll unswear.

Othello.　　　　　　　　What hath he said?

Iago. Why, that he did—I know not what he did.

Othello. What? what?

Iago. Lie——

Othello. With her?

35　*Iago.*　　　　　With her, on her; what you will.

Othello. Lie with her? Lie on her?—We say lie on her
　　when they belie her.—Lie with her! Zounds, that's
　　fulsome.°—Handkerchief—confessions—handker-
　　chief!—To confess, and be hanged for his labor—
40　　first to be hanged, and then to confess! I tremble at
　　it. Nature would not invest herself in such shadow-
　　ing passion without some instruction.° It is not
　　words that shakes me thus.—Pish! Noses, ears, and

21 **raven** (a harbinger of death)　25 **abroad** i.e., in the world　27 **voluntary dotage** weakness of the will　28 **Convincèd or supplied** persuaded or
gratified (the mistress)　38 **fulsome** foul, repulsive　41–42 **Nature ... instruction** i.e., my mind would not become so darkened (with anger) unless
there were something in this (accusation); (it should be remembered that Othello believes in the workings of magic and supernatural forces)

lips? Is't possible?—Confess?—Handkerchief?—O
devil!   *Falls in a trance.*   45

Iago. Work on.
  My med'cine works! Thus credulous fools are
    caught,
  And many worthy and chaste dames even thus,
  All guiltless, meet reproach.° What, ho! My lord!
  My lord, I say! Othello!

                    Enter Cassio.
                        How now, Cassio?   50

Cassio. What's the matter?

Iago. My lord is fall'n into an epilepsy.
  This is his second fit; he had one yesterday.

Cassio. Rub him about the temples.

Iago. The lethargy° must have his quiet course.   55
  If not, he foams at mouth, and by and by
  Breaks out to savage madness. Look, he stirs.
  Do you withdraw yourself a little while.
  He will recover straight. When he is gone,
  I would on great occasion° speak with you.   60

                        [*Exit Cassio.*]
  How is it, general? Have you not hurt your head?

Othello. Dost thou mock° me?

Iago.   I mock you not, by heaven.
  Would you would bear your fortune like a man.

Othello. A hornèd man's a monster and a beast.

Iago. There's many a beast then in a populous city,   65
  And many a civil° monster.

Othello. Did he confess it?

Iago.   Good, sir, be a man.
  Think every bearded fellow that's but yoked
  May draw° with you. There's millions now alive

49 **reproach** shame   55 **lethargy** coma   60 **great occasion** very important
matter   62 **mock** (Othello takes Iago's comment as a reference to his
horns—which it is)   66 **civil** city-dwelling   69 **draw** i.e., like the horned
ox

70　　　That nightly lie in those unproper° beds
　　　Which they dare swear peculiar.° Your case is
　　　　　better.
　　　O, 'tis the spite of hell, the fiend's arch-mock,
　　　To lip a wanton in a secure couch,
　　　And to suppose her chaste. No, let me know;
75　　　And knowing what I am, I know what she shall be.

Othello. O, thou art wise! 'Tis certain.

Iago.　　　　　　　　　　　Stand you awhile apart;
　　　Confine yourself but in a patient list.°
　　　Whilst you were here, o'erwhelmèd with your
　　　　　grief—
　　　A passion most unsuiting such a man—
80　　　Cassio came hither. I shifted him away°
　　　And laid good 'scuses upon your ecstasy;°
　　　Bade him anon return, and here speak with me;
　　　The which he promised. Do but encave° yourself
　　　And mark the fleers,° the gibes, and notable°
　　　　　scorns
85　　　That dwell in every region of his face.
　　　For I will make him tell the tale anew:
　　　Where, how, how oft, how long ago, and when
　　　He hath, and is again to cope your wife.
　　　I say, but mark his gesture. Marry patience,
90　　　Or I shall say you're all in all in spleen,°
　　　And nothing of a man.

Othello.　　　　　　　Dost thou hear, Iago?
　　　I will be found most cunning in my patience;
　　　But—dost thou hear?—most bloody.

Iago.　　　　　　　　　　That's not amiss;
　　　But yet keep time in all. Will you withdraw?

[*Othello moves to one side, where his remarks are not
　　　　　　　　audible to Cassio and Iago.*]

70 **unproper** i.e., not exclusively the husband's　71 **peculiar** their own
alone　77 **a patient list** the bounds of patience　80 **shifted him away** got
rid of him by a stratagem　81 **ecstasy** trance (the literal meaning, "outside
one-self," bears on the meaning of the change Othello is undergoing)　83 **en-
cave** hide　84 **fleers** mocking looks or speeches　84 **notable** obvious　90
spleen passion, particularly anger

Now will I question Cassio of Bianca,   95
A huswife° that by selling her desires
Buys herself bread and cloth. It is a creature
That dotes on Cassio, as 'tis the strumpet's plague
To beguile many and be beguiled by one.
He, when he hears of her, cannot restrain   100
From the excess of laughter. Here he comes.

Enter Cassio.

As he shall smile, Othello shall go mad;
And his unbookish° jealousy must conster°
Poor Cassio's smiles, gestures, and light behaviors
Quite in the wrong. How do you, lieutenant?   105

Cassio. The worser that you give me the addition°
Whose want even kills me.

Iago. Ply Desdemona well, and you are sure on't.
Now, if this suit lay in Bianca's power,
How quickly should you speed!

Cassio.   Alas, poor caitiff!°   110

Othello. Look how he laughs already!

Iago. I never knew woman love man so.

Cassio. Alas, poor rogue! I think, i' faith, she loves me.

Othello. Now he denies it faintly, and laughs it out.

Iago. Do you hear, Cassio?

Othello.   Now he importunes him   115
To tell it o'er. Go to! Well said, well said!

Iago. She gives it out that you shall marry her.
Do you intend it?

Cassio. Ha, ha, ha!

Othello. Do ye triumph, Roman? Do you triumph?   120

Cassio. I marry? What, a customer?° Prithee bear

96 **huswife** housewife (but with the special meaning here of "prostitute")
103 **unbookish** ignorant 103 **conster** construe 106 **addition** title 110
caitiff wretch 121 **customer** one who sells, a merchant (here, a prostitute)

some charity to my wit; do not think it so unwhole-
some. Ha, ha, ha!

Othello. So, so, so, so. They laugh that win.

125 *Iago.* Why, the cry goes that you marry her.

Cassio. Prithee, say true.

Iago. I am a very villain else.

Othello. Have you scored° me? Well.

Cassio. This is the monkey's own giving out. She is
130 persuaded I will marry her out of her own love and
flattery, not out of my promise.

Othello. Iago beckons me; now he begins the story.

[*Othello moves close enough to hear.*]

Cassio. She was here even now; she haunts me in every
place. I was the other day talking on the sea bank
135 with certain Venetians, and thither comes the
bauble,° and falls me thus about my neck——

Othello. Crying "O dear Cassio!" as it were. His gesture imports it.

Cassio. So hangs, and lolls, and weeps upon me; so
140 shakes and pulls me! Ha, ha, ha!

Othello. Now he tells how she plucked him to my
chamber. O, I see that nose of yours, but not that
dog I shall throw it to.

Cassio. Well, I must leave her company.

145 *Iago.* Before me!° Look where she comes.

Enter Bianca.

Cassio. 'Tis such another fitchew!° Marry a perfumed
one? What do you mean by this haunting of me?

Bianca. Let the devil and his dam haunt you! What did
you mean by that same handkerchief you gave me
150 even now? I was a fine fool to take it. I must take

---

128 **scored** marked, defaced   136 **bauble** plaything   145 **Before me!** (an
exclamation of surprise)   146 **fitchew** polecat, i.e., strong-smelling creature

out the work? A likely piece of work that you should
find it in your chamber and know not who left it
there! This is some minx's token, and I must take
out the work? There! [*She throws down the handkerchief.*] Give it your hobbyhorse.° Wheresoever   155
you had it, I'll take out no work on't.

Cassio. How now, my sweet Bianca? How now? how
now?

Othello. By heaven, that should be my handkerchief!

Bianca. If you'll come to supper tonight, you may; if   160
you will not, come when you are next prepared
for.°   *Exit.*

Iago. After her, after her!

Cassio. Faith, I must; she'll rail in the streets else.

Iago. Will you sup there?   165

Cassio. Yes, I intend so.

Iago. Well, I may chance to see you, for I would very
fain speak with you.

Cassio. Prithee come. Will you?

Iago. Go to, say no more.   [*Exit Cassio.*]   170

Othello. [*Comes forward.*] How shall I murder him,
Iago?

Iago. Did you perceive how he laughed at his vice?

Othello. O Iago!

Iago. And did you see the handkerchief?   175

Othello. Was that mine?

Iago. Yours, by this hand! And to see how he prizes
the foolish woman your wife! She gave it him, and
he hath giv'n it his whore.

Othello. I would have him nine years a-killing!—A   180
fine woman, a fair woman, a sweet woman?

155 **hobbyhorse** prostitute　　161–62 **next prepared for** next expected—i.e.,
never

Iago. Nay, you must forget that.

Othello. Ay, let her rot, and perish, and be damned
tonight; for she shall not live. No, my heart is turned
185 to stone; I strike it, and it hurts my hand. O, the
world hath not a sweeter creature! She might lie by
an emperor's side and command him tasks.

Iago. Nay, that's not your way.°

Othello. Hang her! I do but say what she is. So deli-
190 cate with her needle. An admirable musician. O, she
will sing the savageness out of a bear! Of so high
and plenteous wit and invention°——

Iago. She's the worse for all this.

Othello. O, a thousand, a thousand times. And then,
195 of so gentle a condition?°

Iago. Ay, too gentle.

Othello. Nay, that's certain. But yet the pity of it,
Iago. O Iago, the pity of it, Iago.

Iago. If you are so fond over her iniquity, give her
200 patent to offend; for if it touch° not you, it comes
near nobody.

Othello. I will chop her into messes!° Cuckold me!

Iago. O, 'tis foul in her.

Othello. With mine officer!

205 *Iago.* That's fouler.

Othello. Get me some poison, Iago, this night. I'll not
expostulate with her, lest her body and beauty unprovide my mind° again. This night, Iago!

Iago. Do it not with poison. Strangle her in her bed,
210 even the bed she hath contaminated.

Othello. Good, good! The justice of it pleases. Very
good!

---

188 **way** proper course   192 **invention** imagination   195 **gentle a condition** (1) well born (2) of a gentle nature   200 **touch** affects   202 **messes**
bits   207–08 **unprovide my mind** undo my resolution

Iago. And for Cassio, let me be his undertaker.° You
   shall hear more by midnight.

Othello. Excellent good!   [*A trumpet.*]
               What trumpet is that same?   *215*

Iago. I warrant something from Venice.

    Enter Lodovico, Desdemona, and Attendants.
                'Tis Lodovico.
   This comes from the Duke. See, your wife's with
   him.

Lodovico. God save you, worthy general.

Othello.   With° all my heart, sir.

Lodovico. The Duke and the senators of Venice greet
   you.   [*Gives him a letter.*]

Othello. I kiss the instrument of their pleasures.   *220*

            [*Opens the letter and reads.*]

Desdemona. And what's the news, good cousin Lodovico?

Iago. I am very glad to see you, signior.
   Welcome to Cyprus.

Lodovico. I thank you. How does Lieutenant Cassio?

Iago.   Lives, sir.

Desdemona. Cousin, there's fall'n between him   and
   my lord   *225*
   An unkind° breach; but you shall make all well.

Othello. Are you sure of that?

Desdemona. My lord?

Othello. [*Reads*] "This fail you not to do, as you
   will——"

Lodovico. He did not call; he's busy in the paper.   *230*
   Is there division 'twixt my lord and Cassio?

---

213 **undertaker** (not "burier" but "one who undertakes to do something")
218 **With** i.e., I greet you with   226 **unkind** unnatural

Desdemona. A most unhappy one. I would do much
    T' atone° them, for the love I bear to Cassio.

Othello. Fire and brimstone!

Desdemona.   My lord?

Othello.   Are you wise?

Desdemona. What, is he angry?

235   *Lodovico.*   May be th' letter moved him;
    For, as I think, they do command him home,
    Deputing Cassio in his government.°

Desdemona. Trust me, I am glad on't.

Othello.   Indeed?

Desdemona.   My lord?

Othello. I am glad to see you mad.

Desdemona.   Why, sweet Othello—

240   *Othello.* Devil!   [*Strikes her.*]

Desdemona. I have not deserved this.

Lodovico. My lord, this would not be believed in
    Venice,
    Though I should swear I saw't. 'Tis very much.
    Make her amends; she weeps.

Othello.   O devil, devil!

245   If that the earth could teem° with woman's tears,
    Each drop she falls° would prove a crocodile.°
    Out of my sight!

Desdemona.   I will not stay to offend you.   [*Going.*]

Lodovico. Truly, an obedient lady.
    I do beseech your lordship call her back.

Othello. Mistress!

Desdemona.   My lord?

250   *Othello.*   What would you with her, sir?

---

233 **atone** reconcile   237 **government** office   245 **teem** conceive   246
falls drops   246 **crocodile** (the crocodile was supposed to shed false tears to
lure its victims)

Lodovico. Who? I, my lord?

Othello. Ay! You did wish that I would make her turn.
    Sir, she can turn, and turn, and yet go on
    And turn again; and she can weep, sir, weep; ·
    And she's obedient; as you say, obedient.   *255*
    Very obedient. Proceed you in your tears.
    Concerning this, sir—O well-painted passion!
    I am commanded home.—Get you away;
    I'll send for you anon.—Sir, I obey the mandate
    And will return to Venice.—Hence, avaunt!   *260*

                            [*Exit Desdemona.*]
    Cassio shall have my place. And, sir, tonight
    I do entreat that we may sup together.
    You are welcome, sir, to Cyprus.—Goats and mon-
        keys!   *Exit.*

Lodovico. Is this the noble Moor whom our full Senate
    Call all in all sufficient? Is this the nature   *265*
    Whom passion could not shake? whose solid virtue
    The shot of accident nor dart of chance
    Could neither graze nor pierce?

Iago.   He is much changed.

Lodovico. Are his wits safe? Is he not light of brain?

Iago. He's that he is; I may not breathe my censure.   *270*
    What he might be (if, what he might, he is not)
    I would to heaven he were!

Lodovico.   What, strike his wife?

Iago. Faith, that was not so well; yet would I knew
    That stroke would prove the worst.

Lodovico.   Is it his use?°
    Or did the letters work upon his blood°   *275* ·
    And new-create his fault?

Iago.   Alas, alas!
    It is not honesty in me to speak
    What I have seen and known. You shall observe
        him,

274 **use** habit   275 **blood** passion

And his own courses° will denote him so
280   That I may save my speech. Do but go after
And mark how he continues.

Lodovico. I am sorry that I am deceived in him.

Exeunt.

Scene 2. [*The citadel.*]

Enter Othello and Emilia.

Othello. You have seen nothing then?

Emilia. Nor ever heard, nor ever did suspect.

Othello. Yes, you have seen Cassio and she together.

Emilia. But then I saw no harm, and then I heard
5   Each syllable that breath made up° between them.

Othello. What, did they never whisper?

Emilia.   Never, my lord.

Othello. Nor send you out o' th' way?

Emilia. Never.

Othello. To fetch her fan, her gloves, her mask, nor
nothing?

10   *Emilia.* Never, my lord.

Othello. That's strange.

Emilia. I durst, my lord, to wager she is honest,
Lay down my soul at stake.° If you think other,
Remove your thought. It doth abuse your bosom.
15   If any wretch have put this in your head,
Let heaven requite it with the serpent's curse,°
For if she be not honest,° chaste, and true,

---

279 **courses** actions   4.2.5 **that breath made up** spoken   13 **at stake** as
the wager   16 **serpent's curse** (God's curse on the serpent after the fall in
Eden)   17 **honest** chaste

There's no man happy. The purest of their wives
Is foul as slander.

Othello. Bid her come hither. Go.

Exit Emilia.

She says enough; yet she's a simple bawd°   20
That cannot say as much. This is a subtle whore,
A closet lock and key of villainous secrets,
And yet she'll kneel and pray; I have seen her do't.

Enter Desdemona and Emilia.

Desdemona. My lord, what is your will?

Othello. Pray you, chuck, come hither.

Desdemona. What is your pleasure?

Othello. Let me see your eyes.   25
Look in my face.

Desdemona. What horrible fancy's this?

Othello. [*To Emilia*] Some of your function,° mistress:
Leave procreants alone and shut the door;
Cough or cry hem if anybody come.
Your mystery,° your mystery! Nay, dispatch!   30

Exit Emilia.

Desdemona. Upon my knee, what doth your speech import?
I understand a fury in your words.°

Othello. Why, what art thou?

Desdemona. Your wife, my lord; your true
And loyal wife.

Othello. Come, swear it, damn thyself;
Lest, being like one of heaven, the devils themselves   35
Should fear to seize thee. Therefore be double-damned:
Swear thou art honest.

Desdemona. Heaven doth truly know it.

---

20 **bawd** procuress   27 **Some of your function** do your proper work (as the operator of a brothel)   30 **mystery** trade   32 **words** (Q1 adds to this line, "But not the words")

Othello. Heaven truly knows that thou art false as hell.

Desdemona. To whom, my lord? With whom? How am
    I false?

40   *Othello.* Ah, Desdemon! Away! Away! Away!

Desdemona. Alas the heavy day! Why do you weep?
    Am I the motive° of these tears, my lord?
    If haply° you my father do suspect
    An instrument of this your calling back,
45   Lay not your blame on me. If you have lost him,
    I have lost him too.

Othello.   Had it pleased heaven
    To try me with affliction, had they rained
    All kinds of sores and shames on my bare head,
    Steeped° me in poverty to the very lips,
50   Given to captivity me and my utmost hopes,
    I should have found in some place of my soul
    A drop of patience. But, alas, to make me
    The fixèd figure for the time of scorn°
    To point his slow and moving finger at.
55   Yet could I bear that too, well, very well.
    But there where I have garnered up my heart,
    Where either I must live or bear no life,
    The fountain from the which my current runs
    Or else dries up—to be discarded thence,
60   Or keep it as a cistern for foul toads,
    To knot and gender° in—turn thy complexion there,
    Patience, thou young and rose-lipped cherubin!
    I here look grim as hell!°

Desdemona. I hope my noble lord esteems me honest.

65   *Othello.* O, ay, as summer flies are in the shambles,°
    That quicken even with blowing.° O thou weed,

42 **motive** cause 43 **haply** by chance 49 **Steeped** submerged 53 **The
... scorn** the very image of scorn in our time 61 **knot and gender**
twist in bunches and procreate 61–63 **turn ... hell** (the rough sense
would seem to be, "even Patience would grow pale, turn complexion, at
Desdemona's perfidy, but that Othello looks grimly on") 65 **shambles**
abattoirs 66 **quicken even with blowing** become impregnated as soon as
they lay their eggs

Who art so lovely fair, and smell'st so sweet,
That the sense aches at thee, would thou hadst never
   been born!

Desdemona. Alas, what ignorant° sin have I committed?

Othello. Was this fair paper, this most goodly book,   *70*
Made to write "whore" upon? What committed?
Committed? O thou public commoner,°
I should make very forges of my cheeks
That would to cinders burn up modesty,
Did I but speak thy deeds. What committed?   *75*
Heaven stops the nose at it, and the moon winks;°
The bawdy wind that kisses all it meets
Is hushed within the hollow mine of earth
And will not hear 't. What committed?

Desdemona. By heaven, you do me wrong!   *80*

Othello. Are not you a strumpet?

Desdemona.   No, as I am a Christian!
If to preserve this vessel for my lord
From any other foul unlawful touch
Be not to be a strumpet, I am none.

Othello. What, not a whore?

Desdemona.   No, as I shall be saved!   *85*

Othello. Is't possible?

Desdemona. O, heaven forgive us!

Othello.   I cry you mercy° then.
I took you for that cunning whore of Venice
That married with Othello. [*Calling*] You, mistress,

             Enter Emilia.

That have the office opposite to Saint Peter   *90*
And keep the gate of hell! You, you, ay, you!
We have done our course; there's money for your
   pains.   [*Throws her some coins.*]

---

69 **ignorant** unknowing   72 **commoner** prostitute   76 **winks** closes its eyes (the moon was the symbol of chastity)   87 **cry you mercy** ask your pardon

I pray you turn the key and keep your counsel.

Exit.

Emilia. Alas, what does this gentleman conceive?
95 How do you, madam? How do you, my good lady?

Desdemona. Faith, half asleep.

Emilia. Good madam, what's the matter with my lord?

Desdemona. With who?

Emilia. Why, with my lord, madam.

Desdemona. Who is thy lord?

100 *Emilia.*   He that is yours, sweet lady.

Desdemona. I have none. Do not talk to me, Emilia.
I cannot weep, nor answers have I none
But what should go by water.° Prithee tonight
Lay on my bed my wedding sheets, remember;
And call thy husband hither.

105 *Emilia.*   Here's a change indeed!

Exit.

Desdemona. 'Tis meet I should be used so, very meet.
How have I been behaved, that he might stick
The small'st opinion on my least misuse?°

Enter Iago and Emilia.

Iago. What is your pleasure, madam? How is't with
you?

Desdemona. I cannot tell. Those that do teach young
babes
110 Do it with gentle means and easy tasks.
He might have chid me so; for, in good faith,
I am a child to chiding.

Iago.   What is the matter, lady?

Emilia. Alas, Iago, my lord hath so bewhored her,

103 **water** tears   107–08 **stick ... misuse** base any doubt on my smallest
fault

Thrown such despite° and heavy terms upon her   *115*
That true hearts cannot bear it.

Desdemona. Am I that name, Iago?

Iago.   What name, fair lady?

Desdemona. Such as she said my lord did say I was.

Emilia. He called her whore. A beggar in his drink
Could not have laid such terms upon his callet.°   *120*

Iago. Why did he so?

Desdemona. I do not know; I am sure I am none such.

Iago. Do not weep, do not weep. Alas the day.

Emilia. Hath she forsook so many noble matches,
Her father and her country, and her friends,   *125*
To be called whore? Would it not make one weep?

Desdemona. It is my wretched fortune.

Iago.   Beshrew° him for 't!
How comes this trick upon him?

Desdemona.   Nay, heaven doth know.

Emilia. I will be hanged if some eternal villain,
Some busy and insinuating rogue,   *130*
Some cogging,° cozening slave, to get some office,
Have not devised this slander. I will be hanged else.

Iago. Fie, there is no such man! It is impossible.

Desdemona. If any such there be, heaven pardon him.

Emilia. A halter pardon him! And hell gnaw his bones!   *135*
Why should he call her whore? Who keeps her com-
    pany?
What place? What time? What form? What likeli-
    hood?
The Moor's abused by some most villainous knave,
Some base notorious knave, some scurvy fellow.
O heavens, that such companions° thou'dst unfold,°   *140*
And put in every honest hand a whip
To lash the rascals naked through the world
Even from the east to th' west!

115 **despite** abuse   120 **callet** slut   127 **Beshrew** curse   131 **cogging**
cheating   140 **companions** fellows, rogues   140 **unfold** disclose

Iago.   Speak within door.°

Emilia. O, fie upon them! Some such squire° he was
145   That turned your wit the seamy side without
      And made you to suspect me with the Moor.

Iago. You are a fool. Go to.

Desdemona.   Alas, Iago,
      What shall I do to win my lord again?
      Good friend, go to him, for, by this light of heaven,
150   I know not how I lost him. Here I kneel:
      If e'er my will did trespass 'gainst his love
      Either in discourse of thought° or actual deed,
      Or that mine eyes, mine ears, or any sense
      Delighted them in any other form;
155   Or that I do not yet, and ever did,
      And ever will (though he do shake me off
      To beggarly divorcement) love him dearly,
      Comfort forswear me. Unkindness may do much,
      And his unkindness may defeat° my life,
160   But never taint my love. I cannot say "whore."
      It does abhor me now I speak the word;
      To do the act that might the addition earn
      Not the world's mass of vanity could make me.

Iago. I pray you be content. 'Tis but his humor.°
165   The business of the state does him offense.

Desdemona. If 'twere no other.

Iago.   It is but so, I warrant.

                          [*Trumpets within.*]
      Hark how these instruments summon to supper.
      The messengers of Venice stay the meat.°
      Go in, and weep not. All things shall be well.

                          [*Exeunt Desdemona and Emilia.*]
                    Enter Roderigo.
170   How now, Roderigo?

143 **within door** more quietly and moderately   144 **squire** (a term of contempt)   152 **discourse of thought** thinking   159 **defeat** destroy   164 **humor** mood   168 **stay the meat** await the meal

Roderigo. I do not find that thou deal'st justly with me.

Iago. What in the contrary?

Roderigo. Every day thou daff'st° me with some device,° Iago, and rather, as it seems to me now,
keep'st from me all conveniency° than suppliest me   *175*
with the least advantage of hope. I will indeed no
longer endure it; nor am I yet persuaded to put up°
in peace what already I have foolishly suffered.

Iago. Will you hear me, Roderigo?

Roderigo. I have heard too much, and your words   *180*
and performances are no kin together.

Iago. You charge me most unjustly.

Roderigo. With naught but truth. I have wasted myself out of my means. The jewels you have had from
me to deliver Desdemona would half have corrupted   *185*
a votarist.° You have told me she hath received
them, and returned me expectations and comforts
of sudden respect° and acquaintance; but I find
none.

Iago. Well, go to; very well.   *190*

Roderigo. Very well? Go to? I cannot go to, man; nor
'tis not very well. Nay, I think it is scurvy, and begin
to find myself fopped° in it.

Iago. Very well.

Roderigo. I tell you 'tis not very well. I will make my-   *195*
self known to Desdemona. If she will return me
my jewels, I will give over my suit and repent my
unlawful solicitation. If not, assure yourself I will
seek satisfaction of you.

Iago. You have said now?   *200*

Roderigo. Ay, and said nothing but what I protest°
intendment of doing.

---

173 **daff'st** put off   173–74 **device** scheme   175 **conveniency** what is
needful   177 **put up** accept   186 **votarist** nun   188 **sudden respect** immediate consideration   193 **fopped** duped   201 **protest** aver

Iago. Why, now I see there's mettle° in thee, and even
from this instant do build on thee a better opinion
205 than ever before. Give me thy hand, Roderigo. Thou
hast taken against me a most just exception;° but
yet I protest I have dealt most directly° in thy
affair.

Roderigo. It hath not appeared.

210 *Iago.* I grant indeed it hath not appeared, and your
suspicion is not without wit and judgment. But,
Roderigo, if thou hast that in thee indeed which I
have greater reason to believe now than ever—I
mean purpose, courage, and valor—this night show
215 it. If thou the next night following enjoy not Desdemona, take me from this world with treachery and
devise engines for° my life.

Roderigo. Well, what is it? Is it within reason and
compass?°

220 *Iago.* Sir, there is especial commission come from
Venice to depute Cassio in Othello's place.

Roderigo. Is that true? Why, then Othello and Desdemona return again to Venice.

Iago. O, no; he goes into Mauritania and taketh away
225 with him the fair Desdemona, unless his abode be
lingered here by some accident; wherein none can
be so determinate° as the removing of Cassio.

Roderigo. How do you mean, removing him?

Iago. Why, by making him uncapable of Othello's
230 place—knocking out his brains.

Roderigo. And that you would have me to do?

Iago. Ay, if you dare do yourself a profit and a right.
He sups tonight with a harlotry,° and thither will I
go to him. He knows not yet of his honorable for-
235 tune. If you will watch his going thence, which I

203 **mettle** spirit   206 **exception** objection   207 **directly** straightforwardly
217 **engines for** schemes against   219 **compass** possibility   227 **determi-
nate** effective   233 **harlotry** female

will fashion to fall out° between twelve and one,
you may take him at your pleasure. I will be near
to second° your attempt, and he shall fall between
us. Come, stand not amazed at it, but go along with
me. I will show you such a necessity in his death   240
that you shall think yourself bound to put it on him.
It is now high supper time, and the night grows
to waste. About it.

Roderigo. I will hear further reason for this.

Iago. And you shall be satisfied.   *Exeunt.*   245

Scene 3. [The citadel.]

*Enter Othello, Lodovico, Desdemona, Emilia, and
Attendants.*

Lodovico. I do beseech you, sir, trouble yourself no
further.

Othello. O, pardon me; 'twill do me good to walk.

Lodovico. Madam, good night. I humbly thank your
ladyship.

Desdemona. Your honor is most welcome.

Othello. Will you walk, sir? O, Desdemona.   5

Desdemona. My lord?

Othello. Get you to bed on th' instant; I will be returned forthwith. Dismiss your attendant there.
Look't be done.

Desdemona. I will, my lord.   10

        Exit [Othello, with Lodovico and Attendants].

Emilia. How goes it now? He looks gentler than he did.

236 **fall out** occur   238 **second** support

Desdemona. He says he will return incontinent,°
    And hath commanded me to go to bed,
    And bade me to dismiss you.

Emilia.   Dismiss me?

15 *Desdemona.* It was his bidding; therefore, good Emilia,
    Give me my nightly wearing, and adieu.
    We must not now displease him.

Emilia. I would you had never seen him!

Desdemona. So would not I. My love doth so approve
       him
    That even his stubbornness, his checks,° his
20   frowns—
    Prithee unpin me—have grace and favor.

Emilia. I have laid these sheets you bade me on the
    bed.

Desdemona. All's one.° Good Father, how foolish
    are our minds!
    If I do die before, prithee shroud me
    In one of these same sheets.

25 *Emilia.*   Come, come! You talk.

Desdemona. My mother had a maid called Barbary.
    She was in love; and he she loved proved mad
    And did forsake her. She had a song of "Willow";
    An old thing 'twas, but it expressed her fortune,
30 And she died singing it. That song tonight
    Will not go from my mind; I have much to do
    But to go hang my head all at one side
    And sing it like poor Barbary. Prithee dispatch.

Emilia. Shall I go fetch your nightgown?

35 *Desdemona.* No, unpin me here.
    This Lodovico is a proper man.

Emilia. A very handsome man.

Desdemona. He speaks well.

4.3.12 **incontinent** at once   20 **checks** rebukes   23 **All's one** no matter

Emilia. I know a lady in Venice would have walked
   barefoot to Palestine for a touch of his nether lip.   *40*

Desdemona. [*Sings*]
      "The poor soul sat singing by a sycamore tree,
         Sing all a green willow;
      Her hand on her bosom, her head on her knee,
         Sing willow, willow, willow.
      The fresh streams ran by her and murmured
            her moans;   *45*
         Sing willow, willow, willow;
      Her salt tears fell from her, and soft'ned the
         stones—
         Sing willow, willow, willow—"
   Lay by these.   [*Gives Emilia her clothes.*]
      "Willow, Willow"——   *50*
   Prithee hie° thee; he'll come anon.°
      "Sing all a green willow must be my garland.
      Let nobody blame him; his scorn I approve"——
   Nay, that's not next. Hark! Who is't that knocks?

Emilia. It is the wind.   *55*

Desdemona. [*Sings*]
      "I called my love false love; but what said he
            then?
         Sing willow, willow, willow:
      If I court moe° women, you'll couch with moe
         men."
   So, get thee gone; good night. Mine eyes do itch.
   Doth that bode weeping?

Emilia.   'Tis neither here nor there.   *60*

Desdemona. I have heard it said so. O, these men,
   these men.
   Dost thou in conscience think, tell me, Emilia,
   That there be women do abuse their husbands
   In such gross kind?

Emilia.   There be some such, no question

51 **hie** hurry   51 **anon** at once   58 **moe** more

Desdemona. Wouldst thou do such a deed for all the
65 world?

Emilia. Why, would not you?

Desdemona.   No, by this heavenly light!

Emilia. Nor I neither by this heavenly light.
I might do't as well i' th' dark.

Desdemona. Wouldst thou do such a deed for all the
world?

70 *Emilia.* The world's a huge thing; it is a great price for
a small vice.

Desdemona. In troth, I think thou wouldst not.

Emilia. In troth, I think I should; and undo't when I
had done. Marry, I would not do such a thing for
75 a joint-ring,° nor for measures of lawn,° nor for
gowns, petticoats, nor caps, nor any petty exhibition,° but for all the whole world? Why, who
would not make her husband a cuckold to make him
a monarch? I should venture purgatory for't.

80 *Desdemona.* Beshrew me if I would do such a wrong
for the whole world.

Emilia. Why, the wrong is but a wrong i' th' world;
and having the world for your labor, 'tis a wrong
in your own world, and you might quickly make
85 it right.

Desdemona. I do not think there is any such woman.

Emilia. Yes, a dozen; and as many to th' vantage as
would store° the world they played for.
But I do think it is their husbands' faults
90 If wives do fall. Say that they slack their duties
And pour our treasures into foreign° laps;
Or else break out in peevish jealousies,
Throwing restraint upon us; or say they strike us,

---

75 **joint-ring** (a ring with two interlocking halves)   75 **lawn** fine linen
76–77 **exhibition** payment   87–88 **to . . . store** in addition as would fill   91
foreign alien, i.e., other than the wife

Or scant our former having in despite°—
Why, we have galls; and though we have some
　grace,　　　　　　　　　　　　　　　　　　　　*95*
Yet have we some revenge. Let husbands know
Their wives have sense like them. They see, and
　smell,
And have their palates both for sweet and sour,
As husbands have. What is it that they do
When they change° us for others? Is it sport?　　*100*
I think it is. And doth affection° breed it?
I think it doth. Is't frailty that thus errs?
It is so too. And have not we affections?
Desires for sport? and frailty? as men have?
Then let them use us well; else let them know,　　*105*
The ills we do, their ills instruct us so.°

Desdemona. Good night, good night. Heaven me such
　uses° send,
　Not to pick bad from bad, but by bad mend. *Exeunt.*

---

94 scant ... despite reduce, in spite, our household allowance (?)　**100
change** exchange　**101 affection** strong feeling, desire　**106 instruct us so**
teach us to do likewise　**107 uses** practices

ACT 5

Scene 1. [*A street.*]

Enter Iago and Roderigo.

Iago. Here, stand behind this bulk;° straight will he
    come.
    Wear thy good rapier bare, and put it home.
    Quick, quick! Fear nothing; I'll be at thy elbow.
    It makes us, or it mars us, think on that,
5   And fix most firm thy resolution.

Roderigo. Be near at hand; I may miscarry in't.

Iago. Here, at thy hand. Be bold, and take thy stand.

                           [*Moves to one side.*]

Roderigo. I have no great devotion to the deed,
    And yet he hath given me satisfying reasons.
10   'Tis but a man gone. Forth my sword! He dies!

Iago. I have rubbed this young quat° almost to the
    sense,°
    And he grows angry. Now, whether he kill Cassio,
    Or Cassio him, or each do kill the other,
    Every way makes my gain. Live Roderigo,
15   He calls me to a restitution large
    Of gold and jewels that I bobbed° from him
    As gifts to Desdemona.
    It must not be. If Cassio do remain,

5.1.1 **bulk** projecting stall of a shop   11 **quat** pimple   11 **to the sense** raw
16 **bobbed** swindled

He hath a daily beauty in his life
That makes me ugly; and besides, the Moor   20
May unfold me to him; there stand I in much peril.
No, he must die. But so, I hear him coming.

Enter Cassio.

Roderigo. I know his gait. 'Tis he. Villain, thou diest!

[*Thrusts at Cassio.*]

Cassio. That thrust had been mine enemy indeed
But that my coat° is better than thou know'st.   25
I will make proof of thine.   [*Fights with Roderigo.*]

Roderigo.   O, I am slain!°

Cassio. I am maimed forever. Help, ho! Murder!
Murder!

Enter Othello [*to one side*].

Othello. The voice of Cassio. Iago keeps his word.

Roderigo. O, villain that I am!

Othello.   It is even so.

Cassio. O help, ho! Light! A surgeon!   30

Othello. 'Tis he. O brave Iago, honest and just,
That hast such noble sense of thy friend's wrong!
Thou teachest me. Minion,° your dear lies dead,
And your unblest° fate hies.° Strumpet, I come.
Forth of my heart those charms, thine eyes, are
blotted.   35
Thy bed, lust-stained, shall with lust's blood be
spotted.

Exit Othello.

25 **coat** i.e., a mail shirt or bulletproof vest   26 **slain** (most editors add here a stage direction which has Iago wounding Cassio in the leg from behind, but remaining unseen. However, nothing in the text requires this, and Cassio's wound can be given him in the fight with Roderigo, for presumably when Cassio attacks Roderigo the latter would not simply accept the thrust but would parry. Since Iago enters again at line 46, he must exit at some point after line 22)   33 **Minion** hussy, i.e., Desdemona   34 **unblest** unsanctified   34 **hies** approaches swiftly

Enter Lodovico and Gratiano.

Cassio. What, ho? No watch? No passage?° Murder!
　　Murder!

Gratiano. 'Tis some mischance. The voice is very
　　direful.

Cassio. O, help!

40　*Lodovico.* Hark!

Roderigo. O wretched villain!

Lodovico. Two or three groan. 'Tis heavy night.
　　These may be counterfeits. Let's think't unsafe
　　To come into the cry without more help.

45　*Roderigo.* Nobody come? Then shall I bleed to death.

Lodovico. Hark!

　　　　　Enter Iago [with a light].

Gratiano. Here's one comes in his shirt, with light and
　　weapons.

Iago. Who's there? Whose noise is this that cries on
　　murder?

Lodovico. We do not know.

Iago.　　　　　　　　Do not you hear a cry?

Cassio. Here, here! For heaven's sake, help me!

50　*Iago.*　　　　　　　　What's the matter?

Gratiano. This is Othello's ancient, as I take it.

Lodovico. The same indeed, a very valiant fellow.

Iago. What are you here that cry so grievously?

Cassio. Iago? O, I am spoiled, undone by villains.
55　　Give me some help.

Iago. O me, lieutenant! What villains have done this?

Cassio. I think that one of them is hereabout
　　And cannot make away.

37 **passage** passersby

Iago.　　　　　　　O treacherous villains!
　　[*To Lodovico and Gratiano*] What are you there?
　　　Come in, and give some help.

Roderigo. O, help me there!　　　　　　　　　　60

Cassio. That's one of them.

Iago.　　　　　　　　O murd'rous slave! O vil-
　　lain!　　　　　　　　　　[*Stabs Roderigo.*]

Roderigo. O damned Iago! O inhuman dog!

Iago. Kill men i' th' dark?—Where be these bloody
　　thieves?—
　　How silent is this town!—Ho! Murder! Murder!—
　　What may you be? Are you of good or evil?　　65

Lodovico. As you shall prove us, praise us.

Iago. Signior Lodovico?

Lodovico. He, sir.

Iago. I cry you mercy. Here's Cassio hurt by villains.

Gratiano. Cassio?　　　　　　　　　　　　　70

Iago. How is't, brother?

Cassio. My leg is cut in two.

Iago.　　　　　　　　Marry, heaven forbid!
　　Light, gentlemen. I'll bind it with my shirt.

Enter Bianca.

Bianca. What is the matter, ho? Who is't that cried?

Iago. Who is't that cried?　　　　　　　　　75

Bianca. O my dear Cassio! My sweet Cassio!
　　O Cassio, Cassio, Cassio!

Iago. O notable strumpet!—Cassio, may you suspect
　　Who they should be that have thus mangled you?

Cassio. No.　　　　　　　　　　　　　　80

Gratiano. I am sorry to find you thus. I have been to
　　seek you.

Iago. Lend me a garter. So. O for a chair
　　To bear him easily hence.

Bianca. Alas, he faints! O Cassio, Cassio, Cassio!

85 *Iago.* Gentlemen all, I do suspect this trash
To be a party in this injury.—
Patience awhile, good Cassio.—Come, come.
Lend me a light. Know we this face or no?
Alas, my friend and my dear countryman
90 Roderigo? No.—Yes, sure.—Yes, 'tis Roderigo!

Gratiano. What, of Venice?

Iago. Even he, sir. Did you know him?

Gratiano.   Know him? Ay.

Iago. Signior Gratiano? I cry your gentle pardon.
These bloody accidents must excuse my manners
That so neglected you.

95 *Gratiano.*   I am glad to see you.

Iago. How do you, Cassio?—O, a chair, a chair!

Gratiano. Roderigo?

Iago. He, he, 'tis he! [*A chair brought in.*] O, that's
well said;° the chair.
Some good man bear him carefully from hence.
I'll fetch the general's surgeon. [*To Bianca*] For you,
100 mistress,
Save you your labor. [*To Cassio*] He that lies slain
here, Cassio,
Was my dear friend. What malice was between you?

Cassio. None in the world; nor do I know the man.

Iago. What, look you pale?—O, bear him out o' th'
air.   [*Cassio is carried off.*]
Stay you, good gentlemen.—Look you pale, mis-
105 tress?
Do you perceive the gastness° of her eye?
Nay, if you stare, we shall hear more anon.
Behold her well; I pray you look upon her.

98 **well said** well done   106 **gastness** terror

Do you see, gentlemen? Nay, guiltiness will speak,
Though tongues were out of use.°   *110*

[*Enter Emilia.*]

Emilia. Alas, what is the matter? What is the matter,
    husband?

Iago. Cassio hath here been set on in the dark
    By Roderigo and fellows that are scaped.
    He's almost slain, and Roderigo quite dead.

Emilia. Alas, good gentleman! Alas, good Cassio!   *115*

Iago. This is the fruits of whoring. Prithee, Emilia,
    Go know of Cassio where he supped tonight.
    [*To Bianca*] What, do you shake at that?

Bianca. He supped at my house; but I therefore shake
    not.

Iago. O, did he so? I charge° you go with me.   *120*

Emilia. Oh fie upon thee, strumpet!

Bianca. I am no strumpet, but of life as honest
    As you that thus abuse me.

Emilia.   As I? Fie upon thee!

Iago. Kind gentlemen, let's go see poor Cassio
    dressed.°
    [*To Bianca*] Come, mistress, you must tell's another
    tale.   125
    Emilia, run you to the citadel
    And tell my lord and lady what hath happed.

                              [*Exit Emilia.*]
Will you go on afore?   *Exeunt* [*all but Iago*].
                    This is the night
That either makes me or fordoes me quite.°   [*Exit.*]

110 **tongues were out of use** men no longer spoke 120 **charge** command
124 **dressed** bandaged 129 **fordoes me quite** completely ruins me

Scene 2. [*Desdemona's chamber.*]

*Enter Othello [with a light]; and Desdemona
in her bed.*

Othello. It is the cause, it is the cause, my soul.
Let me not name it to you, you chaste stars.
It is the cause. Yet I'll not shed her blood,
Nor scar that whiter skin of hers than snow,
5 And smooth as monumental alabaster.
Yet she must die, else she'll betray more men.
Put out the light, and then put out the light.
If I quench thee, thou flaming minister,°
I can again thy former light restore,
10 Should I repent me; but once put out thy light,
Thou cunning'st° pattern of excelling nature,
I know not where is that Promethean heat°
That can thy light relume.° When I have plucked
the rose,
I cannot give it vital° growth again;
15 It needs must wither. I'll smell thee on the tree.
[He kisses her.]
O balmy breath, that dost almost persuade
Justice to break her sword. One more, one more!
Be thus when thou art dead, and I will kill thee,
And love thee after. One more, and that's the last!
20 So sweet was ne'er so fatal. I must weep,
But they are cruel tears. This sorrow's heavenly;
It strikes where it doth love. She wakes.

Desdemona. Who's there? Othello?

Othello.   Ay, Desdemona.

5.2.8 **minister** worker, servant 11 **cunning'st** most intricate and skillfully
wrought (by nature excelling itself) 12 **Promethean heat** divine fire
(Prometheus is the Titan who stole fire from heaven and gave it to man) 13
relume relight 14 **vital** living

Desdemona. Will you come to bed, my lord?

Othello. Have you prayed tonight, Desdemon?

Desdemona.   Ay, my lord.   25

Othello. If you bethink yourself of any crime
   Unreconciled as yet to heaven and grace,
   Solicit for it straight.

Desdemona. Alack, my lord, what may you mean by
      that?

Othello. Well, do it, and be brief; I will walk by.°   30
   I would not kill thy unprepared spirit.
   No, heavens forfend! I would not kill thy soul.

Desdemona. Talk you of killing?

Othello.   Ay, I do.

Desdemona.   Then heaven
   Have mercy on me!

Othello.   Amen, with all my heart.

Desdemona. If you say so, I hope you will not kill me.   35

Othello. Humh.

Desdemona. And yet I fear you; for you're fatal then
   When your eyes roll so. Why I should fear I know
      not,
   Since guiltiness I know not; but yet I feel I fear.

Othello. Think on thy sins.

Desdemona.   They are loves I bear to you.   40

Othello. Ay, and for that thou diest.

Desdemona. That death's unnatural that kills for
      loving.
   Alas, why gnaw you so your nether lip?
   Some bloody passion shakes your very frame.
   These are portents; but yet I hope, I hope,   45
   They do not point on me.

Othello.   Peace and be still.

30 **by** nearby

Desdemona. I will so. What's the matter?

Othello. That handkerchief which I so loved and gave
   thee,
  Thou gav'st to Cassio.

Desdemona.   No, by my life and soul!
  Send for the man and ask him.

50 *Othello.*   Sweet soul, take heed,
  Take heed of perjury; thou art on thy deathbed.

Desdemona. Ay, but not yet to die.

Othello.   Presently.°
  Therefore confess thee freely of thy sin,
  For to deny each article° with oath
55   Cannot remove nor choke the strong conception
  That I do groan withal. Thou art to die.

Desdemona. Then Lord have mercy on me.

Othello.   I say, amen.

Desdemona. And have you mercy too. I never did
  Offend you in my life; never loved Cassio
60   But with such general warranty° of heaven
  As I might love. I never gave him token.

Othello. By heaven, I saw my handkerchief in's hand!
  O perjured woman! thou dost stone° my heart,
  And mak'st me call what I intend to do
65   A murder, which I thought a sacrifice.
  I saw the handkerchief.

Desdemona.   He found it then.
  I never gave it him. Send for him hither.
  Let him confess a truth.

Othello.   He hath confessed.

Desdemona. What, my lord?

Othello. That he hath used thee.

Desdemona.   How? Unlawfully?

52 **Presently** immediately   54 **article** item (of the charge of adultery. Othello makes heavy use of legal terms in this scene)   60 **warranty** allowance
63 **stone** turn to stone

Othello.　　　　　　　　　　　　　　　　Ay.　70

Desdemona. He will not say so.

Othello.　　　　　　　　No, his mouth is stopped.
　　Honest Iago hath ta'en order for't.°

Desdemona. O, my fear interprets. What, is he dead?

Othello. Had all his hairs been lives, my great revenge
　　Had stomach° for them all.　75

Desdemona. Alas, he is betrayed, and I undone!

Othello. Out, strumpet! Weep'st thou for him to my
　　face?

Desdemona. O, banish me, my lord, but kill me not!

Othello. Down, strumpet!

Desdemona. Kill me tomorrow; let me live tonight!　80

Othello. Nay, if you strive——

Desdemona. But half an hour!

Othello.　　　　　　Being done, there is no pause.

Desdemona. But while I say one prayer!

Othello.　　　　　　　　　　　It is too late.
　　　　　　　　　　　　　　　　Smothers her.
　　　　　　　　Emilia at the door.

Emilia. [*Calls within.*] My lord, my lord! What, ho, my
　　lord, my lord!

Othello. What noise is this? Not dead? Not yet quite
　　dead?　85
　　I that am cruel am yet merciful;
　　I would not have thee linger in thy pain.
　　So, so.

Emilia. [*Within*] What, ho! My lord, my lord!

Othello.　　　　　　　　　　　Who's there?

Emilia. [*Within*] O, good my lord, I would speak a
　　word with you.

72 **ta'en order for't** make sure of it　75 **stomach** appetite

90 *Othello.* Yes, 'tis Emilia.—By and by.—She's dead.—
       'Tis like she comes to speak of Cassio's death.
       The noise was high.° Ha! No more moving?
       Still as the grave.—Shall she come in? Were't
          good?—
       I think she stirs again. No.—What's best to do?
95   If she come in, she'll sure speak to my wife.
       My wife! My wife! What wife? I have no wife.
       O, insupportable! O heavy hour!
       Methinks it should be now a huge eclipse
       Of sun and moon, and that th' affrighted globe
       Should yawn° at alteration.

100 *Emilia.*   [*Within*] I do beseech you
       That I may speak with you, O good my lord!

   Othello. I had forgot thee. O, come in, Emilia.
       Soft, by and by.—Let me the curtains draw.—

   [*Draws the bed hangings and then opens the door.*]
       Where art thou?

                         Enter Emilia.
                      What's the matter with thee now?

105 *Emilia.* O my good lord, yonder's foul murders done!

   Othello. What? Now?

   Emilia. But now, my lord.

   Othello. It is the very error° of the moon.
       She comes more nearer earth than she was wont
110   And makes men mad.

   Emilia. Cassio, my lord, hath killed a young Venetian
       Called Roderigo.

   Othello.   Roderigo killed?
       And Cassio killed?

92 **high** loud (Q1 reads "here")   98–100 **Methinks . . . alteration** (the Elizabethans believed that great changes in human affairs were reflected by disorders in nature)   100 **yawn** gape open (as in an earthquake)   108 **error**
wandering out of regular course (disorders in the heavens were believed by
some to cause disorders on earth, as well as vice versa)

Emilia.   No, Cassio is not killed.

Othello. Not Cassio killed? Then murder's out of tune,
  And sweet revenge grows harsh.   115

Desdemona. O, falsely, falsely murdered!

Emilia.   O Lord! What cry is that?

Othello. That? What?

Emilia. Out and alas! that was my lady's voice.
  Help! Help, ho! Help! O lady, speak again!
  Sweet Desdemona! O sweet mistress, speak!   120

Desdemona. A guiltless death I die.

Emilia. O, who hath done this deed?

Desdemona. Nobody—I myself. Farewell.
  Commend me to my kind lord. O, farewell!

                                    [*She dies.*]

Othello. Why, how should she be murd'red?

Emilia.   Alas, who knows? 125

Othello. You heard her say herself, it was not I.

Emilia. She said so. I must needs report the truth.

Othello. She's like a liar gone to burning hell!
  'Twas I that killed her.

Emilia.   O, the more angel she,
  And you the blacker devil!   130

Othello. She turned to folly, and she was a whore.

Emilia. Thou dost belie her, and thou art a devil.

Othello. She was false as water.

Emilia.   Thou art rash as fire to say
  That she was false. O, she was heavenly true!

Othello. Cassio did top her. Ask thy husband else. 135
  O, I were damned beneath all depth in hell
  But that I did proceed upon just grounds
  To this extremity. Thy husband knew it all.

Emilia. My husband?

Othello.   Thy husband.

Emilia.   That she was false to wedlock?

140   *Othello.* Ay, with Cassio. Had she been true,
    If heaven would make me such another world
    Of one entire and perfect chrysolite,°
    I'd not have sold her for it.

Emilia.   My husband?

Othello. Ay, 'twas he that told me on her first.
145   An honest man he is, and hates the slime
    That sticks on filthy deeds.

Emilia.   My husband?

Othello. What needs this iterance? Woman, I say thy
    husband.

Emilia. O mistress, villainy hath made mocks with
    love!
    My husband say she was false?

Othello.   He, woman.
150   I say, thy husband. Dost understand the word?
    My friend, thy husband; honest, honest Iago.

Emilia. If he say so, may his pernicious soul
    Rot half a grain a day! He lies to th' heart.
    She was too fond of her most filthy bargain.

155   *Othello.* Hah?

Emilia. Do thy worst.
    This deed of thine is no more worthy heaven
    Than thou wast worthy her.

Othello.   Peace, you were best.°

Emilia. Thou hast not half that pow'r to do me harm
160   As I have to be hurt. O gull! O dolt!
    As ignorant as dirt! Thou hast done a deed—
            [*Othello moves to draw his sword.*]
    I care not for thy sword; I'll make thee known,
    Though I lost twenty lives. Help! Help! Ho! Help!
    The Moor hath killed my mistress! Murder! murder!

---

142 **chrysolite** topaz   158 **Peace, you were best** i.e., you had better be
silent

Enter Montano, Gratiano, and Iago [and Others].

Montano. What is the matter? How now, general?   165

Emilia. O, are you come, Iago? You have done well,
   That men must lay their murders on your neck.

Gratiano. What is the matter?

Emilia. Disprove this villain, if thou be'st a man.
   He says thou told'st him that his wife was false.   170
   I know thou didst not; thou'rt not such a villain.
   Speak, for my heart is full.

Iago. I told him what I thought, and told no more
   Than what he found himself was apt and true.

Emilia. But did you ever tell him she was false?   175

Iago. I did.

Emilia. You told a lie, an odious damnèd lie!
   Upon my soul, a lie! A wicked lie!
   She false with Cassio? Did you say with Cassio?

Iago. With Cassio, mistress. Go to, charm° your
   tongue.   180

Emilia. I will not charm my tongue; I am bound to
   speak:
   My mistress here lies murdered in her bed.

All. O heavens forfend!

Emilia. And your reports have set the murder on.

Othello. Nay, stare not, masters. It is true indeed.   185

Gratiano. 'Tis a strange truth.

Montano. O monstrous act!

Emilia.   Villainy, villainy, villainy!
   I think upon't—I think I smell't!—O villainy!
   I thought so then.—I'll kill myself for grief.—
   O villainy, villainy!   190

Iago. What, are you mad? I charge you get you home.

Emilia. Good gentlemen, let me have leave to speak.

180 **charm** control

'Tis proper I obey him, but not now.
Perchance, Iago, I will ne'er go home.

Othello. O! O! O!   [*Falls on the bed.*]

195 *Emilia.*   Nay, lay thee down and roar,
For thou hast killed the sweetest innocent
That e'er did lift up eye.

Othello.   O, she was foul!   [*Rises.*]
I scarce did know you, uncle. There lies your niece,
Whose breath, indeed, these hands have newly
      stopped.
200 I know this act shows horrible and grim.

Gratiano. Poor Desdemon! I am glad thy father's dead.
Thy match was mortal to him, and pure grief
Shore his old thread in twain. Did he live now,
This sight would make him do a desperate turn;
205 Yea, curse his better angel from his side,
And fall to reprobation.°

Othello. 'Tis pitiful; but yet Iago knows
That she with Cassio hath the act of shame
A thousand times committed. Cassio confessed it;
210 And she did gratify his amorous works
With that recognizance and pledge of love,
Which I first gave her. I saw it in his hand.
It was a handkerchief, an antique token
My father gave my mother.

215 *Emilia.* O God! O heavenly God!

Iago. Zounds, hold your peace!

Emilia.   'Twill out, 'twill out! I peace?
No, I will speak as liberal as the north.°
Let heaven and men and devils, let them all,
All, all, cry shame against me, yet I'll speak.

Iago. Be wise, and get you home.

220 *Emilia.*   I will not.

                    [*Iago draws and threatens Emilia.*]

206 **reprobation** damnation   217 **liberal as the north** freely (and bitingly)
as the north wind blows

Gratiano. Fie! Your sword upon a woman?

Emilia. O thou dull Moor, that handkerchief thou
speak'st of
I found by fortune, and did give my husband;
For often with a solemn earnestness—
More than indeed belonged to such a trifle—   225
He begged of me to steal't.

Iago.   Villainous whore!

Emilia. She give it Cassio? No, alas, I found it,
And I did give't my husband.

Iago.   Filth, thou liest!

Emilia. By heaven, I do not, I do not, gentlemen.
O murd'rous coxcomb! What should such a fool   230
Do with so good a wife?

Othello.   Are there no stones° in heaven
But what serves for the thunder? Precious villain!
[*The Moor runs at Iago, but is disarmed by Montano.
Iago kills his wife.*]

Gratiano. The woman falls. Sure he hath killed his
wife.

Emilia. Ay, ay. O, lay me by my mistress' side.

[*Exit Iago.*]

Gratiano. He's gone, but his wife's killed.   235

Montano. 'Tis a notorious° villain. Take you this
weapon,
Which I have recovered from the Moor.
Come, guard the door without. Let him not pass,
But kill him rather. I'll after that same villain,
For 'tis a damnèd slave.

            Exit [*with all but Othello and Emilia*].

Othello.   I am not valiant neither;   240
But every puny whipster° gets my sword.
But why should honor outlive honesty?
Let it go all.

231 **stones** thunderbolts   236 **notorious** out-and-out   241 **puny whipster**
small top-whipping boy (?)

Emilia.   What did thy song bode, lady?
Hark, canst thou hear me? I will play the swan,
245 And die in music. [*Sings*] "Willow, willow, willow."
Moor, she was chaste. She loved thee, cruel Moor,
So come my soul to bliss as I speak true.
So speaking as I think, alas, I die.   [*She dies.*]

Othello. I have another weapon in this chamber;
250 It was a sword of Spain, the ice-brook's temper.
O, here it is.—Uncle, I must come forth.

Gratiano. [*Within*] If thou attempt it, it will cost thee
  dear.
Thou hast no weapon, and perforce must suffer.

Othello. Look in upon me then and speak with me,
255 Or, naked as I am, I will assault thee.

[*Enter Gratiano.*]

Gratiano. What is the matter?

Othello.   Behold, I have a weapon;
A better never did itself sustain
Upon a soldier's thigh. I have seen the day
That with this little arm and this good sword
260 I have made my way through more impediments
Than twenty times your stop. But O vain boast!
Who can control his fate? 'Tis not so now.
Be not afraid, though you do see me weaponed.
Here is my journey's end, here is my butt,°
265 And very seamark of my utmost sail.°
Do you go back dismayed? 'Tis a lost fear.
Man but a rush° against Othello's breast,
And he retires. Where should Othello go?
Now, how dost thou look now? O ill-starred wench!
270 Pale as thy smock! When we shall meet at compt,°
This look of thine will hurl my soul from heaven,
And fiends will snatch at it. Cold, cold, my girl?
Even like thy chastity.
O cursèd, cursèd slave! Whip me, ye devils,

264 **butt** target, stopping place 265 **seamark of my utmost sail** marker
of my farthest journey 267 **Man but a rush** attack with only a reed 270
compt Judgment Day

From the possession of° this heavenly sight!   275
Blow me about in winds! roast me in sulfur!
Wash me in steep-down gulfs of liquid fire!
O Desdemon! Dead Desdemon; dead. O! O!
    Enter Lodovico, Cassio, Montano, and Iago
      [as prisoner,] with Officers.

Lodovico. Where is this rash and most unfortunate
   man?

Othello. That's he that was Othello; Here I am.   280

Lodovico. Where is that viper? Bring the villain forth.

Othello. I look down towards his feet°—but that's a
   fable.
If that thou be'st a devil, I cannot kill thee.

                      [Wounds Iago.]

Lodovico. Wrench his sword from him.

                   [Othello is disarmed.]

Iago.   I bleed, sir, but not killed.

Othello. I am not sorry neither. I'd have thee live;   285
For in my sense, 'tis happiness to die.

Lodovico. O thou Othello that was once so good,
Fall'n in the practice° of a cursèd slave,
What shall be said to thee?

Othello.   Why, anything:
An honorable murderer, if you will;   290
For naught I did in hate, but all in honor.

Lodovico. This wretch hath part confessed his villainy.
Did you and he consent in Cassio's death?

Othello. Ay.

Cassio. Dear general, I never gave you cause.   295

Othello. I do believe it, and I ask your pardon.
Will you, I pray, demand that demi-devil
Why he hath thus ensnared my soul and body?

---

275 **the possession of** being possessed by   282 **towards his feet** i.e., for
his cloven hoofs   288 **practice** plotting

Iago. Demand me nothing. What you know, you know.
From this time forth I never will speak word.

Lodovico. What, not to pray?

Gratiano.   Torments will ope your lips.

Othello. Well, thou dost best.

Lodovico. Sir, you shall understand what hath befall'n,
Which, as I think, you know not. Here is a letter
Found in the pocket of the slain Roderigo;
And here another. The one of them imports
The death of Cassio to be undertook
By Roderigo.

Othello. O villain!

Cassio.   Most heathenish and most gross!

Lodovico. Now here's another discontented paper
Found in his pocket too; and this, it seems,
Roderigo meant t' have sent this damnèd villain;
But that, belike, Iago in the interim
Came in and satisfied him.

Othello.   O thou pernicious caitiff!
How came you, Cassio, by that handkerchief
That was my wife's?

Cassio.   I found it in my chamber;
And he himself confessed it but even now
That there he dropped it for a special purpose
Which wrought to his desire.

Othello.   O fool! Fool! Fool!

Cassio. There is besides in Roderigo's letter,
How he upbraids Iago that he made him
Brave me upon the watch; whereon it came
That I was cast; and even but now he spake,
After long seeming dead—Iago hurt him,
Iago set him on.

Lodovico. You must forsake this room and go with
us.
Your power and your command is taken off,
And Cassio rules in Cyprus. For this slave,

If there be any cunning cruelty
That can torment him much and hold him long,   *330*
It shall be his. You shall close prisoner rest
Till that the nature of your fault be known
To the Venetian state. Come, bring away.

Othello. Soft you, a word or two before you go.
I have done the state some service, and they know't. *335*
No more of that. I pray you, in your letters,
When you shall these unlucky deeds relate,
Speak of me as I am. Nothing extenuate,
Nor set down aught in malice. Then must you speak
Of one that loved not wisely, but too well;   *340*
Of one not easily jealous, but, being wrought,
Perplexed in the extreme; of one whose hand,
Like the base Judean,° threw a pearl away
Richer than all his tribe; of one whose subdued
   eyes,
Albeit unusèd to the melting mood,   *345*
Drops tears as fast as the Arabian trees
Their med'cinable gum. Set you down this.
And say besides that in Aleppo once,
Where a malignant and a turbaned Turk
Beat a Venetian and traduced the state,   *350*
I took by th' throat the circumcisèd dog
And smote him—thus.   [*He stabs himself.*]

Lodovico. O bloody period!°

Gratiano.   All that is spoke is marred.

Othello. I kissed thee ere I killed thee. No way but this,
Killing myself, to die upon a kiss.   *355*

        [*He falls over Desdemona and dies.*]

Cassio. This did I fear, but thought he had no weapon;
For he was great of heart.

Lodovico.   [*To Iago*] O Spartan dog,
More fell° than anguish, hunger, or the sea!

343 **Judean** (most editors use the Q1 reading, "Indian," here, but F is clear; both readings point toward the infidel, the unbeliever)   353 **period** end   358 **fell** cruel

Look on the tragic loading of this bed.
360 This is thy work. The object poisons sight;
Let it be hid.   [*Bed curtains drawn.*]
        Gratiano, keep° the house,
And seize upon the fortunes of the Moor,
For they succeed on you. To you, lord governor,
Remains the censure of this hellish villain,
365 The time, the place, the torture. O, enforce it!
Myself will straight aboard, and to the state
This heavy act with heavy heart relate.   *Exeunt.*

                        FINIS

361 **keep** remain in

Textual Note

Othello contains some of the most difficult editorial problems of any Shakespearean play. The play was entered in *The Stationer's Register* on 6 October, 1621, and printed in a quarto edition, Q1, by Thomas Walkley in 1622, some eighteen or nineteen years after it was first staged. More curiously, at the time that Walkley printed his quarto edition, the plans for printing the folio edition of Shakespeare's collected works were completed and printing was well along. The Folio, F, appeared in late 1623, and the text of *Othello* included in it differs considerably from Q1. A second quarto, Q2, was printed from F in 1630. The chief differences between the two major texts, Q1 and F, are: (1) There are 160 lines in F that are not in Q1; some of these omissions affect the sense in Q1, but others seem to be either intentional cuts in Q1 or additions in F. (2) There are a number of oaths in Q1 that are not in F; this fact can be interpreted in a number of ways, but all arguments go back to the prohibition in 1606 of swearing on stage—but apparently not in printed editions. (3) The stage directions in Q1 are much fuller than in F. (4) There are a large number of variant readings in the two texts, in single words, in phrases, and in lineation; where Q1, for example, reads "toged" (i.e., wearing a toga), F reads "tongued"; where Q1 reads "Worships," F reads "Moorships."

These may seem petty problems, but they present an editor with a series of most difficult questions about what to print at any given point where the two texts are in disagreement. The usual solution in the past has been for the editor to include all material in F and Q1, and where the two texts are in disagreement to select the reading he prefers. The result is what is known as an eclectic text. But modern bibliographical studies have demonstrated that it is possible to proceed, in some cases at least, in a more precise manner by examining the conflicting texts carefully in order to arrive at something like a reasonable judgment about their relative authority. Shakespearean bibliography has become a most elaborate affair, however, and in most cases it has become necessary to take the word of specialists on these matters. Unfortunately, in the case of *Othello* the experts are not in agreement, and none of their arguments has the ring of certainty. Here is, however, the most general opinion of how the two different texts came into being and how they are related.

After Shakespeare wrote the play, his original draft, usually termed "foul papers," was copied, around 1604, by a scribe and made into what is known as the "promptbook," the official copy of the play used in the theater as the basis for production. This promptbook was the property of the players' company, the King's Men in this case, and remained in their possession to be used, and perhaps revised, whenever they produced *Othello*. Being a repertory company they would present a play for a few performances, then drop it for a time, and then present it again when conditions seemed favorable. At some time around 1620, another copy was made of the original foul papers, or some later copy of them, and this served as the basis for the 1622 Quarto. Later, when the publishers of the Folio got around to printing *Othello*, they took a copy of Q1 and corrected it by the original promptbook, and this corrected copy was then given to the compositors who were setting type for F. There are genuine objections to this theory, the most telling raised by M. R. Ridley, in *The Arden Shakespeare* edition of *Othello*; but the theory does explain certain difficult facts, and most bibliographers seem to accept some version of it.

Since 1964, and Nevill Coghill's *Shakespeare's Professional Skills*, however, editors have increasingly returned to a much earlier view that the successive editions of *Othello* represent not two different versions of a hypothetical original play but are two somewhat differing plays, each complete in itself, though containing errors. This "two-play theory" has been advanced most forcefully for *King Lear*, but the quarto and folio versions of *Othello* have been argued to be different playhouse versions produced by Shakespeare to update and adjust his play in ways thought best for performance. The full argument for this view is presented by E. J. A. Honigman, "Shakespeare's Revised Plays: *King Lear* and *Othello*," *The Library* 6, 4:2 (1982): 142–73.

The end of this line of argument is to establish fairly reasonably the authority of the F text as being the closest either to what Shakespeare wrote originally or to the play as he finally left it after playhouse revisions. This agrees with what most scholars find in reading the two texts. Sir Walter Greg puts this common belief in the superiority of F in the strongest terms: "In the great majority of cases there can be no doubt that F has preserved the more Shakespearean reading." (*The Shakespeare First Folio*, Oxford, 1955, p. 365.) For practical purposes what this means is that where an F reading makes sense, then an editor has no choice but to accept it—even though he "likes" the Q reading better and would have used it if he had *written,* instead of only edited, the play. But while an editor may be aided and comforted by the bibliographers' decision that F is more authoritative than Q1, his problems are by no means solved. There are places where F does not make sense but Q1 does, places where F is deficient in some way and Q is clear and complete, and places where both fail to make sense or seem to point to a common failure to transcribe correctly their original. When this occurs an editor must try to understand how the trouble occurred and then fall back on his judgment. This will force him to try to reconstruct the original manuscript from which we are told Q and F both derive, and he must attempt to deduce the original reading which both scribes mangled or which the typesetters in the different printing houses misread or made a mistake in setting.

This editorial process is endlessly complicated, but the general basis of this edition is as follows: F is taken for the copy text and its readings are preserved wherever they make sense. Oaths and stage directions are, however, taken from Q1, since they were presumably part of the original manuscript, but were deleted by the promptbook transcriber to comply with the prohibition against swearing on stage and because the prompt copy did not require such elaborate stage directions as a reading version—somewhat contrary to common sense, this last, but the bibliographers insist upon it. Where mislineation occurs in F, but Q1 has it correctly, the Q1 lineation is used on the theory that it has a better chance of being the original than any hypothetical reconstruction of my own. Finally, where F and Q1 both produce nonsense, changes, based on the above theory about the transmission of the text and on the work of previous editors, have been made.

Where F is deficient, the reading adopted and printed in this text is given below first in italics; unless otherwise stated it is taken from Q1. The original F reading that has been changed follows in roman. Obvious typographical errors in F, expansions of abbreviations, spelling variants ("murder," "murther"), and changes in punctuation and lineation are not noted. The act and scene divisions are translated from Latin, and the division at 2.3 is from the Globe edition rather than from F; otherwise the divisions of F and the Globe edition are identical. "The Names of the Actors," here printed at the beginning of the play, in F follows the play.

1.1.1 *Tush! Never* Never 4 *'Sblood, but* But 26 *other* others 27 *Christian* Christen'd 30 *God bless* blesse 63 *full* fall *thick-lips* Thicks-lips 83 *Zounds, sir* Sir 105 *Zounds, sir* Sir 111 *germans* Germaines 143 *produced* producted 151 *hell pains* (emendation) hell apines [hells paines Q1]

1.2.33 *Duke* Dukes 37 *Even* enen 49 *carack* (emendation) Carract [Carrick Q1] 50 *he's made* he' made 57 *Come* Cme 67 *darlings* Deareling 74 *weaken* weakens 83 *Whither* Whether 86 *if I do* if do

1.3.53 *nor* hor 74 *your* yonr 99 *maimed* main'd 106 *Duke* [F omits] 107 *overt test* oer Test 110 *First Senator* Sen. 122 *till* tell 138 *travel's* trauellours 140 *rocks, and hills* Rocks, Hills *heads* head 142 *other* others 146 *thence* hence 154 *intentively* instinctively 203 *preserved* presern'd 227 *couch* (emendation) Coach [Cooch Q1] 229 *alacrity* Alacartie 259 *me* my [F and Q1] 273 *First Senator* Sen. 286 *First Senator* Sen. 321–22 *balance* braine 328 *scion* (emendation) Seyen [seyen Q1] 376 *snipe* snpe 379 *H'as* She ha's

2.1.9 *mortise* (emendation) morties [morties Q1] 33 *prays* praye 40 *Third Gentleman* Gent. 53 *First Gentleman* Gent. 56 *Second Gentleman* Gent. 59 *Second Gentleman* Gent. 65 *ingener* Ingeniuer 66 *Second Gentleman* Gent. 94 *Second Gentleman* Gent. 168 *gyve* (emendation) giue [catch Q1] 173 *an* and 175 *clyster* cluster 212 *hither* thither 242 *has* he's 261 *mutualities* mutabilities 299 *wife* wist 307 *nightcap* Night-Cape

2.3.39 *unfortunate* infortunate 57 *to put* put to 61 *God* heauen 72 *God* Heauen 77 *Englishman* Englishmen 93 *thine* thy 95 *'Fore God* Why 99 *God's* heauen's 108 *God forgive* Forgiue 141 *Within . . . help* [F omits; Q1 reads "Helpe, helpe, within"] 142 *Zounds, you* You 156 *God's will* Alas 160 *God's will* Fie, fie 162 *Zounds, I* I 217 *leagued* (emendation) [league F and Q1] 260 *God* Heauen 274 *to* ro 288 *O God* Oh 343 *were 't* were to 362 *enmesh* en-mash 378 *By the mass* In troth

3.1.1s.d [F includes the Clown] 20 *Exeunt Musicians* Exit Mu. 25 *general's wife* Generall 30 *Cassio* [no speech ascription in F]

3.2.6 *We'll* Well

3.3.74 *By'r Lady* Trust me 94 *you* he 106 *By heaven* Alas 135 *free to* free 136 *vile* vild 139 *But some* Wherein 148 *Shape* (emendation) Shapes 162 *By heaven I'll* Ile 170 *fondly* (emendation) soundly [strongly Q1] 175 *God* heauen 182 *exsufflicate* (emendation) exufflicate (F and Q1) *blown* blowd 217 *my* your 222 *vile* vilde 248 *hold him* him 258 *qualities* Quantities 259 *human* humane 281 *to* too 335 *of* in 347 *make* makes 372 *b' wi'* buy 392 *supervisor* supervision 437 *that was* (Malone's emendation) it was [F and Q1]

3.4.77 *God* Heauen 81 *Heaven* Blesse 97 *I'faith* In sooth 170 *I'faith* Indeed 186 *by my faith* in good troth

4.1.21 *infected* infectious 37 *Zounds, that's* that's 79 *unsuiting* resulting 103 *conster* conserue 109 *power* dowre 113 *i'faith* indeed 124 *win* winnes 132 *beckons* becomes 164 *Faith, I* I 218 *God save* Save 248 *an obedient* obedient

4.2.16 *requite* requit 30 *Nay* May 48 *kinds* kind 154 *in* [Q2] or 168 *stay* stays

4.3.14 *bade* bid 51 *hie* high

5.1.1 *bulk* Barke 22 *hear* heard 34 *hies* highes 35 *Forth* For 50 *heaven's* heauen 104 *out o' th'* o' th'

5.2.13 *the rose* thy Rose 35 *say so* say 57 *Then Lord* O Heauen 100 *Should* Did 116 *O Lord* Alas 126 *heard* heare 206 *reprobation* Reprobance 215 *O God! O heavenly God* O Heauen! Oh heauenly powres 216 *Zounds* Come

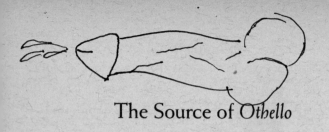

The Source of *Othello*

Shakespeare's play is based on a story in Giraldi Cinthio's *Hecatommithi* (III, 7), a collection of a hundred tales printed in Italy in the sixteenth century. So far as is known, there was no English translation of the source story in Shakespeare's time, and while he may have read it in a French translation of Gabriel Chappuys, it seems probable that he read the original Italian. For a discussion of the evidence for this view and a good comparison of the story and the play, see Kenneth Muir, *Shakespeare's Sources* (London, 1957), Vol. I, "Comedies and Tragedies," pp. 122–23. The translation reprinted here is that of J. E. Taylor, done in 1855.

Selection from Giraldi Cinthio
Hecatommithi

There once lived in Venice a Moor, who was very valiant and of a handsome person; and having given proofs in war of great skill and prudence, he was highly esteemed by the Signoria of the Republic, who in rewarding deeds of valor advanced the interests of the state.

It happened that a virtuous lady of marvelous beauty, named Disdemona, fell in love with the Moor, moved thereto by his valor; and he, vanquished by the beauty and the noble character of Disdemona, returned her love; and their affection was so mutual that, although the parents of the lady strove all they could to induce her to take another husband, she consented to marry the Moor; and they lived in such harmony and peace in Venice that no word ever passed between them that was not affectionate and kind.

Now it happened at this time that the Signoria of Venice made a change in the troops whom they used to maintain in Cyprus, and they appointed the Moor commander of the soldiers whom they dispatched thither. Joyful as was the Moor at the honor proffered him, such dignity being only conferred on men of noble rank and well-tried faith, and who had displayed bravery in arms—yet his pleasure was lessened when he reflected on the length and dangers of the voyage, fearing that Disdemona would be pained at his absence. But Disdemona, who had no other happiness in the world than the Moor, and who rejoiced to witness the testimony of his valor her husband had received from so powerful and noble a republic, was all impatient that he should embark with his troops, and longed to accompany him to so honorable a post. And all the more it vexed her to see the Moor so troubled; and not knowing what could be the reason, one day, when they were at dinner, she said to him, "How is it, O Moor, that when so honorable a post has been conferred on you by the Signoria, you are thus melancholy?"

The Moor answered Disdemona, "My pleasure at the honor I have received is disturbed by the love I bear you; for I see that of necessity one of two things must happen—either that I take you with me to encounter the perils of the sea, or, to save you from this danger, I must leave you here in Venice. The first could not be otherwise than serious to me, for all the toil you would have to bear and every danger that might befall you would cause me extreme anxiety and pain, yet, were I to leave you behind me, I should be hateful to myself, since in parting from you I should part from my own life."

Disdemona, on hearing this, replied: "My husband, what thoughts are these that wander through your mind? Why let such things disturb you? I will accompany you whithersoe'er you go, were it to pass through fire, as now to cross the water in a safe and well-provided ship; if indeed there are toils and perils to encounter, I will share them with you. And in truth I should think you loved me little were you to leave me here in Venice, denying me to bear you company, or could believe that I would liefer bide in safety here than share the dangers that await you. Prepare then for the voyage with all the readiness which the dignity of the post you hold deserves."

The Moor, in the fullness of his joy, threw his arms around his wife's neck, and with an affectionate and tender kiss exclaimed, "God keep you long in such love, dear wife!" Then speedily donning his armor, and having prepared everything for his expedition, he embarked on board the galley with his wife and all his troops, and, setting sail, they pursued their voyage, and with a perfectly tranquil sea arrived safely at Cyprus.

Now amongst the soldiery there was an Ensign, a man of handsome figure, but of the most depraved nature in the world. This man was in great favor with the Moor, who had not the slightest idea of his wickedness; for, despite the malice lurking in his heart, he cloaked with proud and valorous speech and with a specious presence the villainy of his soul with such art that he was to all outward show another Hector or Achilles. This man had likewise taken with him his wife to Cyprus, a young, and fair, and virtuous lady; and being of Italian birth she was much loved by Disdemona, who spent the greater part of every day with her.

In the same Company there was a certain Captain of a troop, to whom the Moor was much affectioned. And Disdemona, for this cause, knowing how much her husband valued him, showed him proofs of the greatest kindness, which was all very grateful to the Moor. Now the wicked Ensign, regardless of the faith that he had pledged his wife, no less than of the friendship, fidelity, and obligation which he owed the Moor, fell passionately in love with Disdemona, and bent all his thoughts to achieve his conquest; yet he dared not to declare his passion openly, fearing that, should the Moor perceive it, he would at once kill him. He therefore sought in various ways, and with secret guile, to betray his passion to the lady; but she, whose every wish was centered in the Moor, had no thought for this Ensign more than for any other man; and all the means he tried to gain her love had no more effect than if he had not tried them. But the Ensign imagined that the cause of his ill success was that Disdemona loved the Captain of the troop; and he pondered how to remove him from her sight. The love which he had borne the lady now changed into the bitterest hate, and, having failed in his purposes, he devoted all his thoughts to plot the death of the Captain of the troop and to divert the affection of the Moor from Disdemona. After revolving in his mind various schemes, all alike wicked, he at length resolved to accuse her of unfaithfulness to her husband, and to represent the Captain as her paramour. But knowing the singular love the Moor bore to Disdemona, and the friendship which he had for the Captain, he was well aware that, unless he practiced an artful fraud upon the Moor, it were impossible to make him give ear to either accusation; wherefore he resolved to wait until time and circumstance should open a path for him to engage in his foul project.

Not long afterwards it happened that the Captain, having drawn his sword upon a soldier of the guard, and struck him, the Moor deprived him of his rank; whereat Disdemona was deeply grieved, and endeavored again and again to reconcile her husband to the man. This the Moor told to the wicked Ensign, and how his wife importuned him so much about the Captain that he feared he should be forced at last to receive him back to service. Upon this hint the Ensign resolved to act, and began to work his web of intrigue. "Perchance," said he, "the lady Disdemona may have good reason to look kindly on him."

"And wherefore?" said the Moor.

"Nay, I would not step 'twixt man and wife," replied the Ensign, "but let your eyes be witness to themselves."

In vain the Moor went on to question the officer—he would proceed no further; nevertheless, his words left a sharp, stinging thorn in the Moor's heart, who could think of nothing else, trying to guess their meaning and lost in melancholy. And one day, when his wife had been endeavoring to pacify his anger toward the Captain, and praying him not to be unmindful of ancient services and friendship for one small fault, especially since peace had been made between the Captain and the soldier he had struck, the Moor was

angered, and exclaimed, "Great cause have you, Disdemona, to care so anxiously about this man! Is he a brother,
or your kinsman, that he should be so near your heart?"

The lady, with all gentleness and humility, replied, "Be
not angered, my dear lord; I have no other cause to bid me
speak than sorrow that I see you lose so dear a friend as, by
your own words, this Captain has been to you; nor has he
done so grave a fault that you should bear him so much
enmity. Nay, but you Moors are of so hot a nature that every
little trifle moves you to anger and revenge."

Still more enraged at these words, the Moor replied, "I
could bring proofs—by heaven it mocks belief! but for the
wrongs I have endured revenge must satisfy my wrath."

Disdemona, in astonishment and fright, seeing her husband's anger kindled against her, so contrary to his wont,
said humbly and with timidity, "None save a good intent
has led me thus to speak with you, my lord; but to give cause
no longer for offense, I'll never speak a word more on the
subject."

The Moor, observing the earnestness with which his wife
again pleaded for the Captain, began to guess the meaning of
the Ensign's words; and in deep melancholy he went to seek
that villain and induce him to speak more openly of what he
knew. Then the Ensign, who was bent upon injuring the
unhappy lady, after feigning at first great reluctance to say
aught that might displease the Moor, at length pretended to
yield to his entreaties, and said, "I can't deny it pains me to
the soul to be thus forced to say what needs must be more
hard to hear than any other grief; but since you will it so, and
that the regard I owe your honor compels me to confess the
truth, I will no longer refuse to satisfy your questions and my
duty. Know, then, that for no other reason is your lady vexed
to see the Captain in disfavor than the pleasure that she has
in his company whenever he comes to your house, and all
the more since she has taken an aversion to your blackness."

These words went straight to the Moor's heart; but in
order to hear more (now that he believed true all that the
Ensign had told him) he replied, with a fierce glance, "By
heavens, I scarce can hold this hand from plucking out that
tongue of thine, so bold, which dares to speak such slander
of my wife!"

"Captain," replied the Ensign, "I looked for such reward for these my faithful officers—none else; but since my duty, and the jealous care I bear your honor, have carried me thus far, I do repeat, so stands the truth, as you have heard it from these lips; and if the lady Disdemona hath, with a false show of love for you, blinded your eyes to what you should have seen, this is no argument but that I speak the truth. Nay, this same Captain told it me himself, like one whose happiness is incomplete until he can declare it to another; and, but that I feared your anger, I should have given him, when he told it me, his merited reward, and slain him. But since informing you of what concerns you more than any other man brings me so undeserved a recompense, would I had held my peace, since silence might have spared me your displeasure."

Then the Moor, burning with indignation and anguish, said, "Make thou these eyes self-witnesses of what thou tell'st, or on thy life I'll make thee wish thou hadst been born without a tongue."

"An easy task it would have been," replied the villain, "when he was used to visit at your house; but now that you have banished him, not for just cause, but for mere frivolous pretext, it will be hard to prove the truth. Still, I do not forgo the hope to make you witness of that which you will not credit from my lips."

Thus they parted. The wretched Moor, struck to the heart as by a barbed dart, returned to his home, and awaited the day when the Ensign should disclose to him the truth which was to make him miserable to the end of his days. But the evil-minded Ensign was, on his part, not less troubled by the chastity which he knew the lady Disdemona observed inviolate; and it seemed to him impossible to discover a means of making the Moor believe what he had falsely told him; and, turning the matter over in his thoughts in various ways, the villain resolved on a new deed of guilt.

Disdemona often used to go, as I have already said, to visit the Ensign's wife, and remained with her a good part of the day. Now, the Ensign observed that she carried about with her a handkerchief, which he knew the Moor had given her, finely embroidered in the Moorish fashion, and which was precious to Disdemona, nor less so to the Moor. Then he conceived the plan of taking this kerchief from her secretly, and thus laying the snare for her final ruin. The Ensign had a little daughter, a child three years of age, who was much loved by Disdemona, and one day, when the unhappy lady had gone to pay a visit at the house of this vile man, he took the little child up in his arms and carried her to Disdemona, who took her and pressed her to her bosom; whilst at the same instant this traitor, who had extreme dexterity of hand, drew the kerchief from her sash so cunningly that she did not notice him, and overjoyed he took his leave of her.

Disdemona, ignorant of what had happened, returned home, and, busy with other thoughts, forgot the hand-kerchief. But a few days afterwards, looking for it and not finding it, she was in alarm, lest the Moor should ask her for it, as he oft was wont to do. Meanwhile, the wicked Ensign, seizing a fit opportunity, went to the Captain of the troop, and with crafty malice left the handkerchief at the head of his bed without his discovering the trick, until the following morning, when, on his getting out of bed, the handkerchief fell upon the floor, and he set his foot upon it. And not being able to imagine how it had come to his house, knowing that it belonged to Disdemona, he resolved to give it to her; and waiting until the Moor had gone from home, he went to the back door and knocked. It seemed as if fate conspired with the Ensign to work the death of the unhappy Disdemona. Just at that time the Moor returned home, and hearing a knocking at the back door, he went to the window, and in a rage exclaimed, "Who knocks there?" The Captain, hearing the Moor's voice, and fearing lest he should come down-stairs and attack him, took to flight without answering a word. The Moor went down, and opening the door hastened into the street and looked about, but in vain. Then, return-ing into the house in great anger, he demanded of his wife who it was that had knocked at the door. Disdemona replied, as was true, that she did not know; but the Moor said, "It seemed to me the Captain."

"I know not," answered Disdemona, "whether it was he or another person."

The Moor restrained his fury, great as it was, wishing to do nothing before consulting the Ensign, to whom he has-tened instantly, and told him all that had passed, praying him to gather from the Captain all he could respecting the affair.

The Ensign, overjoyed at the occurrence, promised the Moor to do as he requested, and one day he took occasion to speak with the Captain when the Moor was so placed that he could see and hear them as they conversed. And whilst talking to him of every other subject than of Disdemona, he kept laughing all the time aloud, and feigning astonishment, he made various movements with his head and hands, as if listening to some tale of marvel. As soon as the Moor saw the Captain depart, he went up to the Ensign to hear what he had said to him. And the Ensign, after long entreaty, at length said, "He has hidden from me nothing, and has told me that he has been used to visit your wife whenever you went from home, and that on the last occasion she gave him this handkerchief which you presented to her when you married her."

The Moor thanked the Ensign, and it seemed now clear to him that, should he find Disdemona not to have the handkerchief, it was all true that the Ensign had told to him. One day, therefore, after dinner, in conversation with his wife on various subjects, he asked her for the kerchief. The unhappy lady, who had been in great fear of this, grew red as fire at this demand; and to hide the scarlet of her cheeks, which was closely noted by the Moor, she ran to a chest and pretended to seek the handkerchief, and after hunting for it a long time, she said, "I know not how it is—I cannot find it; can you, perchance, have taken it?"

"If I had taken it," said the Moor, "why should I ask it of you? but you will look better another time."

On leaving the room, the Moor fell to meditating how he should put his wife to death, and likewise the Captain of the troop, so that their deaths should not be laid to his charge. And as he ruminated over this day and night, he could not prevent his wife's observing that he was not the same towards her as he had been wont; and she said to him again and again, "What is the matter? What troubles you? How comes it that you, who were the most lighthearted man in the world, are now so melancholy?"

The Moor feigned various reasons in reply to his wife's questioning, but she was not satisfied, and, although conscious that she had given the Moor no cause, by act or deed, to be so troubled, yet she feared that he might have grown wearied of her; and she would say to the Ensign's wife, "I know not what to say of the Moor; he used to be all love towards me; but within these few days he has become another man; and much I fear that I shall prove a warning to young girls not to marry against the wishes of their parents, and that the Italian ladies may learn from me not to wed a man whom nature and habitude of life estrange from us. But as I know the Moor is on such terms of friendship with your husband, and communicates to him all his affairs, I pray you, if you have heard from him aught that you may tell me of, fail not to befriend me." And as she said this, she wept bitterly.

The Ensign's wife, who knew the whole truth (her husband wishing to make use of her to compass the death of Disdemona), but could never consent to such a project, dared not, from fear of her husband, disclose a single circumstance: all she said was, "Beware lest you give any cause of suspicion to your husband, and show to him by every means your fidelity and love."—"Indeed I do so," replied Disdemona, "but it is all of no avail."

Meanwhile the Moor sought in every way to convince himself of what he fain would have found untrue, and he prayed the Ensign to contrive that he might see the handkerchief in the possession of the Captain. This was a difficult matter to the wicked Ensign; nevertheless, he promised to use every means to satisfy the Moor of the truth of what he said.

Now, the Captain had a wife at home who worked the most marvelous embroidery upon lawn, and seeing the handkerchief, which belonged to the Moor's wife, she resolved, before it was returned to her, to work one like it. As she was engaged in this task, the Ensign observed her standing at a window, where she could be seen by all the passers-by in the street, and he pointed her out to the Moor, who was now perfectly convinced of his wife's guilt. Then he arranged with the Ensign to slay Disdemona and the Captain of the troop, treating them as it seemed they both deserved. And the Moor prayed the Ensign that he would kill the Captain, promising eternal gratitude to him. But the Ensign at first refused to undertake so dangerous a task, the Captain being a man of equal skill and courage; until at length, after much entreating and being richly paid, the Moor prevailed on him to promise to attempt the deed.

Having formed this resolution, the Ensign, going out one dark night, sword in hand, met the Captain on his way to visit a courtesan, and struck him a blow on his right thigh, which cut off his leg and felled him to the earth. Then the Ensign was on the point of putting an end to his life, when the Captain, who was a courageous man and used to the sight of blood and death, drew his sword, and, wounded as he was, kept on his defense, exclaiming with a loud voice, "I'm murdered!" Thereupon the Ensign, hearing the people come running up, with some of the soldiers who were lodged thereabouts, took to his heels to escape being caught; then turning about again, he joined the crowd, pretending to have been attracted by the noise. And when he saw the Captain's leg cut off, he judged that, if not already dead, the blow must, at all events, end his life; and whilst in his heart he was rejoiced at this, he yet feigned to compassionate the Captain as he had been his brother.

The next morning the tidings of this affair spread through the whole city, and reached the ears of Disdemona; whereat she, who was kindhearted and little dreamed that any ill would betide her, evinced the greatest grief at the calamity. This served but to confirm the Moor's suspicions, and he went to seek for the Ensign, and said to him, "Do you know that my wife is in such grief at the Captain's accident that she is well nigh gone mad."

"And what could you expect, seeing he is her very soul?" replied the Ensign.

"Ay, soul forsooth!" exclaimed the Moor; "I'll draw the soul from out her body; call me no man if that I fail to shut the world upon this wretch."

Then they consulted of one means and another—poison and daggers—to kill poor Disdemona, but could resolve on nothing. At length the Ensign said, "A plan comes to my mind, which will give you satisfaction and raise cause for no suspicion. It is this: the house in which you live is very old, and the ceiling of your chamber has many cracks; I propose we take a stocking, filled with sand, and beat Disdemona with it till she dies; thus will her body bear no signs of violence. When she is dead we can pull down a portion of the ceiling, and thus make it seem as if a rafter falling on her head had killed the lady. Suspicion cannot rest on you, since all men will impute her death to accident."

This cruel counsel pleased the Moor, and he only waited for a fitting time to execute the plot. One night, when he and Disdemona had retired to bed, the Ensign, whom the Moor had concealed in a closet which opened into the chamber, raised a noise in the closet, according to a concerted plan; whereat the Moor said to his wife, "Did you not hear that noise?"

"Indeed I heard it," she replied.

"Rise," said the Moor, "and see what 'tis."

The unhappy Disdemona rose from bed, and the instant she approached the closet, out rushed the Ensign, and being strong and of stout nerve, he beat her cruelly with the bag of sand across her back; upon which Disdemona fell to the ground, scarce able to draw her breath; but with the little voice she had left, she called upon the Moor for aid. But the Moor, leaping from bed, exclaimed, "Thou wickedest of women, thus has thy falseness found its just reward, the recompense to wives who, counterfeiting love, place horns upon their husbands' brows."

The wretched lady, hearing these words, and feeling that she was near her end (for the Ensign had given her another blow), appealed to the justice of Heaven, since justice here had failed her, in proof of her fidelity and truth; and as she was thus calling Heaven to witness, the wicked Ensign inflicted a third blow, under which she sank lifeless on the floor.

Then the Ensign and the Moor, laying Disdemona on the bed and wounding her head, pulled down part of the ceiling of the chamber, as they had arranged; whereupon the Moor began to call aloud for help, exclaiming that the house was falling. Hearing this uproar, the neighbors all came running up, and there found Disdemona lying dead beneath a rafter—a sight which, from the good life of that poor lady, did fill all hearts with sorrow.

On the following day Disdemona was buried, followed to the grave by the universal grief of the people. But Heaven, the just regarder of all hearts, willed not that so wicked a deed should go unpunished. Ere long the Moor, whom Dis-

demona had loved more than her own life, began to feel
such sorrow at her loss that he went wandering about as one
bereft of reason, searching in every part of the house. And
reflecting in his thoughts that the Ensign had been the cause
that he had lost, with Disdemona, all joy in life, he conceived
so deep a hatred to that wicked man he could not bear to set
eyes on him, and had it not been for his fear of the inviolable
justice of the Signoria of Venice, he would have slain him
openly. But being unable to do this with safety, he deprived
him of his rank, and would not allow him to remain in his
Company; whereat such an enmity arose between the two
that no greater or more deadly can be imagined.

The Ensign, that wickedest of all bad men, now turned his
thoughts to injuring the Moor; and seeking out the Captain,
whose wound was by this time healed, and who went about
with a wooden leg in place of the one that had been cut off,
he said to him, " 'Tis time you should be avenged for your
lost limb; and if you will come with me to Venice, I'll tell
you who the malefactor is, whom I dare not mention to you
here for many reasons; and I will bring you proofs."

The Captain of the troop, whose anger returned fiercely,
but without knowing why, thanked the Ensign, and went
with him to Venice. On arriving there the Ensign told him
that it was the Moor who had cut off his leg, on account of
the suspicion he had formed of Disdemona's conduct with
him; and for that reason he had slain her, and then spread the
report that the ceiling had fallen and killed her. Upon
hearing which, the Captain accused the Moor to the Signoria, both of having cut off his leg and killed his wife, and
called the Ensign to witness the truth of what he said. The
Ensign declared both charges to be true, for that the Moor
had disclosed to him the whole plot, and had tried to persuade him to perpetrate both crimes; and that, having afterwards killed his wife out of jealousy he had conceived, he
had narrated to him the manner in which he had perpetrated
her death.

The Signoria of Venice, when they heard of the cruelty
inflicted by a barbarian upon a lady of their city, commanded
that the Moor's arms should be pinioned in Cyprus, and
he be brought to Venice, where, with many tortures, they
sought to draw from him the truth. But the Moor, bearing

with unyielding courage all the torment, denied the whole charge so resolutely that no confession could be drawn from him. But, although by his constancy and firmness he escaped death, he was, after being confined for several days in prison, condemned to perpetual banishment, in which he was eventually slain by the kinsfolk of Disdemona, as he merited. The Ensign returned to his own country, and, following up his wonted villainy, he accused one of his companions of having sought to persuade him to kill an enemy of his, who was a man of noble rank; whereupon this person was arrested and put to the torture; but when he denied the truth of what his accuser had declared, the Ensign himself was likewise tortured to make him prove the truth of his accusations; and he was tortured so that his body ruptured, upon which he was removed from prison and taken home, where he died a miserable death. Thus did Heaven avenge the innocence of Disdemona; and all these events were narrated by the Ensign's wife, who was privy to the whole, after his death, as I have told them here.

Commentaries

The three critical writings reprinted here give some idea of the range of *Othello* criticism and at the same time provide various insights into the play and critical guidelines for approaching it. Thomas Rymer's discussion of *Othello* from his *A Short View of Tragedy* (1693), is a famous attack on the play by a determined neoclassicist and realist. Rymer's smugness and lack of understanding of the nature of dramatic poetry are ridiculous, but his absurd, and at times infuriating, misinterpretations force a reader to formulate and thus become conscious of his own assumptions about the nature of poetry and drama. The Romantic movement in literature had as one of its by-products a great revival of interest in and a new approach to Shakespeare, and Samuel Taylor Coleridge, besides being a great poet, was the first modern Shakespearean critic. Keats, Byron, Lamb, Hazlitt, and Coleridge were all particularly fascinated by the plays, but it was Coleridge who in several series of public lectures brought Romantic theories of art to bear on Shakespeare and began to create that enthusiasm for the plays so characteristic of the nineteenth century. Coleridge never wrote a book on Shakespeare and his lectures were never printed, but notes and newspaper reports of them have survived, and these along with various marginalia from his books and reports of his "table talk" make it possible to put together at least the outline of his views. Modern criticism grows out of Romantic criticism, though it differs in many of its assumptions about the nature of poetry and in its working techniques. The two pieces of modern criticism here reprinted are distinguished interpretations of *Othello* which offer two different, but complementary, critical approaches. Maynard Mack's "The Jacobean Shakespeare" explores the individual tragedies by defining the "vertebrate characteristics" they share with other Shakespearean tragedies. Mack seeks the common constituent elements and the basic patterns of development of Shakespearean tragedy.

SAMUEL TAYLOR COLERIDGE

[Comments on *Othello*]

The admirable preparation, so characteristic of Shakespeare, in the introduction of Roderigo as the dupe on whom
Iago first exercises his art, and in so doing displays his own
character. Roderigo is already fitted and predisposed [to be
a dupe] by his own passions—without any fixed principle or
strength of character (the want of character and the power of
the passions—like the wind loudest in empty houses—form
his character)—but yet not without the moral notions and
sympathies with honor which his rank, connections, had
hung upon him. The very three first lines happily state the
nature and foundation of the friendship—the purse—as well
as the contrast of Roderigo's intemperance of mind with
Iago's coolness, the coolness of a preconceiving experi-
menter. The mere language of protestation in

> If ever I did dream of such a matter,
> Abhor me—

which, fixing the associative link that determines Roderigo's continuation of complaint—

> Thou told'st me thou didst hold him in thy hate—

elicits a true feeling of Iago's—the dread of contempt
habit[ual] to those who encourage in themselves and have

From *Shakespearean Criticism* by Samuel Taylor Coleridge. 2nd ed., ed.
Thomas Middleton Raysor. (New York: E. P. Dutton and Company, Inc.,
1960; London: J. M. Dent & Sons, Ltd., 1961. 2 vols.)

their keenest pleasure in the feeling and expression of contempt for others. His high self-opinion—and how a wicked man employs his real feelings as well as assumes those most alien from his own, as instruments of his purpose.

> *Iago.* Virtue! a fig! 'tis in ourselves that we are thus or thus.

Iago's passionless character, all will in intellect; therefore a bold partisan here of a truth, but yet of a truth converted into falsehood by absence of all the modifications by the frail nature of man. And the last sentiment—

> . . . our raging motions, our carnal stings, our unbitted lusts;
> whereof I take this, that you call love, to be a sect or scion—

There lies the Iagoism of how many! And the repetition, "Go make money!"—a pride in it, of an anticipated dupe, stronger than the love of lucre.

> *Iago.* Go to, farewell, put money enough in your purse: Thus do
> I ever make my fool my purse.

The triumph! Again, "put money," after the effect has been fully produced. The last speech [Iago's soliloquy], the motive-hunting of motiveless malignity—how awful! In itself fiendish; while yet he was allowed to bear the divine image, too fiendish for his own steady view. A being next to devil, only not quite devil—and this Shakespeare has attempted—executed—without disgust, without scandal!
[5.2.349–51. Othello's death-speech.]

> . . . of one whose hand,
> Like the base Indian, threw a pearl away
> Richer than all his tribe.

Following, in part, a suggestion of the scholar Warburton, Theobald, in his edition of the play, defends the reading of the first Folio, *Iudean,* which he alters to *Judian.*
Thus it is for no-poets to comment on the greatest of poets! To make Othello say that he, who had killed his wife, was like Herod, who had killed his! Oh, how many beauties

in this one line were impenetrable by the *thought*-swarming, ever *idea*less Warburton! Othello wishes to excuse himself—to excuse himself by accusing. This struggle of feeling is finely conveyed in the word "base," which is applied to the *rude* Indian not in his own character, but as the momentary representative of Othello. "Indian" means American or Carib, a savage *in genere.* Othello's *belief* is not caused by jealousy; it is forced upon him by Iago, and is such as any man would and must feel who had believed in Iago as Othello did. His great mistake is that *we* know Iago for a villain from the first moment.

MAYNARD MACK

The Jacobean Shakespeare

Some Observations on the Construction of the Tragedies

This chapter aims at being a modest supplement (I cannot too much stress the adjective) to A. C. Bradley's pioneering analysis of the construction of Shakespearean tragedy, the second of his famous lectures, published some fifty-five years ago. Bradley's concern was with what would probably today be called the clearer outlines of Shakespearean practice—the management of exposition, conflict, crisis, catastrophe; the contrasts of pace and scene; the over-all patterns of rise-and-fall, variously modulated; the slackened tension after the crisis and Shakespeare's devices for countering this; and the faults.

Bradley is quite detailed about the faults. Sometimes, he says, there are too rapid shiftings of scene and *dramatis personae,* as in the middle section of *Antony and Cleopatra.* Sometimes there is extraneous matter, not required for plot or character development, like the player's speech in *Hamlet* about the murder of Priam, or Hamlet's advice later to the same player on speaking in the theater. Sometimes there are soliloquies too obviously expositional, as when Edgar disguises to become Poor Tom in *King Lear.* Or there is contradiction and inconsistency, as the double time in

From *Stratford-upon-Avon Studies: Jacobean Theatre* (Vol. I), ed. John Russell Brown and Bernard Harris. (London: Edward Arnold [Publishers] Ltd., 1960; New York: St. Martin's Press, Inc., 1961.) © Edward Arnold (Publishers) Ltd., 1960. Reprinted by permission of the publishers.

Othello. Or flatulent writing: "obscure, inflated, tasteless," or "pestered with metaphors." Or "gnomic" insertions, like the Duke's couplet interchange with Brabantio in *Othello,* used "more freely than, I suppose, a good playwright now would care to do." And finally, to make an end, there is too often sacrificing of dramatic appropriateness to get something said that the author wants said. Thus the comments of the Player King and Claudius on the instability of human purpose arise because Shakespeare "wishes in part simply to write poetry, and partly to impress on the audience thoughts which will help them to understand, not the player-king nor yet King Claudius, but Hamlet himself." These failings, Bradley concludes, belong to an art of drama imperfectly developed, which Shakespeare inherited from his predecessors and acquiesced in, on occasion, from "indifference or want of care."

Though Bradley's analysis is still the best account we have of the outward shape of Shakespearean tragedy, a glance at his list of faults and, especially, his examples reminds us that a vast deal of water has got itself under the critical bridges since 1904. It is not simply that most of the faults he enumerates would no longer be regarded as such, but would, instead, be numbered among the characteristic practices of Shakespearean dramaturgy, even at its most triumphant. Still more striking is the extent to which our conception of the "construction" of the tragedies has itself changed. The matters Bradley described have not ceased to be important—far from it: several of our current interpreters, one feels, would benefit if, like Bottom of Master Mustardseed, they were to desire him "of more acquaintance." Still, it is impossible not to feel that Bradley missed something—that there is another kind of construction in Shakespeare's tragedies than the one he designates, more inward, more difficult to define, but not less significant. This other structure is not, like his, generated entirely by the interplay of plot and character. Nor is it, on the other hand, though it is fashionable nowadays to suppose so, ultimately a verbal matter. It is poetic, but it goes well beyond what in certain quarters today is called (with something like a lump in the throat) "the poetry." Some of its elements arise from the playwright's visualizing imagination, the consciousness of groupings, gestures, entrances, exits. Others may even be prior to language, in the sense that they appear to belong to a paradigm of tragic "form" that was consciously or unconsciously part of Shakespeare's inheritance and intuition as he worked.

At any rate, it is into this comparatively untraveled and uncharted territory of inward structure that I should like to launch a few tentative explorations. I shall occasionally look backward as far as *Julius Caesar* (1599), *Richard II* (1595–1600), and even *Romeo and Juliet* (1595–6); but in the main I shall be concerned with the tragedies of Shakespeare's prime, from *Hamlet* (1600–1) to *Coriolanus* (1607–8). In these seven or eight years, Shakespeare's golden period, he consolidated a species of tragic structure that for suggestiveness and flexibility has never been matched.[1] I do not anticipate being able to return with a map of this obscure terrain. I hope only to convince better travelers that there is something out there to be known.

First, the hero. The Shakespearean tragic hero, as everybody knows, is an overstater. His individual accent will vary with his personality, but there is always a residue of hyperbole. This, it would seem, is for Shakespeare the authentic tragic music, mark of a world where a man's reach must always exceed his grasp and everything costs not less than everything.

> Wert thou as far
> As that vast shore wash'd with the farthest sea,
> I would adventure for such merchandise.
>
> (*Romeo*, 2.2.82–84)

> 'Swounds, show me what thou'lt do:
> Woo't weep? woo't fight? woo't fast? woo't tear thyself?
> Woo't drink up eisel? eat a crocodile
> I'll do't.
>
> (*Hamlet*, 5.1.276–79)

> Ay, . . . had she been true,
> If heaven would make me such another world

[1] The flexibility of the structure is witnessed by the amazing differences between the tragedies, of which it is, however, the lowest common multiple. In my discussion, I shall necessarily take the differences between the tragedies for granted and stress simply the vertebrate characteristics they share.

Of one entire and perfect chrysolite,
I'ld not have sold her for it.   (*Othello*, 5.2.140–43)

Death, traitor! nothing could have subdued nature
To such a lowness but his unkind daughters,   (*Lear*, 3.4.70–71)

Will all great Neptune's ocean wash this blood
Clean from my hand?   (*Macbeth*, 2.2.59–60)

                I, that with my sword
Quarter'd the world, and o'er green Neptune's back
With ships made cities, . . .   (*Antony*, 4.14.57–59)

              I go alone,
Like to a lonely dragon, that his fen
Makes fear'd and talk'd of more than seen.
                        (*Coriolanus*, 4.1.29–31)

This idiom is not, of course, used by the hero only. It is the language he is dressed in by all who love him, and often by those who do not:

This was the noblest Roman of them all: . . .
His life was gentle, and the elements
So mix'd in him that Nature might stand up
And say to all the world, "This was a man!"
                     (*Caesar*, 5.5.68, 73–75)

The courtier's, soldier's, scholar's, eye, tongue, sword;
The expectancy and rose of the fair state,
The glass of fashion and the mold of form,
The observed of all observers, . . .   (*Hamlet*, 3.1.154–57)

Can he be angry? I have seen the cannon,
When it hath blown his ranks into the air,
And, like the devil, from his very arm
Puff'd his own brother:—and is he angry?   (*Othello*, 3.4.134–37)

            On the Alps
It is reported thou didst eat strange flesh,
Which some did die to look on.
                   (*Antony*, 1.4.66–68)

> Let me twine
> Mine arms about that body, where against
> My grainèd ash an hundred times hath broke,
> And scarr'd the moon with splinters. (*Coriolanus*, 4.5.110–13)

But by whomever used, it is a language that depends for its vindication—for the redemption of its paper promises into gold—upon the hero, and any who stand, heroically, where he does. It is the mark of his, and their, commitment to something beyond "the vast waters / Of the petrel and the porpoise," as Mr. Eliot has it in *East Coker*, a commitment to something—not merely death—which shackles accidents and bolts up change and palates no dung whatever.

Thus the hyperbole of tragedy stands at the opposite end of a tonal scale from the hyperbole of comedy, which springs from and nourishes detachment:

> When I was about thy years, Hal, I was not an eagle's talet in the waist; I could have crept into any alder-man's thumb-ring
> (*I Henry IV*, 2.4.330–32)

> O, she misused me past the endurance of a block! an oak but with one green leaf on it would have answered her; my very visor began to assume life, and scold with her. (*Much Ado*, 2.1.237–40)

> He has a son, who shall be flayed alive; then 'nointed over with honey, set on the head of a wasp's nest; then stand till he be three quarters and a dram dead; then recovered again with aqua-vitae or some other hot infusion; then, raw as he is, and in the hottest day prognostication proclaims, shall he be set against a brick-wall, the sun looking with a southward eye upon him, where he is to behold him with flies blown to death. (*Winter's Tale*, 4.4.790–98)

Comic overstatement aims at being preposterous. Until it becomes so, it remains flat. Tragic overstatement, on the other hand, aspires to be believed, and unless in some sense it is so, remains bombast.

Besides the hyperbolist, in Shakespeare's scheme of things, there is always the opposing voice, which belongs to the hero's foil. As the night the day, the idiom of absoluteness demands a vocabulary of a different intensity, a different rhetorical and moral wave length, to set it off. This other idiom is not necessarily understatement, though it often takes the form of a deflating accent and very often involves colloquialism—or perhaps merely a middling sort of speech—expressive of a suppler outlook than the hero's, and of other and less upsetting ways of encountering experience than his hyperbolic, not to say intransigent, rigorism. " 'Twere to consider too curiously to consider so" (5.1.207), says Horatio of Hamlet's equation between the dust of Alexander and a bunghole, and this enunciates perfectly the foil's role. There is no tragedy in him because he does not consider "curiously"; there are always more things in earth and heaven than are dreamt of in his philosophy.

Each of the Shakespearean tragedies contains at least one personage to speak this part, which is regularly assigned to someone in the hero's immediate entourage—servitor, wife, friend. In *Romeo and Juliet*, it is of course Mercutio, with his witty resolution of all love into sex. In *Julius Caesar*, it is Cassius, whose restless urgent rhythms, full of flashing images, swirl about Brutus's rounder and abstracter speech, like dogs that bay the moon:

> *Brutus.* I do believe that these applauses are
>   For some new honors that are heap'd on Caesar.
>
> *Cassius.* Why, man, he doth bestride the narrow world
>   Like a Colossus, and we petty men
>   Walk under his huge legs and peep about
>   To find ourselves dishonorable graves.   (1.2.133–38)

In the famous forum speeches, this second voice is taken over temporarily by Antony, and there emerges a similar but yet more powerful contrast between them. Brutus's prose—in which the actuality of the assassination is intellectualized and held at bay by the strict patterns of an obtrusively formal rhetoric, almost as though corporal death were transubstantiated to "a ballet of bloodless categories"— gives way to Antony's sinewy verse about the "honorable men" (3.2.85), which draws the deed, and its consequence the dead Caesar, ever closer till his own vengeful emotions are kindled in the mob.

In *Hamlet*, the relation of foil to hero undergoes an

unusual adaptation. Here, since the raciest idiom of the play belongs to the hero himself, the foil, Horatio, is given a quite conventional speech, and, to make the contrast sharper (Hamlet being of all the heroes the most voluble), as little speech as may be. Like his stoicism, like his "blood and judgment" (3.2.71)—

> so well commeddled,
> That they are not a pipe for Fortune's finger
> To sound what stop she please—   (71–73)

Horatio's "Here, sweet lord" (55), "O, my dear lord" (58), "Well, my lord" (89) are, presumably (as the gentleman in *Lear* says of Cordelia's tears), "a better way" (4.3.20) than Hamlet's self-lacerating virtuosities and verbosities. But of course we do not believe this and are not meant to: who would be Horatio if he could be Hamlet?

Plainly, this is one of the two questions that all the tragic foils exist to make us ask (the other we shall come to presently). Who, for instance, would be Enobarbus, clear-sighted as he is, in preference to Antony? His brilliant sardonic speech, so useful while he can hold his own career and all about him in the comic focus of detachment, withers in the face of his engagement to ultimate issues, and he dies speaking with imagery, accent, and feeling which are surely meant to identify him at the last with the absoluteness of the heroic world, the more so since his last syllables anticipate Cleopatra's:

> Throw my heart
> Against the flint and hardness of my fault;
> Which, being dried with grief, will break to powder,
> And finish all foul thoughts. O Antony,
> Nobler than my revolt is infamous,
> Forgive me in thine own particular;
> But let the world rank me in register
> A master-leaver and a fugitive:
> O Antony! O Antony!   (4.9.15–23)

Such unequivocal judgments are a change indeed on the part of one who could earlier rally cynically with

Menas about "two thieves kissing" (2.6.97) when their hands meet.

King Lear is given two foils. The primary one is obviously the Fool, whose rhymes and riddles and jets of humor in the first two acts set off both the old king's brooding silences and his massively articulated longer speeches when aroused. But in the storm scenes, and occasionally elsewhere, one is almost as keenly conscious of the relief into which Lear's outrageous imprecations are thrown by the mute devoted patience of his servant Kent. For both foils—and this of course is their most prominent function as representatives of the opposing voice—the storm itself is only a storm, to be stoically endured, in the one case, and, in the other, if his master would but hear reason, eschewed:

> O nuncle, court holy-water in a dry house is better than this rain-water out o' door. Good nuncle, in, ask thy daughters' blessing: . . .
>
> (3.2.10–12)

Doubtless the Fool does not wish to be taken quite *au pied de la lettre* in this—his talk is always in the vein of the false daughters', his action quite other. But neither for him nor for Kent does facing the thunder have any kind of transcendent meaning. In Lear's case, it has; the thunder he hears is like the thunder heard over Himavant in *The Waste Land*; it has what the anthropologists call "mana"; and his (and our) consuming questions are what it means—and if it means—and whose side it is on.

In my view, the most interesting uses of the opposing voice occur in *Macbeth* and *Othello*. In *Macbeth*, Shakespeare gives it to Lady Macbeth, and there was never, I think, a more thrilling tragic counterpoint set down for the stage than that in the scene following the murder of Duncan, when her purely physical reading of what has happened to them both is met by his metaphysical intuitions. His "noise" (2.2.14) to her is just the owl screaming and the crickets' cry. The voice of one crying "sleep no more" (40) is only his "brain-sickly" (45) fear. The blood on his hands is what "a little water clears us of" (66). "Consider it not so deeply"

(29), she says at one point, with an echo of Horatio in the graveyard. "These deeds must not be thought / After these ways" (32–33). But in the tragic world, which always opens on transcendence, they must; and this she herself finds before she dies, a prisoner to the deed, endlessly washing the damned spot that will not out. "What's done cannot be undone" (5.1.71) is a language that like Enobarbus she has to learn.

Othello's foil of course is Iago, about whose imagery and speech there hangs, as recent commentators have pointed out, a constructed air, an ingenious, hyperconscious generalizing air, essentially suited to one who, as W. H. Clemen has said, "seeks to poison . . . others with his images" (*The Development of Shakespeare's Imagery,* p. 122). Yet Iago's poison does not work more powerfully through his images than through a corrosive habit of abstraction applied in those unique relations of love and faith where abstraction is most irrelevant and most destructive. Iago has learned to "sickly o'er" the central and irreducible individual with the pale cast of class and kind:

> Blessed fig's end! The wine she drinks is made of grapes. . . .
> (2.1.251)

> These Moors are changeable in their wills. . . . If sanctimony and a frail vow betwixt an erring barbarian and supersubtle Venetian be not too hard for my wits . . .   (1.3.342–43, 350–53)

> Come on, come on; you are pictures out of door,
> Bells in your parlors, wildcats in your kitchens,
> Saints in your injuries, devils being offended,
> Players in your housewifery, and housewives in your
>   beds.   (2.1.108–11)

> I know our country disposition well;
> In Venice they do let heaven see the pranks
> They dare not show their husbands.   (3.3.201–03)

Othello's downfall is signaled quite as clearly when he drifts into this rationalized dimension—

> O curse of marriage,
> That we can call these delicate creatures ours,
> And not their appetites—   (267–69)

leaving behind his true vernacular, the idiom of "My life upon her faith!", as when his mind fills with Iago's copulative imagery. Shakespeare seems to have been well aware that love (especially such love as can be reflected only in the union of a black man with a white woman, East with West) is the mutual knowing of uniqueness:

> Reason, in itself confounded,
> Saw division grow together,
> To themselves yet either neither,
> Simple were so well compounded,
>
> That it cried, How true a twain
> Seemeth this concordant one!
> Love hath reason, reason none,
> If what parts can so remain.
>
> Whereupon it made this threne
> To the phoenix and the dove,
> Co-supremes and stars of love,
> As chorus to their tragic scene.
>   (*The Phoenix and the Turtle*, 41)

And also that there are areas of experience where, as a great saint once said, one must first believe in order that one may know.

To one who should ask why these paired voices seem to be essential ingredients of Shakespearean tragedy, no single answer can, I think, be given. They occur partly, no doubt, because of their structural utility, the value of complementary personalities in a work of fiction being roughly analogous to the value of thesis and antithesis in a discursive work. Partly too, no doubt, because in stage performance, the antiphonal effects of the two main vocabularies, strengthened by diversity in manner, costume, placing on the stage, supply variety of mood and gratify the eye and ear. But these are superficial considerations. Perhaps we come to something more satisfactory when we consider that these two voices apparently answer to reverberations which reach far back in the human past. *Mutatis mutandis*, Coriolanus and Menenius, Antony and Enobarbus, Macbeth and Lady Macbeth, Lear and his Fool, Othello and Iago, Hamlet and Horatio, Brutus and Cassius, Romeo and Mercutio exhibit a kind of duality that is also exhibited in Oedipus and Jocasta (as well as Creon), Antigone and Ismene, Prometheus and Oceanus, Phaedra and her nurse—and also, in many instances in Greek tragedy, by the protagonist and the chorus.

If it is true, as can be argued, that the Greek chorus functions in large measure as spokesman for the values of the community, and the first actor, in large measure, for the passionate life of the individual, we can perhaps see a philosophical basis for the long succession of opposing voices. What matters to the community is obviously accommodation—all those adjustments and resiliences that enable it to survive; whereas what matters to the individual, at least in his heroic mood, is just as obviously integrity—all that enables him to remain an *individual*, one thing not many. The confrontation of these two outlooks is therefore a confrontation of two of our most cherished instincts, the instinct to be resolute, autonomous, free, and the instinct to be "realistic," adaptable, secure. If it is also true, as I think most of us believe, that tragic drama is in one way or other a record of man's affair with transcendence (whether this be defined as gods, God, or, as by Malraux, the human "fate," which men must "question" even if they cannot control), we can see further why the hero must have an idiom—such as hyperbole—that establishes him as moving to measures played above, or outside, our normal space and time. For the *reductio ad absurdum* of the tragic confrontation is the comic one, exemplified in Don Quixote and his Sancho, where the comedy arises precisely from the fact that the hero only *imagines* he moves to measures above and outside our normal world; and where, to the extent that we come to identify with his faith, the comedy slides towards pathos and even the tragic absolute.

These considerations, however, remain speculative. What is not in doubt is that dramaturgically the antiphony of two voices and two vocabularies serves Shakespeare well, and in one of its extensions gives rise to a phenomenon as peculiar and personal to him as his signature. Towards the close of a tragic play, or if not towards the close, at the climax, will normally appear a short scene or episode (sometimes more than one) of spiritual cross purposes: a scene in which the line of tragic speech and feeling generated by commitment is crossed by an alien speech and feeling very much detached. Bradley, noting such of these episodes as are "humorous or semi-humorous," places them among Shakespeare's devices for sustaining interest after the crisis, since their introduction "affords variety and relief, and also heightens by contrast the tragic feelings." Another perceptive critic has noted that though such scenes afford "relief," it is not by laughter. "We return for a moment to simple people, a gravedigger, a porter, a countryman, and to the goings on of every day, the feeling for bread and cheese, and when we go back to the high tragic mood we do so with a heightened sense that we are moving in a world fully realized" (F. P. Wilson, *Elizabethan and Jacobean*, p. 122). To such comments, we must add another. For the whole effect of these episodes does not come simply from variety, or from the juxtaposition of bread and cheese with the high tragic mood, though these elements are certainly present in it.

It arises, in the main, I think, from the fact that Shakespeare here lays open to us, in an especially poignant form, what I take to be the central dialogue of tragic experience. It is a dialogue of which the Greek dialogue of individual with community, the seventeenth-century dialogue of soul with body, the twentieth-century dialogue of self with soul are perhaps all versions in their different ways: a dialogue in which each party makes its case in its own tongue, incapable of wholly comprehending what the other means. And Shakespeare objectifies it for us on his stage by the encounter of those by whom, "changed, changed utterly," a terrible beauty has been born, with those who are still players in life's casual comedy. Hamlet and the gravediggers, Desdemona and Emilia, Cleopatra and the clown

afford particularly fine examples of Shakespeare's technique in this respect.

In the first instance, the mixture of profoundly imaginative feelings contained in Hamlet's epitaph for Yorick—

> I knew him, Horatio: a fellow of infinite jest, of most excellent
> fancy; he hath borne me on his back a thousand times; and now,
> how abhorred in my imagination it is! my gorge rises at it. Here
> hung those lips that I have kissed I know not how oft. Where be
> your gibes now? your gambols? your songs? your flashes of mer-
> riment, that were wont to set the table on a roar? Not one now, to
> mock your own grinning? quite chap-fallen? Now get you to my
> lady's chamber, and tell her, let her paint an inch thick, to this
> favor she must come; make her laugh at that—   (5.1.186–97)

is weighed over against the buffoon literalism of the
clown—

> *Hamlet.* What man dost thou dig it for?
>
> *First Clown.* For no man, sir.
>
> *Hamlet.* What woman, then?
>
> *First Clown.* For none, neither.
>
> *Hamlet.* Who is to be buried in 't?
>
> *First Clown.* One that was a woman, sir; but, rest her
> soul, she's dead—   (132–38)

and against his uncompromising factualism too, his hard dry
vocabulary of detachment, without overtones, by which he
cuts his métier down to a size that can be lived with:

> Faith, if 'a be not rotten before 'a die, . . . 'a will last you some eight
> year or nine year: a tanner will last you nine year.   (166, 168–69)

But in this scene Hamlet's macabre thoughts are not
allowed to outweigh the clown. A case is made for factualism and literalism. Horatio is seen to have a point in
saying it is to consider too curiously to consider as Hamlet

does. A man must come to terms with the graveyard; but
how long may he linger in it with impunity, or allow it
to linger in him? Such reckonings the opposing voice,
whether spoken by the primary foil or by another, is calculated to awake in us: this is the second kind of question that
it exists to make us ask.

In a sense, then, the implicit subject of all these episodes
is the predicament of being human. They bring before us the
grandeur of man's nature, which contains, potentially, both
voices, both ends of the moral and psychic spectrum. They
bring before us the necessity of his choice, because it is
rarely given to him to go through any door without closing
the rest. And they bring before us the sadness, the infinite
sadness of his lot, because, short of the "certain certainties"
that tragedy does not deal with, he has no sublunar way of
knowing whether defiant "heroism" is really more to be
desired than suppler "wisdom." The alabaster innocence of
Desdemona's world shines out beside the crumpled bed-
sitters of Emilia's—

Desdemona. Wouldst thou do such a deed for all the world?

Emilia. Why, would not you?

Desdemona.   No, by this heavenly light!

Emilia. Nor I neither by this heavenly light;
    I might do't as well i' the dark.

Desdemona. Wouldst thou do such a deed for all the world?

Emilia. The world's a huge thing: it is a great price
    For a small vice.

Desdemona. In troth, I think thou wouldst not.

Emilia. In troth, I think I should . . . who would not make her
    husband a cuckold to make him a monarch? I should venture
    purgatory for 't.

Desdemona. Beshrew me, if I would do such a wrong
    For the whole world.

Emilia. Why, the wrong is but a wrong i' the world; and having

the world for your labor, 'tis a wrong in your own world, and
you might quickly make it right.

Desdemona. I do not think there is any such woman—

                                                        (4.3.65–86)

but the two languages never, essentially, commune—and,
for this reason, the dialogue they hold can never be finally
adjudicated.

The same effect may be noted in Cleopatra's scene with
the countryman who brings her the asps. Her exultation casts
a glow over the whole scene of her death. But her language
when the countryman has gone would not have the tragic
resonance it has, if we could not hear echoing between the
lines the gritty accents of the opposing voice:

Give me my robe, put on my crown; I have
Immortal longings in me.   (5.2.280–81)

> Truly, I have him: but I would not be the party that should
> desire you to touch him, for his biting is immortal; those that do
> die of it do seldom or never recover.   (245–48)

The stroke of death is as a lover's pinch,
Which hurts, and is desired.   (295–96)

> I heard of one of them no longer than yesterday: a very honest
> woman, but something given to lie; as a woman should not do,
> but in the way of honesty: how she died of the biting of it, what
> pain she felt.   (250–54)

                    Peace, peace!
Dost thou not see my baby at my breast,
That sucks the nurse asleep?   (308–10)

> Give it nothing, I pray you, for it is not worth the feeding.
>   (269–70)

The "worm" (255)—or "my baby" (309); the Antony
Demetrius and Philo see—or the Antony whose face is as

the heavens; the "small vice" (*Othello*, 4.3.71) of Emilia—
or the deed one would not do for the whole world; the skull
knocked about the mazzard by a sexton's spade—or the
skull which "had a tongue in it and could sing once"
(*Hamlet*, 5.1.76–77): these are incommensurables, which
human nature nevertheless must somehow measure, reconcile, and enclose.

We move now from "character" to "action," and to
the question: what happens in a Shakespearean tragedy?
Bradley's traditional categories—exposition, conflict, crisis, catastrophe, etc.—give us one side of this, but, as we
noticed earlier, largely the external side, and are in any case
rather too clumsy for the job we try to do with them. They
apply as well to potboilers of the commercial theater as to
serious works of art, to prose as well as poetic drama. What
is worse, they are unable to register the unique capacity of
Shakespearean dramaturgy to hint, evoke, imply, and, in
short, by indirections find directions out. The nature of
some of Shakespeare's "indirections" is a topic we must
explore before we can hope to confront the question posed
above with other terms than Bradley's.

To clarify what I mean by indirection, let me cite an
instance from *King Lear*. Everybody has noticed, no doubt,
that Lear's Fool (apart from being the King's primary foil)
gives voice during the first two acts to notations of topsi-
turviness that are not, one feels, simply his own responses to
the inversions of order that have occurred in family and
state, but a reflection of the King's; or, to put the matter
another way, the situation is so arranged by Shakespeare that
we are invited to apply the Fool's comments to Lear's inner
experience, and I suspect that most of us do so. The Fool
thus serves, to some extent, as a screen on which Shakespeare flashes, as it were, readings from the psychic life of
the protagonist, possibly even his subconscious life, which
could not otherwise be conveyed in drama at all. Likewise,
the Fool's *idée fixe* in this matter, his apparent obsession
with one idea (often a clinical symptom of incipient
insanity) is perhaps dramatic shorthand, and even sleight-of-
hand, for goings-on in the King's brain that only occasionally bubble to the surface in the form of conscious

apprehensions: "O let me not be mad, not mad sweet heaven" (1.5.46). "O fool, I shall go mad" (2.4.285). Conceivably, there may even be significance in the circumstance that the Fool does not enter the play as a speaking character till after King Lear has behaved like a fool, and leaves it before he is cured.

Whatever the truth of this last point, the example of the Fool in *Lear* introduces us to devices of play construction and ways of recording the progress of inward "action," which, though the traditional categories say nothing about them, are a basic resource of Shakespeare's playwriting, and nowhere more so than in the tragedies. We may now consider a few of them in turn.

First, there are the figures, like the Fool, some part of whose consciousness, as conveyed to us at particular moments, seems to be doing double duty, filling our minds with impressions analogous to those which we may presume to be occupying the conscious or unconscious mind of the hero, whether he is before us on the stage or not. A possible example may be Lady Macbeth's sleepwalking scene. Macbeth is absent at this juncture, has gone "into the field" (5.1.4)—has not in fact been visible during two long scenes and will not be visible again till the next scene after this. In the interval, the slayings at Macduff's castle and the conversations between Malcolm and Macduff keep him before us in his capacity as tyrant, murderer, "hell-kite" (4.3.217), seen from the outside. But Lady Macbeth's sleepwalking is, I think, Shakespeare's device for keeping him before us in his capacity as tragic hero and sufferer. The "great perturbation in nature" (5.1.10) of which the doctor whispers ("to receive at once the benefit of sleep, and do the effects of watching" (10–12)), the "slumbery agitation" (12), the "thick-coming fancies That keep her from her rest" (5.3.38–9): these, by a kind of poetical displacement, we may apply to him as well as to her; and we are invited to do so by the fact that from the moment of the first murder all the play's references to sleep, and its destruction, have had reference to Macbeth himself. We are, of course, conscious as we watch the scene, that this is Lady Macbeth suffering the metaphysical aspects of murder that she did not believe in; we may also be conscious that the remorse pictured here tends to distinguish her from her husband, who for some time has been giving his "initiate fear" the "hard use" (3.4.144) he said it lacked, with dehumanizing consequences. Yet in some way the pity of this situation suffuses him as well as her, the more so because in every word she utters his presence beside her is supposed; and if we allow this to be true, not only will Menteith's comment in the following scene—

> Who then shall blame
> His pester'd senses to recoil and start,
> When all that is within him does condemn
> Itself for being there—   (5.2.22–25)

evoke an image of suffering as well as retribution, but we shall better understand Macbeth's striking expression, at his next appearance, in words that we are almost bound to feel have some reference to himself, of corrosive griefs haunting below the conscious levels of the mind:

> Canst thou not minister to a mind diseased,
> Pluck from the memory a rooted sorrow,
> Raze out the written troubles of the brain
> And with some sweet oblivious antidote
> Cleanse the stuff'd bosom of that perilous stuff
> Which weighs upon the heart?   (5.3.40–45)

Such speeches as this, and as Lady Macbeth's while sleepwalking—which we might call umbrella speeches, since more than one consciousness may shelter under them—are not uncommon in Shakespeare's dramaturgy, as many critics have pointed out. *Lear* affords the classic examples: in the Fool, as we have seen, and also in Edgar. Edgar's speech during the storm scenes projects in part his role of Poor Tom, the eternal outcast; in part, Edmund (and also Oswald), the vicious servant, self-seeking, with heart set on lust and proud array; possibly in part, Gloucester, whose arrival with a torch the Fool appropriately announces (without knowing it) in terms related to Edgar's themes: "Now a little fire in a wide field were like an old lecher's heart" (3.4.113–14); and surely, in some part too,

the King, for the chips and tag-ends of Edgar's speech
reflect, as if from Lear's own mind, not simply mental disintegration, but a strong sense of a fragmented moral order:
"Obey thy parents; keep thy word justly; swear not; commit
not with man's sworn spouse. . . ." (80–82)

But in my view, the most interesting of all the umbrella
speeches in the tragedies is Enobarbus's famous description
of Cleopatra in her barge. The triumvirs have gone offstage,
Antony to have his first view of Octavia. When we see him
again, his union with Octavia will have been agreed on all
parts (though not yet celebrated), and he will be saying to
her, with what can hardly be supposed to be insincerity:

> My Octavia,
> Read not my blemishes in the world's report:
> I have not kept my square; but that to come
> Shall all be done by the rule. Good night, dear lady.
>
> (2.3.4–7)

Then the soothsayer appears, reminds Antony that his
guardian angel will always be overpowered when Caesar's
is by, urges him to return to Egypt; and Antony, left alone
after the soothsayer has gone, meditates a moment on the
truth of the pronouncement and then says abruptly:

> I will to Egypt:
> And though I make this marriage for my peace,
> I' the east my pleasure lies.   (39–41)

There is plainly a piece of prestidigitation here. It is performed in part by means of the soothsayer's entry, which is
evidently a kind of visual surrogate for Antony's own personal intuition. ("I see it in my motion, have it not in my
tongue" [14–15], the soothsayer says, when asked for the
reasons he wishes Antony to return; and that is presumably
the way Antony sees it too: in his "motion," i.e., in-
voluntarily, intuitively.) But a larger part is played by
Enobarbus's account of Cleopatra. Between the exit of the
triumvirs and the reappearance of Antony making unso-
licited promises to Octavia, this is the one thing that inter-
venes. And it is the only thing that needs to. Shakespeare

has made it so powerful, so colored our imaginations with
it, that we understand the promises of Antony, not in the
light in which he understands them as he makes them,
but in the riotous brilliance of Enobarbus's evocation of
Cleopatra. The psychic gap, in Antony, between "My Octavia" (4) and "Good night, dear lady" (7), on the one hand,
and "I will to Egypt" (39), on the other, is filled by a vision,
given to us, of irresistible and indeed quasi-unearthly
power, of which the soothsayer's intuition is simply a more
abstract formulation. Here again, by indirection, Shakespeare finds direction out.

Not all mirror situations in the tragedies involve reflection
of another consciousness. Some, as is well known, empha-
size the outlines of an action by recapitulating it, as when
Edgar's descent to Poor Tom and subsequent gradual re-
ascent to support the gored state echoes the downward and
upward movement in the lives of both King Lear and
Gloucester; or as when Enobarbus's defection to, and again
from, the bidding of his practical reason repeats that which
Antony has already experienced, and Cleopatra will experience (at least in one way of understanding Act 5) between
Antony's death and her own. *Hamlet*, complex in all respects, offers an unusually complex form of this. The three
sons, who are, in various senses, all avengers of dead fathers,
are all deflected, temporarily, from their designs by the
maneuvers of an elder (Claudius for Laertes and Hamlet; the
King of Norway, inspired by Claudius, for Fortinbras), who
in two cases is the young man's uncle. There are of course
important differences between these three young men which
we are not to forget; but with respect to structure, the images
in the mirror are chiefly likenesses. Hamlet, outmaneuvered
by Claudius, off to England to be executed, crosses the
path of Fortinbras, who has also been outmaneuvered by
Claudius (working through his uncle), and is off to Poland to
make mouths at the invisible event, while at the same
moment Laertes, clamoring for immediate satisfaction in the
King's palace, is outmaneuvered in his turn. Likewise, at the
play's end, all three young men are "victorious," in ways
they could hardly have foreseen. The return of Fortinbras,
having achieved his objective in Poland, to find his "rights"
in Denmark achieved without a blow, is timed to coincide

with Hamlet's achieving his objective in exposing and killing the King, and Laertes' achieving his objective of avenging his father's death on Hamlet. When this episode is
played before us in the theater, there is little question, to my
way of thinking, but that something of the glow and martial
upsurge dramatized in Fortinbras's entrance associates itself
to Hamlet, even as Fortinbras's words associate Hamlet to a
soldier's death. Meantime, Laertes, who has been trapped
by the King and has paid with his life for it, gives us an alter-
native reflection of the Prince, which is equally a part of the
truth.

Fortinbras's arrival at the close of *Hamlet* is an instance
of an especially interesting type of mirroring to be found
everywhere in Shakespeare's work—the emblematic entrance, and exit. Sometimes such exits occur by death, as the
death of Gaunt, who takes a sacramental view of kingship
and nation, in *Richard II*, at the instant when Richard has
destroyed, by his personal conduct and by "farming" his
realm, the sacramental relationships which make such a
view possible to maintain. Gaunt has to die, we might say,
before a usurpation like his son's can even be imagined;
and it is, I take it, not without significance that the first
word of Bolingbroke's return comes a few seconds after we
have heard (from the same speaker, Northumberland) that
Gaunt's tongue "is now a stringless instrument." Something
similar, it seems clear, occurs with the death of Mamillius in
The Winter's Tale. Sickening with his father's sickening
mind, Mamillius dies in the instant that his father repudiates
the message of the oracle; and though, in the end, all else is
restored to Leontes, Mamillius is not.

In the tragedies, emblematic entrances and exits assume a
variety of forms, ranging from those whose significance is
obvious to those where it is uncertain, controversial, and
perhaps simply a mirage. One entrance whose significance
is unmistakable occurs in the first act of *Macbeth*, when
Duncan, speaking of the traitor Cawdor, whom he has slain,
laments that there is no art to find the mind's construction
in the face, just as the new Cawdor, traitor-to-be, appears
before him. Equally unmistakable is the significance of the
King's exit, in the first scene of *Lear*, with the man who like

himself has put externals first. "Come, noble Burgundy" (1.1.68), he says, and in a pairing that can be made profoundly moving on the stage, the two men go out together.

But what are we to say to Antony's freedman Eros, who enters for the first time (at least by name) just before his master's suicide and kills himself rather than kill Antony. This is all from his source, Plutarch's life of Antony; but why did Shakespeare include it? Did Eros's name mean something to him? Are we to see here a shadowing of the other deaths for love, or not? And the carrying off of Lepidus, drunk, from the feast aboard Pompey's galley. Does this anticipate his subsequent fate? and if it does, what does the intoxication signify which in this scene all the great men are subject to in their degree. Is it ordinary drunkenness; or is it, like the drunkenness that afflicts Caliban, Trinculo, and Stephano in *The Tempest*, a species of self-intoxication, Shakespeare's subdued comment on the thrust to worldly power? Or again, what of the arrival of the players in *Hamlet*? Granted their role in the plot, does Shakespeare make no other profit from them? Are such matters as the speech on Priam's murder and the advice on acting interesting excrescences, as Bradley thought, or does each mirror something that we are to appropriate to our understanding of the play: in the first instance, the strange confederacy of passion and paralysis in the hero's mind,[2] in the second, the question that tolls on all sides through the castle at Elsinore: when is an act not an "act"?[3]

These are questions to which it is not always easy to give a sound answer. The ground becomes somewhat firmer underfoot, I think, if we turn for a concluding instance to Bianca's pat appearances in *Othello*. R. B. Heilman suggests that in rushing to the scene of the night assault on Cassio, when she might have stayed safely within doors, and so exposing herself to vilification as a "notable strumpet" (5.1.78), Bianca acts in a manner "thematically relevant, because Othello has just been attacking Desdemona as a strumpet"—both "strumpets," in other words, are faithful

[2]See an important comment on this by H. Levin, in *Kenyon Review* (1950): 273–96.

[3]I have touched on this point in *Tragic Themes in Western Literature*, ed. C. Brooks (1953).

(*Magic in the Web*, p. 180). Whether this is true or not, Bianca makes two very striking entrances earlier, when in each case she may be thought to supply in living form on the stage the prostitute figure that Desdemona has become in Othello's mind. Her second entrance is notably expressive. Othello here is partially overhearing while Iago rallies Cassio about Bianca, Othello being under the delusion that the talk is of Desdemona. At the point when, in Othello's mental imagery, Desdemona becomes the soliciting whore—"she tells him how she plucked him to my chamber" (4.1.141)—Bianca enters in the flesh, and not only enters, but flourishes the magic handkerchief, now degenerated, like the love it was to ensure, to some "minx's" (153) some "hobby-horse's" (155) token, the subject of jealous bickering. In the theater, the emblematic effect of this can hardly be ignored.[4]

Further types of mirroring will spring to every reader's mind. The recapitulation of a motif, for instance, as in the poisoning episodes in *Hamlet*. *Hamlet* criticism has too much ignored, I think, the fact that a story of poisoning forms the climax of the first act, a mime and "play" of poisoning the climax of the third, and actual poisoning, on a wide scale, the climax of the fifth. Surely this repetition was calculated to keep steady for Shakespeare's Elizabethan audiences the political and moral bearings of the play? We may say what we like about Hamlet's frailties, which are real, but we can hardly ignore the fact that in each of the poisoning episodes the poisoner is the King. The King, who ought to be like the sun, giving warmth, radiance, and fertility to his kingdom, is actually its destroyer. The "leperous distilment" (1.5.64) he pours into Hamlet's father's ear, which courses through his body with such despatch, has coursed just as swiftly through the body politic, and what we see in Denmark as a result is a poisoned kingdom, containing one corruption upon another of Renaissance ideals: the "wise councilor," who is instead a tedious windbag; the young "man of honor," who has no trust in another's honor, as his advice to his sister shows, and none of his own, as his

<hr/>

[4]Another emblematic entrance is the first entrance of the soothsayer in *Julius Caesar*; see "The Teaching of Drama," *Essays on the Teaching of English*, ed. E. J. Gordon and E. S. Noyes (1960).

own treachery to Hamlet shows; the "friends" (2.2.227), who are not friends but spies; the loved one, the "mistress" (434), who proves disloyal (a decoy, however reluctant, for villainy), and goes mad—through poison also, "the poison of deep grief" (4.5.75); the mother and Queen, who instead of being the guardian of the kingdom's matronly virtues has set a harlot's blister on love's forehead and made marriage vows "as false as dicers' oaths" (3.4.46); and the Prince, the "ideal courtier," the Renaissance man—once active, energetic, now reduced to anguished introspection; a glass of fashion, now a sloven in antic disarray; a noble mind, now partly unhinged, in fact as well as seeming; the observed of all observers, now observed in a more sinister sense; the mold of form, now capable of obscenities, cruelty, even treachery, mining below the mines of his school friends to hoist them with their own petard. All this, in one way or another, is the poison of the King, and in the last scene, lest we miss the point, we are made to see the spiritual poison become literal and seize on all those whom it has not already destroyed.

> a Prince's Court
> Is like a common Fountaine, whence should flow
> Pure silver-droppes in generall: But if 't chance
> Some curs'd example poyson't neere the head,
> Death, and diseases through the whole land spread.

The lines are Webster's, but they state with precision one of the themes of Shakespeare's play.

Finally, in the tragedies as elsewhere in Shakespeare, we have the kinds of replication that have been specifically called "mirror scenes,"[5] or (more in Ercles' vein) scenes of "analogical probability."[6] The most impressive examples here are frequently the opening scenes and episodes. The witches of *Macbeth*, whose "foul is fair" (1.1.10) and battle that is "won *and* lost" (4) anticipate so much to come. The

---

[5]By H. T. Price, in *Joseph Quincy Adams Memorial Studies*, ed. J. McManaway (1948), pp. 101 ff.

[6]See P. J. Aldus, *Shakespeare Quarterly* (1955): 397 ff. Aldus deals suggestively with the opening scene of *Julius Caesar*.

"great debate" in *Antony and Cleopatra,* initiated in the comments of Philo and the posturings of the lovers, and reverberating thereafter within, as well as around, the lovers till they die. The watchmen on the platform in *Hamlet,* feeling out a mystery—an image that will re-form in our minds again and again as we watch almost every member of the *dramatis personae* engage in similar activity later on. The technique of manipulation established at the outset of *Othello,* the persuading of someone to believe something he is reluctant to believe and which is not true in the sense presented—exemplified in Iago's management of both Roderigo and Brabantio, and prefiguring later developments even to the detail that the manipulator operates by preference through an instrument.

Lear offers perhaps the best of all these instances. Here the "Nature" (1.2.5) of which the play is to make so much, ambiguous, double-barreled, is represented in its normative aspect in the hierarchies on the stage before us—a whole political society from its *primum mobile,* the great King, down to lowliest attendant, a whole family society from father down through married daughters and sons-in-law to a third daughter with her wooers—and, in its appetitive aspect, which Edmund will formulate in a few moments, in the overt self-will of the old King and the hidden self-will, the "plighted cunning" (1.1.282), of the false daughters. As the scene progresses, in fact, we can see these hierarchies of the normative nature, which at first looked so formidable and solid, crumble away in the repudiation of Cordelia, the banishment of Kent, the exit of Lear and Burgundy, till nothing is left standing on the stage but Nature red in tooth and claw as the false daughters lay their heads together.

I have dwelt a little on these effects of "indirection" in the tragedies because I believe that most of us as playgoers are keenly conscious of their presence. I have perhaps described them badly, in some instances possibly misconceived them; but they are not my invention; this kind of thing has been pointed to more and more widely during the past fifty years by reputable observers. In short, these effects, in some important sense, are "there." And if they are, the question we must ask is, Why? What are they for? How are they used?

I return then to the query with which this section began: what *does* happen in a Shakespearean tragedy? Is it possible to formulate an answer that will, while not repudiating the traditional categories so far as they are useful, take into account the matters we have been examining? In the present state of our knowledge I am not convinced that this is possible: we have been too much concerned in this century with the verbal, which is only part of the picture. Nevertheless, I should like to make a few exploratory gestures.

Obviously the most important thing that happens in a Shakespearean tragedy is that the hero follows a cycle of change, which is, in part, psychic change. And this seems generally to be constituted in three phases. During the first phase, corresponding roughly to Bradley's exposition, the hero is delineated. Among other things, he is placed in positions that enable him to sound the particular timbre of his tragic music:

> Not so, my lord; I am too much i' the sun.   (*Hamlet*, 1.2.67)

> Seems, madam? nay, it is; I know not "seems."   (76)

> My father's brother, but no more like my father
> Than I to Hercules.   (152–53)

>   My fate cries out,
> And makes each petty artery in this body
> As hardy as the Nemean lion's nerve.   (1.4.81–83)

Chiming against this we are also permitted to hear the particular timbre of the opposing voice, spoken by the foil as well as others:

>   If it be,
> Why seems it so particular with thee?   (1.2.74–75)

> For what we know must be and is as common
> As any the most vulgar thing to sense,
> Why should we in our peevish opposition
> Take it to heart?   (98–101)

What if it tempt you toward the flood, my lord,
Or to the dreadful summit of the cliff
That beetles o'er his base into the sea,
And there assume some other horrible form,
Which might deprive your sovereignty of reason
And draw you into madness?   (1.4.69–74)

From now on, as we saw, these are the differing attitudes
towards experience that will supply the essential dialogue of
the play.

The second phase is much more comprehensive. It contains the conflict, crisis, and falling action—in short, the
heart of the matter. Here several interesting developments
occur. The one certain over-all development in this phase
is that the hero tends to become his own antithesis. We
touched on this earlier in the case of Hamlet, in whom
"the courtier's, soldier's, scholar's, eye, tongue, sword"
(3.1.154) suffer some rather savage violations before the
play is done. Likewise, Othello the unshakable, whose original composure under the most trying insults and misrepre-
sentations almost takes the breath away, breaks in this phase
into furies, grovels on the floor in a trance, strikes his wife
publicly. King Lear, "the great image of authority" (4.6.160)
both by temperament and position, becomes a helpless
crazed old man crying in a storm, destitute of everything but
one servant and his Fool. Macbeth, who would have "holily"
(1.5.22) what he would have "highly" (21), who is too full of
the milk of human kindness to catch the nearest way, whose
whole being revolts with every step he takes in his own
revolt—his hair standing on end, his imagination filling
with angels "trumpet-tongued" (1.7.19), his hands (after the
deed) threatening to pluck out his own eyes—turns into the
numbed usurper, "supped full with horrors" (5.5.13), who is
hardly capable of responding even to his wife's death. The development is equally plain in Antony and Coriolanus. "The
greatest prince o' th' world, / The noblest" (4.15.54–55),
finds his greatness slipped from him, and his nobility
debased to the ignominy of having helpless emissaries
whipped. The proud and upright Coriolanus, patriot soldier,
truckles in the market place for votes, revolts to the enemy

he has vanquished, carries war against his own flesh and blood.

This manner of delineating tragic "action," though it may be traced here and there in other drama, seems to be on the whole a property of the Elizabethans and Jacobeans. Possibly it springs from their concern with "whole" personalities on the tragic stage, rather than as so often with the ancients and Racine, just those aspects of personality that guarantee the *dénouement*. In any case, it seems to have become a consistent feature of Shakespeare's dramaturgy, and beautifully defines the sense of psychological alienation and uprootedness that tragic experience in the Elizabethan and Jacobean theater generally seems to embrace. Its distinctively tragic implications stand out the more when we reflect that psychic change in comedy (if indeed comedy can be said to concern itself with psychic change at all) consists in making—or in showing—the protagonist to be more and more what he always was.[7]

In this second phase too, either as an outward manifestation of inward change, or as a shorthand indication that such change is about to begin or end, belong the tragic journeys. Romeo is off to Mantua, Brutus to the Eastern end of the Roman world, Hamlet to England, Othello to Cyprus, Lear and Gloucester to Dover, Timon to the cave, Macbeth to the heath to revisit the witches, Antony to Rome and Athens, Coriolanus to Antium.[8] Such journeys, we rightly say, are called for by the plots. But perhaps we should not be wrong if we added that Shakespearean plotting tends to call for journeys, conceivably for discernible reasons. For one thing, journeys can enhance our impression that psychological changes are taking place, either by emphasizing a lapse of time, or by taking us to new settings, or by both. I suspect we register such effects subconsciously more often than we think.

Furthermore, though it would be foolish to assign to any of the journeys in Shakespeare's tragedies a precise symbolic meaning, several of them have vaguely symbolic

---

[7] I have elaborated this point in an introduction to Fielding's *Joseph Andrews* (1948).

[8] These are merely samples; other journeys occur that I have not named here.

overtones—serving as surrogates either for what can never
be exhibited on the stage, as the mysterious processes
leading to psychic change, which cannot be articulated into
speech, even soliloquy, without losing their formless in-
stinctive character; or for the processes of self-discovery,
the learning processes—a function journeys fulfill in many
of the world's best-known stories (the *Aeneid*, the *Divine
Comedy*, *Tom Jones*, etc.) and in some of Shakespeare's
comedies. Hamlet's abortive journey to England is possibly
an instance of the first category. After his return, and particularly after what he tells us of his actions while at sea, we
are not surprised if he appears, spiritually, a changed man.
Lear's and Gloucester's journey to Dover is perhaps an instance of the second category, leading as it does through
suffering to insight and reconciliation.

During the hero's journey, or at any rate during his over-
all progress in the second phase, he will normally pass
through a variety of mirroring situations of the sort formerly
discussed (though it will be by us and not him that the likeness in the mirror is seen). In some of these, the hero will be
confronted, so to speak, with a version of his own situation,
and his failure to recognize it may be a measure of the nature
of the disaster to ensue. Coriolanus, revolted from Rome and
now its enemy, meets himself in Aufidius's embrace in
Antium. Hamlet meets himself in Fortinbras as the latter
marches to Poland, but does not see the likeness—only the
differences. Lear goes to Goneril's and there meets, as
everyone remembers, images of his own behavior to
Cordelia. Thrust into the night, he meets his own defense-
lessness in Edgar, and is impelled to pray. Encountering in
Dover fields, both Lear and Gloucester confront in each
other an extension of their own experience: blindness that
sees and madness that is wise. Macbeth revisits the witches
on the heath and finds there (without recognizing them) not
only the emblems of his death and downfall to come but his
speciousness and duplicity. Antony encounters in Enobarbus's defection his own; and possibly, in Pompey,
his own later muddled indecision between "honor" and
Realpolitik. Othello hears the innocent Cassio set upon in
the dark, then goes to re-enact that scene in a more figurative darkness in Desdemona's bedroom. Sometimes, alter-

natively or additionally, the hero's way will lie through quasi-symbolic settings or situations. The heath in both *Macbeth* and *King Lear* is infinitely suggestive, even if like all good symbols it refuses to dissipate its *Dinglichkeit* in meaning. The same is true of the dark castle platform in Hamlet, and the graveyard; of the cliff at Dover and Gloucester's leap; of the "monument," where both Antony and Cleopatra die; and of course, as many have pointed out, of the night scenes, the storm, the music, the changes of clothing, the banquets. So much in Shakespeare's tragedies stands on the brink of symbol that for this reason, if no other, the usual terms for describing their construction and mode of action need reinforcement.

After the hero has reached and passed through his own antithesis, there comes a third phase in his development that is extremely difficult to define. It represents a recovery of sorts; in some cases, perhaps even a species of synthesis. The once powerful, now powerless king, will have power again, but of another kind—the kind suggested in his reconciliation with Cordelia and his speech beginning "Come, let's away to prison" (5.3.8); and he will have sanity again, but in a mode not dreamed of at the beginning of the play. Or, to take Othello's case, it will be given the hero to recapture the faith he lost,[9] to learn that the pearl really was richer than all his tribe, and to execute quite another order of justice than the blinkered justice meted out to Cassio and the blind injustice meted out to Desdemona. Or again, to shift to Antony, the man who has so long been thrown into storms of rage and recrimination by the caprices of his unstable mistress receives the last of them without a murmur of reproach, though it has led directly to his death, and dies in greater unison with her than we have ever seen him live.

I believe that some mark of this nature is visible in all the tragedies. Coriolanus, "boy" (2.1.243) though he is and in some ways remains, makes a triumphant choice (detract from his motives as we may), and he knows what it is likely to cost. Moreover, he refuses the way of escape that lies open if he should return now with Volumnia and Vergilia to Rome. "I'll not to Rome, I'll back with you" (5.4.198), he

---

[9]This point is well made in Helen Gardner's *The Noble Moor* (1956).

tells Aufidius, "and pray you / Stand to me in this cause" (198–99). The young man who, after this, dies accused of treachery—by Aufidius's treachery, and the suggestibility of the crowd, as slippery in Corioli as Rome—cannot be thought identical in all respects with the young man who joined Menenius in the play's opening scene. He is that young man, but with the notable difference of his triumphant choice behind him; and there is bound to be more than a military association in our minds when the Second Lord of the Volscians, seeking to quell the mob, cries, "The man is noble, and his fame folds in / This orb o' th' earth" (5.6.124–25); and again too when the First Lord exclaims over his body, "Let him be regarded / As the most noble corse that ever herald / Did follow to his urn" (143–44). Even the monster Macbeth is so handled by Shakespeare, as has been often enough observed, that he seems to regain something at the close—if nothing more, at least some of that *élan* which made him the all-praised Bellona's bridegroom of the play's second scene; and everything Macbeth says, following Duncan's death, about the emptiness of the achievement, the lack of posterity, the sear, the yellow leaf, deprived of "that which should accompany old age, / As honor, love, obedience, troops of friends" (5.3.24–25), affords evidence that the meaning of his experience has not been lost on him.

To say this, I wish to make it clear, is not to say that the Shakespearean tragic hero undergoes an "illumination," or, to use the third term of K. Burke's sequence, a Mathema or perception.[10] This is a terminology that seems to me not very useful to the discussion of tragedy as Shakespeare presents it. It is sufficient for my purposes to say simply that the phase in which we are conscious of the hero as approaching his opposite is followed by a final phase in which we are conscious of him as exhibiting one or more aspects of his original, or—since these may not coincide—his better self: as in the case of Antony's final reunion with Cleopatra, and Coriolanus's decision not to sack Rome. Whether we then go on to give this phenomenon a specific spiritual significance, seeing in it the objective correlative of "perception" or "illu-

[10]*A Grammar of Motives* (1945), pp. 38 ff.

mination," is a question that depends, obviously, on a great many factors, more of them perhaps situated in our own individual philosophies than in the text, and, so, likely to lead us away from Shakespeare rather than towards him. Clearly if Shakespeare wished us to engage in this activity, he was remiss in the provision of clues. Even in *King Lear*, the one play where some sort of regeneration or new insight in the hero has been universally acknowledged, the man before us in the last scene—who sweeps Kent aside, rakes all who have helped him with grapeshot ("A plague upon you, murderers, traitors all. I might have saved her . . .") (5.3.271–72), exults in the revenge he has exacted for Cordelia's death, and dies self-deceived in the thought she still lives—this man is one of the most profoundly human figures ever created in a play; but he is not, certainly, the Platonic idea laid up in heaven, or in critical schemes, of regenerate man.

I have kept to the end, and out of proper order, the most interesting of all the symbolic elements in the hero's second phase. This is his experience of madness. One discovers with some surprise, I think, how many of Shakespeare's heroes are associated with this disease. Only Titus, Hamlet, Lear, and Timon, in various senses, actually go mad; but Iago boasts that he will make Othello mad, and in a way succeeds; Antony, after the second defeat at sea, is said by Cleopatra to be

> more mad,
> Than Telamon for his shield; the boar of Thessaly
> Was never so emboss'd;   (4.13.1–3)

Caithness in *Macbeth* tells us that some say the king is mad, while "others, that lesser hate him, / Do call it valiant fury"; Romeo, rather oddly, enjoins Paris at Juliet's tomb to

> be gone; live, and hereafter say,
> A madman's mercy bade thee run away.   (5.3.66–67)

Even Brutus, by the Antony of *Antony and Cleopatra*, is said to have been "mad."

What (if anything), one wonders, may this mean? Doubtless a sort of explanation can be found in Elizabethan psychological lore, which held that the excess of any passion approached madness, and in the general prevalence, through Seneca and other sources, of the adage: *Quos vult perdere Jupiter dementat prius.*[11] Furthermore, madness, when actually exhibited, was dramatically useful, as Kyd had shown. It was arresting in itself, and it allowed the combination in a single figure of tragic hero and buffoon, to whom could be accorded the license of the allowed fool in speech and action.

Just possibly, however, there was yet more to it than this, if we may judge by Shakespeare's sketches of madness in Hamlet and King Lear. In both these, madness is to some degree a punishment or doom, corresponding to the adage. Lear prays to the heavens that he may not suffer madness, and Hamlet asks Laertes, in his apology before the duel, to overlook his conduct, since "you must needs have heard, how I am punish'd / With a sore distraction" (5.2.229–30). It is equally obvious, however, that in both instances the madness has a further dimension, as insight, and this is true also of Ophelia. Ophelia, mad, is able to make awards of flowers to the King and Queen which are appropriate to frailties of which she cannot be supposed to have conscious knowledge. For the same reason, I suspect we do not need Dover Wilson's radical displacement of Hamlet's entry in 2. 2, so as to enable him to overhear Polonius.[12] It is enough that Hamlet wears, even if it is for the moment self-assumed, the guise of the madman. As such, he can be presumed to have intuitive unformulated awarenesses that reach the surface in free (yet relevant) associations, like those of Polonius with a fishmonger, Ophelia with carrion. Lear likewise is allowed free yet relevant associations. His great speech in Dover fields on the lust of women derives from the designs of Goneril and Regan on Edmund, of which he consciously knows nothing. Moreover, both he and Hamlet can be privileged in madness to say things—Hamlet about the corruption of human nature, and Lear about the corruption of the

[11]"Those whom Jupiter wishes to destroy he first makes mad." [*Editor's note.*]

[12]*What Happens in "Hamlet"* (1935), pp. 103 ff.

Jacobean social system (and by extension about all social systems whatever), which Shakespeare could hardly have risked apart from this license. Doubtless one of the anguishes of being a great artist is that you cannot tell people what they and you and your common institutions are really like—when viewed absolutely—without being dismissed as insane. To communicate at all, you must acknowledge the opposing voice; for there always is an opposing voice, and it is as deeply rooted in your own nature as in your audience's.

Just possibly, therefore, the meaning of tragic madness for Shakespeare approximated the meaning that the legendary figure of Cassandra (whom Shakespeare had in fact put briefly on his stage in the second act of *Troilus and Cressida*) has held for so many artists since his time. Cassandra's madness, like Lear's and Hamlet's—possibly, also, like the madness *verbally* assigned to other Shakespearean tragic heroes—contains both punishment and insight. She is doomed to know, by a consciousness that moves to measures outside our normal space and time; she is doomed never to be believed, because those to whom she speaks can hear only the opposing voice. With the language of the god Apollo sounding in her brain, and the incredulity of her fellow mortals ringing in her ears, she makes an ideal emblem of the predicament of the Shakespearean tragic hero, caught as he is between the absolute and the expedient. And by the same token, of the predicament of the artist—Shakespeare himself, perhaps—who, having been given the power to see the "truth," can convey it only through poetry—what we commonly call a "fiction," and dismiss.

In all these matters, let me add in parenthesis, we would do well to extend more generously our inferences about Shakespeare to the Jacobean playwrights as a group. Some of us have been overlong content with a view of Jacobean tragedy as naïve as those formerly entertained of Restoration comedy, eighteenth-century literature, and modern poetry. But a whole generation of writers does not become obsessed by the sexual feuding of cavalier and citizen, or rhetorical "rules" and social norms, or abrupt images and catapulting rhythms, or outrageous stories of incest, madness, brutality, and lust, because the poetic imagination has suddenly gone "frivolous," or "cold," or "eccentric," or

"corrupt." Such concerns respond to spiritual needs, however dimly apprehended, and one of the prime needs of
Jacobean writers, as the intelligible and on the whole
friendly universe of the Middle Ages failed around them,
was quite evidently to face up to what men are or may be
when stripped to their naked humanity and mortality, and
torn loose from accustomed moorings. Flamineo's phrase in
The White Devil—"this busy trade of life"—offered as a
passing summary of the play's monstrous burden of blood
and madness:

> This busy trade of life appears most vain,
> Since rest breeds rest, where all seek pain by pain—

is characteristically understated and ironic, like Iago's
"Pleasure and action make the hours seem short" (2.3.379).
The creators of Iago and Flamineo, and all the responsible
writers of Jacobean tragedy along with them, knew perfectly
well that it was not in fact the "trade," or habitude, of life to
which they held up art's mirror, but life "on the stretch,"
nature at its farthest reach of possibility. They were fascinated by violence because they were fascinated by the
potencies of the human will: its weaknesses, triumphs, delu-
sions, corruptions, its capacities for destruction and regeneration, its residual dignity when, all else removed, man
stood at his being's limit; and because they knew that in violence lay the will's supreme test, for aggressor and sufferer
alike.

Whatever the themes of individual plays, therefore, the
one pervasive Jacobean theme tends to be the undertaking
and working out of acts of will, and especially (in that
strongly Calvinistic age) of acts of self-will. This is surely
the reason why, in Clifford Leech's happy phrase, these
writers know so little of heaven, so much of hell; and why,
to one conversant with their work so many products of the
century to come seem like fulfillments of ancient prophecy:
Milton's Satan and his "God"—the philosophy embodied in
Leviathan—even, perhaps, the clash of the Civil Wars and
the cleavage in the English spirit reaching from Cavalier and
Puritan to Jacobite and Whig and well beyond. At the very
beginning of the century, these writers had got hold of the

theme that was to exercise it in all departments, political, economic, religious, cultural, till past its close, the problem of anarchic will; and so decisive, so many-sided is their treatment of this problem that even in Milton's massive recapitulation of it in *Paradise Lost* the issue seems sometimes to be losing in vitality what it has gained in clarity, to be fossilizing and becoming formula. The utterances of *his* white devil have more resonance but less complexity and immediacy of feeling than those of Vittoria Corombona, Bosola, Macbeth, or Beatrice Vermandero; and some of them bear a perilous resemblance to the posturings of Restoration heroic tragedy, where the old agonies are heard from still, but now clogged, and put through paces like captive giants in a raree show.

However this may be, I return at the end to the proposition I set out with: there is a lot about the construction of a Shakespearean tragic "action" that we still do not know. My own attempts to get towards it in this chapter are fumbling and may be preposterous: even to myself they sound a little like Bottom's dream. But the interesting thing about Bottom's dream, from my point of view, is that, though he found he was an ass all right, the Titania he tried to tell about was real.

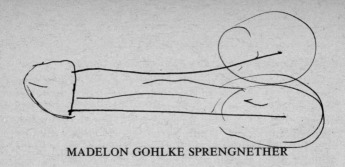

MADELON GOHLKE SPRENGNETHER

"I wooed thee with my sword"
Shakespeare's Tragic Paradigms

> Traditional textual interpretation founds itself on this particular
> understanding of metaphor: a detour to truth. Not only indi-
> vidual metaphors or systems of metaphors, but fiction in gen-
> eral is seen as a detour to a truth that the critic can deliver
> through her interpretation.
>
> —Gayatri Chakravorty Spivak,
>   translator's preface, *Of Grammatology*

Much of what I have to say about Shakespeare and about
the possibility of a feminist psychoanalytic interpretation
of literature, or, for that matter, of culture, depends on a
reading of metaphor. It is metaphor that allows us to sub-
read, to read on the margins of discourse, to analyze what
is latent or implicit in the structures of consciousness or of
a text. A serious feminist critic, moreover, cannot proceed
very far without becoming paranoid, unless she abandons a
strictly intentionalist position. To argue sexism as a conscious conspiracy becomes both foolish and absurd. To
pursue the implications of metaphor, on the other hand, in
terms of plot, character, and possibly even genre, is to adopt
a psychoanalytic strategy that deepens the context of feminist interpretation and reveals the possibility at least of a
feminist psychohistory.

From Madelon Gohlke, " 'I wooed thee with my sword': Shakespeare's
Tragic Paradigms," in *The Woman's Part: Feminist Criticism of Shakespeare*,
ed. Carolyn Ruth Swift Lenz, Gayle Greene, and Carol Thomas Neely
(Urbana, Ill.: University of Illinois, 1980), pp. 150–70.

Metaphor provides a convenient entrance into a text, as it provides a point of departure for psychoanalytic interpretation because of the way in which vehicle consistently outdistances tenor. The following two lines, from *A Midsummer Night's Dream*, for instance, "Hippolyta, I wooed thee with my sword, / And won thy love, doing thee injuries" (1.1.16–17), convey far more than the simple prose explanation offered in my text: "Theseus had captured Hippolyta when he conquered the Amazons."[1] These lines, in which the sword may be the metaphoric equivalent of the phallus, in which love may be either generated or secured by hostility, and in which the two partners take up sadistic and masochistic postures in relation to one another, are not irrelevant to the concerns of the play. They may be seen to reverberate in the exaggerated submission of Helena to Demetrius, in the humiliation of Titania by Oberon, in the penetration by violence of the language of love. They even bear an oblique relation to the "lamentable comedy" of *Pyramis and Thisbe*, the failed marriage plot contained within the larger structure of successful heterosexual union celebrated at the end of the play.

Metaphor may also elucidate character, as in the case of *Much Ado about Nothing*'s Claudio, whose speech is relatively poor in imagery until it erupts into his condemnation of Hero in the middle of the play, where among other things he claims "But you are more intemperate in your blood / Than Venus, or those pamp'red animals / That rage in savage sensuality" (4.1.58–60). It is Claudio's suspicious predisposition which composes this violent and disproportioned outburst. It is no accident that the "solution" to this conflict hinges on the fiction that Claudio has killed Hero through his slander. In this sense the conventional marriage plot of Shakespeare's comedy may also be read metaphorically. The prospect of heterosexual union arouses emotional conflicts which give shape to the plot, unleashing a kind of violence which in the comedies remains symbolic, imagined rather than enacted.

I shall, in the following pages, be considering the uses of metaphor in several related ways. In some instances, I will refer to the function of metaphor in individual discourse, assuming that it is this kind of highly charged imagistic expression that offers the most immediate clues to unconscious awareness. I am assuming furthermore that metaphor may be seen to structure action, so that some features of plot may be regarded as expanded metaphors. Moving outward from this premise, I then want to consider the possibility that certain cultural fictions may be read metaphorically, that is, as expressions of unconsciously held cultural beliefs. I am particularly interested in Shakespeare's tragedies, in what seem to me to be shared fictions on the part of the heroes about femininity and about their own vulnerability in relation to women, fictions interweaving women with violence, generating a particular kind of heterosexual dilemma.

The primacy of metaphor in the structures of individual consciousness, as in the collective fiction of the plot, appears in an early tragedy, *Romeo and Juliet*, where the failure of the play to achieve the generic status of comedy may be read as the result of the way in which heterosexual relations are imagined. In the conversation between the servants Sampson and Gregory, sexual intercourse, through a punning reference to the word "maidenhead," comes to be described as a kind of murder.[2]

> *Sampson.* 'Tis all one. I will show myself a tyrant.
>   When I have fought with the men, I will be civil
>   with the maids—I will cut off their heads.
> *Gregory.* The heads of the maids?
> *Sampson.* Ay, the heads of the maids or their maidenheads. Take
>   it in what sense thou wilt.   (1.1.23–28)

To participate in the masculine ethic of this play is to participate in the feud, which defines relations among men as intensely competitive, and relations with women as controlling and violent, so that women in Sampson's language "being the weaker vessels, are ever thrust to the wall" (17–18). That Romeo initially rejects this ethic would seem to redefine the nature and structure of male/female relationships. What is striking about the relationship between Romeo and Juliet, however, is the extent to which it anticipates and ultimately incorporates violence.

Both lovers have a lively imagination of disaster. While

Romeo ponders "some vile forfeit of untimely death" (1.4.111), Juliet speculates "If he is marrièd, / My grave is like to be my wedding bed" (1.5.136–37). Premonition, for both, has the force of self-fulfilling prophecy. While Romeo seeks danger by courting Juliet, and death by threatening suicide in the wake of Tybalt's death, Juliet, under pressure, exclaims: "I'll to my wedding bed; / And death, not Romeo, take my maidenhead!" (3.2.136–37). Read metaphorically, the plot validates the perception expressed variously in the play that love kills.

The paradigm offered by *Romeo and Juliet*, with some modifications, may be read in the major tragedies as well. Here, the structures of male dominance, involving various strategies of control, expressed in the language of prostitution, rape, and murder, conceal deeper structures of fear, in which women are perceived as powerful, and the heterosexual relation one which is either mutually violent or at least deeply threatening to the man.

Murder in the Bedroom: *Hamlet* and *Othello*

Hamlet's violent behavior in his mother's bedroom expresses some of the violence of his impulses toward her. Obsessed as he is with sexual betrayal, the problem of revenge for him is less a matter of killing Claudius than one of not killing his mother.[3] Hamlet's anger against women, based on his perception of his mother's conduct, finds expression in the language of prostitution in his violent outburst against Ophelia: "I have heard of your paintings, well enough. God hath given you one face, and you make yourselves another. You jig and amble, and you lisp; you nickname God's creatures and make your wantonness your ignorance. Go to, I'll no more on't; it hath made me mad" (3.1.143–48). It is painting which makes women two-faced, which allows them to deceive, to wear the mask of chastity, while lust "Will sate itself in a celestial bed / And prey on garbage" (1.5.56–57). Like whores, all women cannot be trusted.

The paradox of prostitution in the tragedies is based on the masculine perception of the prostitute as not so much the victim as the agent of exploitation. If women are classed as

prostitutes and treated as sexual objects, it is because they
are deeply feared as sexually untrustworthy, as creatures
whose intentions and desires are fundamentally unreadable.
Thus, while Helen in *Troilus and Cressida* is verbally
degraded, as the Trojans discuss her in terms of soiled goods
and contaminated meat, she is, through her infidelity to
Menelaus, the source of the sexual pride and humiliation
that animate the entire conflict between the two warring
nations. Honor among men in this play, though it takes the
form of combat, is ultimately a sexual matter, depending
largely on the fidelity or infidelity of women. For a man to
be betrayed by a woman is to be humiliated or dishonored.
To recover his honor he must destroy the man or woman
who is responsible for his humiliation, for placing him in a
position of vulnerability.

In *Hamlet*, it is the player queen who most clearly articu-
lates the significance attributed to feminine betrayal. "A
second time I kill my husband dead / When second husband
kisses me in bed" (3.2.188–89). It hardly matters whether
Gertrude was implicated in the actual death of the elder
Hamlet. Adultery is itself a form of violence and as great a
crime. Hamlet, who reacts as an injured husband in seeking
revenge against Claudius, also seeks retribution against his
mother. Not having any sanction to kill his mother, however,
he must remind himself to "speak daggers to her, but use
none" (404). That his manner suggests physical violence is
confirmed by Gertrude's response: "What wilt thou do?
Thou wilt not murder me? / Help, ho!" (3.4.22–23). It is at
this point that the violence that Hamlet seeks to contain in
his attitude toward his mother is deflected onto another
object presumed to be appropriate.

This single act of displaced violence, moreover, has further ramifications in terms of Hamlet's relation to Ophelia,
whose conflicted responses to the killing of her father by her
lover increase the burden of double messages she has
already received from the men in the play and culminate in
her madness and death. It is not his mother whom Hamlet
kills (Claudius takes care of that) but Ophelia. Only when
she is dead, moreover, is he clearly free to say that he loved
her. Othello, in whom are more specifically and vividly portrayed the pathology of jealousy, the humiliation and rage

that plague a man supposedly dishonored by the woman he loves, will say of Desdemona late in the play "I will kill thee, / And love thee after" (5.2.18–19).

If I seem to be arguing that the tragedies are largely about the degeneration of heterosexual relationships, or marriages that fail, it is because I am reading the development from the comedies through the problem plays and the major tragedies in terms of an explosion of the sexual tensions that threaten without rupturing the surface of the earlier plays. Throughout, a woman's power is less social or political (though it may have social and political ramifications) than emotional, expressed in her capacity to give or to withhold love. In a figure like Isabella the capacity to withhold arouses lust and a will to power in someone like Angelo, whose enforcing tactics amount to rape. In Portia, the threat of infidelity, however jokingly presented, is a weapon in her struggle with Antonio for Bassanio's allegiance. Male resistance, comic and exaggerated in Benedick, sullen and resentful in Bertram, stems from fears of occupying a position of weakness, taking in essence a "feminine" posture in relation to a powerful woman.

The feminine posture for a male character is that of the betrayed, and it is the man in this position who portrays women as whores. Since Iago occupies this position in relation to Othello, it makes sense that he seeks to destroy him, in the same way that Othello seeks to destroy the agent of his imagined betrayal, Desdemona. There is no reason to suppose, moreover, that Iago's consistently degraded view of women conceals any less hostile attitude in his actual relations with women. He, after all, like Othello, kills his wife. The difference between the two men lies not in their fear and mistrust of women but in the degree to which they are able to accept an emotional involvement. It is Othello, not Iago, who wears his heart on his sleeve, "for daws to peck at" (1.1.62). Were it not for Othello's initial vulnerability to Desdemona he would not be susceptible to Iago's machinations. Having made himself vulnerable, moreover, he attaches an extraordinary significance to the relation. "And when I love thee not, / Chaos is come again" (3.3.91–92). "But there where I have garnered up my heart, / Where either

I must live or bear no life, / The fountain from the which my
current runs / Or else dries up" (4.2.56–59).

Once Othello is convinced of Desdemona's infidelity
(much like Claudio, on the flimsiest of evidence), he regards
her, not as a woman who has committed a single transgres-
sion, but as a whore, one whose entire behavior may be
explained in terms of lust. As such, he may humiliate her in
public, offer her services to the Venetian ambassadors, pass
judgment on her, and condemn her to death. Murder, in this
light, is a desperate attempt to control. It is Desdemona's
power to hurt which Othello seeks to eliminate by ending
her life. While legal and social sanctions may be invoked
against the prostitute, the seemingly virtuous woman suspected of adultery may be punished by death. In either case
it is the fear or pain of victimization on the part of the man
that leads to his victimization of women. It is those who perceive themselves to be powerless who may be incited to the
acts of greatest violence.

The paradox of violence in *Othello*, not unlike that in
Macbeth, is that the exercise of power turns against the hero.
In this case the murder of a woman leads to self-murder, and
the hero dies attesting to the erotic destructiveness at the
heart of his relation with Desdemona. "I kissed thee ere I
killed thee. No way but this, / Killing myself, to die upon a
kiss" (5.2.357–58). If murder may be a loving act, love may
be a murdering act, and consummation of such a love possible only through the death of both parties.

"Of Woman Born": *Lear* and *Macbeth*

The fantasy of feminine betrayal that animates the drama
of *Othello* may be seen to conceal or to be coordinate with
deep fantasies of maternal betrayal in *Macbeth* and *Lear*.[4]
Here the emphasis falls not so much on the adult heterosexual relation (though there are such relations) as on the
mother/son or the fantasy of the mother/son relation. In
these plays, the perception of the masculine consciousness
is that to be feminine is to be powerless, specifically in relation to a controlling or powerful woman. For Lear, rage as
an expression of power acts as a defense against this awareness, while tears threaten not only the dreaded perception

of himself as feminine and hence weak but also the breakdown of his psychic order.

> Life and death, I am ashamed
> That thou hast power to shake my manhood thus!
> That these hot tears, which break from me perforce,
> Should make thee worth them. Blasts and fogs upon thee!
>
> (1.4.298–301)

> You think I'll weep.
> No, I'll not weep.
> I have full cause of weeping, but this heart
> Shall break into a hundred thousand flaws
> Or ere I'll weep. O Fool, I shall go mad!   (2.4.279–83)

> O, let me not be mad, not mad, sweet heaven!
> Keep me in temper, I would not be mad!   (1.5.45–46)

It is not Lear who annihilates his enemies, calling down
curses on the reproductive organs of Goneril and Regan,
but rather Lear who is being banished by the women on
whom he had depended for nurturance. It is they who are
the agents of power and destruction, allied with the storm,
and he like Edgar, who is "unaccommodated man," a
"poor, bare, forked animal" (3.4.105–7), naked and vulnerable. That the condition of powerlessness gives rise to compassion in Lear is part of his dignity as a tragic hero. It does
not, however, alter his perceptions of women as either good
or bad mothers. If the banishment of Cordelia initiates a
process by which Lear becomes psychotic, moreover, it
may be argued that her return is essential to the restoration
of his sanity. The presence or absence of Cordelia, like Othello's faith in Desdemona's fidelity, orders the hero's psychic universe. When Cordelia dies, Lear must either
believe that she is not dead or die with her, being unable to
withstand the condition of radical separation imposed by
death.

The most powerful image of separation in *King Lear*, that
of the child who is banished by his mother, is that of birth.
"We came crying hither: / Thou know'st, the first time that
we smell the air / We wawl and cry" (4.6.178–80). In this

sense, the mother's first act of betrayal may be that of giving
birth, the violent expulsion of her infant into a hostile environment. In other passages, a woman's body itself is perceived as a hostile environment.

> But to the girdle do the gods inherit,
> Beneath is all the fiend's.
> There's hell, there's darkness, there is the sulphurous pit.
>
> (126–29)

> The dark and vicious place where thee he got
> Cost him his eyes.   (5.3.173–74)

Intercourse imaged as violent intrusion into a woman's body
may be designed to minimize the cost.

If it is birth itself, the condition of owing one's life to a
woman and the ambivalence attending an awareness of
dependence on women in general, which structures much of
Lear's relations to his daughters, *Macbeth* may be read in
terms of a systematic attempt on the part of the hero to deny
such an awareness. The world constructed by Macbeth
attempts to deny not only the values of trust and hospitality,
perceived as essentially feminine, but to eradicate femininity itself.[5] Macbeth reads power in terms of a masculine
mystique that has no room for maternal values, as if the conscious exclusion of these values would eliminate all conditions of dependence, making him in effect invulnerable. To
be born of woman, as he reads the witches' prophecy, is
to be mortal. Macbeth's program of violence, involving
murder and pillage in his kingdom and the repression of
anything resembling compassion or remorse within, is designed, like Coriolanus's desperate militarism, to make him
author of himself.

The irony of *Macbeth*, of course, is that in his attempt to
make himself wholly "masculine," uncontaminated, so to
speak, by the womb, he destroys all source of value: honor,
trust, and, to his dismay, fertility itself. It is his deep personal
anguish that he is childless. The values associated with
women and children, which he considers unmanly, come to
be perceived as the source of greatest strength. It is pro-
creation, in this play, rather than violence, which confers

power. "The seeds of Banquo kings!" (3.1.70). To kill a child or to imagine such an act, as Lady Macbeth does in expressing contempt for her husband's vacillations, is to betray not only the bonds of human society, but to betray one's deepest self. To reject the conditions of weakness and the dependence is to make oneself weak and dependent. Macbeth's relentless pursuit of power masks his insecurities, his anxieties, and ultimately his impotence. *Macbeth*, more clearly than any of the other tragedies, with the possible exception of *Coriolanus*, enacts the paradox of power in which the hero's equation of masculinity with violence as a denial or defense against femininity leads to his destruction.

Macbeth's attempt to avoid the perception of Lear that "we cry that we are come / To this great stage of fools" (4.6.182–83), that the human infant is radically defenseless and dependent on the nurturance of a woman, gradually empties his life of meaning, leading to his perception of it as "a tale / Told by an idiot . . . / Signifying nothing" (5.5.26–28). Of all the tragic heroes, moreover, Macbeth is the most isolated in his death, alienated from himself, his countrymen, his queen. He has become what he most feared, the plaything of powerful feminine forces, betrayed by the "instruments of darkness" (1.3.124), the three witches.

"The Heart of Loss": *Antony and Cleopatra*

Interwoven into the patriarchal structure of Shakespeare's tragedies is an equally powerful matriarchal vision. The two are even, I would argue, aspects of one another, both proceeding from the masculine consciousness of feminine betrayal. Both inspire a violence of response on the part of the hero against individual women, but more important, against the hero's ultimately damaging perception of himself as womanish. The concurrence of these themes is particularly evident in *Antony and Cleopatra,* a play that recalls the ritual marriage conclusion of the comedies as it deepens the sexual dilemma of the tragic hero.

Antony's relation both to Cleopatra and to Caesar may be read in terms of his anxieties about dominance, his fear of self-loss in any intimate encounter. Early in the play, Cleopatra uses this perception to her advantage by

suggesting that for Antony to respond to the Roman messengers is to acknowledge his submission either to Caesar or
to Fulvia. Her own tactics, of course, are manipulative and a
form of dominance that Antony himself recognizes. "These
strong Egyptian fetters I must break / Or lose myself in
dotage" (1.1.117–18). The advice of the soothsayer to
Antony concerning his proximity to Caesar is similar in
structure if not in content: "near him thy angel / Becomes
afeard, as being o'erpow'red" (2.3.20–21). When Antony
returns to Egypt, he is in effect "o'erpow'red" by Cleopatra. "O'er my spirit / Thy full supremacy thou knew'st"
(3.11.58–59). "You did know / How much you were my
conqueror, and that / My sword, made weak by my affection,
would / Obey it on all cause" (65–68). Antony, like Romeo
earlier, perceives himself as having been feminized by love.
"O sweet Juliet, / Thy beauty hath made me effeminate / And
in my temper soft'ned valor's steel!" (3.1.115–17). "O, thy
vile lady! / She has robbed me of my sword" (4.14.22–23).

If affection makes Antony weak, it also makes him suspicious of Cleopatra's fidelity. "For I am sure, / Though you
can guess what temperance should be, / You know not what
it is" (3.13.120–22). He falls easy prey to the conviction that
Cleopatra has betrayed him to Caesar, making him the
subject of sexual as well as political humiliation. "O, that I
were / Upon the hill of Basan to outroar / The hornèd herd!"
(126–28). In this light, Cleopatra becomes a "witch," a
"spell," a "triple-turned whore."

> O this false soul of Egypt! This grave charm,
> Whose eye becked forth my wars, and called them home,
> Whose bosom was my crownet, my chief end,
> Like a right gypsy hath at fast and loose
> Beguiled me, to the very heart of loss.
> What, Eros, Eros!   (4.12.25–30)

Antony, under the power of erotic attachment, like Othello
feels himself to have been utterly betrayed. Under the
impact of this loss, moreover, his sense of psychic integrity
begins to disintegrate. "Here I am Antony, / Yet cannot hold
this visible shape, my knave" (4.14.13–14). Chaos is come
again.

While the fiction of Cleopatra's death restores Antony's faith in her love, it does not restore his energy for life. Rather, the withdrawal of her presence destroys any vestige of interest he has in the world of the living. "Now all labor / Mars what it does; yea, very force entangles / Itself with strength" (47–49). It is Cleopatra who not only dominates Antony's emotional life, but who invests his world with meaning. The fact that she, unlike Juliet, Ophelia, Desdemona, Cordelia, and Lady Macbeth, dies so long after her lover, not only reveals her as a complex figure in her own right, but also attests to her power to give imaginative shape to the hero's reality.

Cleopatra in many ways is the epitome of what is hated, loved, and feared in a woman by Shakespeare's tragic heroes. She is, on the one hand, the woman who betrays, a Circe, an Acrasia, an Eve, the Venus of *Venus and Adonis*. To submit to her, or to be seduced by her, is to die. She is the player queen, for whom adultery is also murder. She is a Goneril, a Lady Macbeth, a non-nurturing mother. What she takes, on the other hand, she also has the power to give. She is imaginative, fertile, identified with the procreative processes of the Nile. If Antony lives in our imagination, it is because of her "conception" of him. In this sense, she, like Desdemona and Cordelia, is the hero's point of orientation, his source of signification in the world. Union with her is both celebrated, as a curious comic counterpoint to the tragic structure of double suicide, and portrayed as a literal impossibility. Moreover, for this sexually powerful woman to escape censure, the fate of a Cressida or a Helen, she must negate her own strength, she must die. While Theseus's phallic sword, in Antony's hands, turns against himself, Cleopatra, like Juliet, will accept death "as a lover's pinch, / Which hurts, and is desired" (5.2.295–96). Throughout Shakespeare's tragedies the imagery of heterosexual union involves the threat of mutual or self-inflicted violence.

Looked at from one angle, what Shakespeare's tragedies portray is the anguish and destruction attendant on a fairly conventional and culturally supported set of fictions regarding heterosexual encounter. The tragedies, as I read them, do not themselves support these fictions except to the extent that they examine them with such acute attention. The values that emerge from these plays are, if anything, "feminine," values dissociated from the traditional masculine categories of force and politics, focused instead on the significance of personal relationships, or the fact of human relatedness: the values of feeling, of kinship, of loyalty, friendship, and even romantic love. That the recognition of these values entails the destruction of the hero and everyone who matters to him attests perhaps to a kind of cultural determinism, or at least to the very great difficulty of re-imagining habitual modes of behavior. It is the basis in cultural fictions of certain kinds of heterosexual attitudes to which I now wish to turn.

On the Margins of Patriarchal Discourse

Shakespeare's tragic paradigms offer the possibility of a deconstructive reading of the rape metaphor that informs Theseus's words to his captured queen.[6] Violence against women as an aspect of the structure of male dominance in Shakespeare's plays may be seen to obscure deeper patterns of conflict in which women as lovers, and perhaps more important as mothers, are perceived as radically untrustworthy. In this structure of relation, it is women who are regarded as powerful and men who strive to avoid an awareness of their vulnerability in relation to women, a vulnerability in which they regard themselves as "feminine." It is in this sense that one may speak of a matriarchal substratum or subtext within the patriarchal text. The matriarchal substratum itself, however, is not feminist. What it does in Shakespeare's tragedies is provide a rationale for the manifest text of male dominance while constituting an avenue of continuity between these plays and the comedies in which women more obviously wield power.

The preceding analysis may be seen, moreover, to parallel the movement of psychoanalytic theory from an emphasis on oedipal to pre-oedipal stages of development. Roughly speaking, the shift has occurred in terms of a decrease of concern with father/son relations and a corresponding increase of concern with mother/son relations. (Although the shift from father to mother is clear in the work of such theorists as John Bowlby, Melanie Klein, Margaret Mahler, and

D. W. Winnicott, the child or infant, partly for grammatical reasons, tends to be regarded as male.)[7] Certainly it may be said that the theories of object-relations, narcissism, schizophrenia, and separation-individuation have more to do with the child's early relations with his mother than with his father. Whether or not these theories are read in consonance with Freud's formulation of the Oedipus complex, the shift in focus relocates the discussion of certain issues. This relocation, in turn, reveals new interpretive possibilities. Specifically, it reopens the question of femininity.

A deconstructive reading of the rape metaphor in Shakespeare's tragedies leads directly or indirectly to a discussion of the masculine perception of femininity as weakness. The macho mystique thus becomes a form of "masculine protest," or a demonstration of phallic power in the face of a threatened castration. It is for the male hero, however, that femininity signifies weakness, while actual women are perceived by him as enormously powerful, specifically in their maternal functions. It is not the female herself who is perceived as weak, but rather the feminized male. To project this problem back onto women, as Freud does when in his discussions of femininity he portrays the little girl as perceiving herself castrated, is to present it as incapable of resolution.[8] If femininity itself is defined as the condition of lack, of castration, then there is no way around the masculine equation that to be feminine is to be castrated, or as Antony puts it, to be robbed of one's sword.

It is the masculine consciousness, therefore, that defines femininity as weakness and institutes the structures of male dominance designed to defend against such an awareness. Shakespeare's tragedies, as I read them, may be viewed as a vast commentary on the absurdity and destructiveness of this defensive posture. While Shakespeare may be said to affirm the values of feeling and vulnerability associated with femininity, however, he does not in dramatic terms dispel the anxiety surrounding the figure of the feminized male. At this point, dramatic metaphors, I would say, intersect with cultural metaphors.[9]

Freud's views of femininity may be useful to the extent to which they articulate some deeply held cultural convictions. In one sense, what they do is reveal the basis of some powerful cultural metaphors, so powerful in fact that they continue to find formulation in the midst of our vastly different social and intellectual context. In the midst of profound structural changes in habits of philosophic and scientific thinking, as a culture we cling to the language of presence and absence, language and silence, art and nature, reason and madness to describe the relations between the terms masculine and feminine. It is as though the breakdown of hierarchical modes of thought, of vertical ways of imagining experience, finds its deepest resistance in our habits of imagining the relations between the sexes. Some, like the Jungian James Hillman, would even argue that in order to effect real changes in our intellectual formulations of reality, we must find ways of reimagining femininity.[10] Sexual politics may lie at the heart of human culture, of our constantly shifting and evolving world views.

The preceding discussion, of course, rests on assumptions to which Freud would not have subscribed, chief among which is a hypothesis concerning the relation between cultural metaphors and the concept of a cultural unconscious. What I would like to propose is that the notion of the unconscious may be culture specific, that is to say, that the guiding metaphors of a given society or culture may legitimately be seen to express the structure of its unconscious assumptions, in the same way that the metaphoric structure of individual discourse may be seen to convey some of the unconscious freight of a given life. If Thomas Kuhn is correct in assuming that scientific revolutions are the result of paradigm shifts, or profound changes in our habits of imagining the world, then it may also be possible to consider the unconscious implications of certain habits of imagining.[11] Literary conventions may then be viewed as aspects of these imaginative habits, as codifications of a certain spectrum of unconscious attitudes, at the same time that they change and evolve, live and die according to their relation to the society out of which they arise and to which they respond. Cultural changes, to pursue the implications of Kuhn's argument, are in effect profound metaphoric changes which in turn involve changes in the structuring of the unconscious.

Literary history, may, in this light, be read psychologically. The questions one might ask then would concern the spectrum of psychic needs served by specific conventions and genres. Tracing the uses of a convention would then also yield a literary version of psychohistory. To offer an example close to the subject of this essay, I would like to pursue briefly some of the ramifications of the rhetoric of courtly love.

It is interesting to observe the language of de Rougement, who is so careful to situate the courtly love phenomenon in a historical sense, when he refers to the rhetorical trope of love as war. "There is no need, for example, to invoke Freudian theories in order to see that the war instinct and eroticism are fundamentally allied: it is so perfectly *obvious* from the common figurative use of language."[12] Obvious to whom? Is the war instinct, for instance, perceived as an aspect of the feminine psyche? Here the common (and to many readers unquestioned) assumption that reference to the male of the species includes women may be seen to obscure a process by which a fundamentally "masculine" attitude is proposed as a universal norm. More important, however, is the interpretive process by which de Rougemont reads a metaphor specific to a certain set of conventions, albeit powerful ones, as an inalterable aspect of the unconscious life of the species. "All this confirms the natural— that is to say, the physiological—connexion between the sexual and fighting instincts."[13]

It is this supposedly natural "connexion between the sexual and fighting instincts" that structures the language of the courtly love lyric, as it structures the language of sexual encounter in Shakespeare. To term this rhetoric "conventional" is not to demean it but rather to call attention to its psychological power (which de Rougement himself agrees exists) at the same time that one recognizes its mutability, its historicity. Images of sexual intercourse as an act of violence committed against women run deep in our culture. The depth and persistence of these images, however, may tell us more about the anxieties of a culture in which femininity is conceived as castration and in which women are perceived paradoxically as a source of maternal power than it does about the actual or possible relations between the sexes.

Toward a Feminist Discourse

And, as I have hinted before, deconstruction must also take into account the lack of sovereignty of the critic himself. Perhaps this "will to ignorance" is simply a matter of attitude, a realization that one's choice of evidence is provisional, a self-distrust, a distrust of one's own power, the control of one's vocabulary, a shift from the phallocentric to the hymeneal.

—GAYATRI CHAKRAVORTY SPIVAK,
translator's preface, *Of Grammatology*

Literary history, finally, is an aspect of cultural history. Both attest to changing patterns of awareness, to the constant refiguring of our relation to our specific location in time and space, to our own historicity. If individual history, as Ortega y Gasset writes, may be conceived as a process of casting and living out or living through metaphors of the self, is it not possible to imagine cultural history in similar terms?[14] To interpret these metaphors, to read on the margins of discourse, is not only to engage in a process characteristic of psychoanalytic interpretation but also to become engaged in a fundamentally historical process, that of making what is unconscious conscious and thus altering and displacing the location of the unconscious. This process, obviously akin to that of psychotherapy, is not to be perceived statically as an attempt to eliminate the unconscious but rather as one to dislodge it, to transform its metaphoric base.

Psychoanalytic theory in this sense may also be read in the historical dimension, as a means of reading the unconscious figurings of a given life within a specific cultural moment. As such, it will of course be subject to change and will of course to some extent serve the interests of the society that supports it. I am not arguing here against psychoanalytic theory in any sense but rather *for* a recognition of its historicity.[15] While Freud's elaboration of the Oedipus complex may have served to assuage the neurotic dilemmas of his society, it does not serve the needs of contemporary feminism. In a society like ours in which most women can expect to work outside the home for a significant part of their lives, and to bear fewer than three children, the interpretive myths offered by Freud for women are increasingly pathological. In order to be useful, the theory must bear a demonstrable relation to perceived reality. To argue that the social reality of women should be altered in order to fit the theory is not only reactionary, but naïve. It would make more sense to pursue the directions of contemporary psychoanalytic theory toward a redefinition of femininity, assuming as I do that implicit within the current focus on the mother/child relation is a reawakening of interest in the question of femininity. There are even some theorists, like Dorothy Dinnerstein, who would argue that such a reformulation is necessary for cultural survival, given the destructiveness in political terms of the masculine mystique.[16]

What then, in psychoanalytic terms, would constitute the beginnings of feminist discourse? How is a woman, according to the painful elaborations of Julia Kristeva and others, to avoid the Scylla of silence or madness and the Charybdis of alienated or masculine discourse?[17] Gayatri Spivak has lately been suggesting that what we need is something like a Copernican revolution from the phallocentric formulation of femininity as absence to a gynocentric language of presence.[18] If it makes sense that the male child should perceive his own sex as primary and difference as an inferior version of himself, then it makes as much sense that the little girl should also initially perceive her sex as primary. That each sex should take itself as the norm is perhaps part of the Ptolemaic universe of children which must undergo several stages of decentering before maturity. Not to undergo this process of decentering is to elaborate structures of dominance and submission in which dominance becomes the mask of weakness and submission a subversive strategy in the mutual struggle for power. For a woman to read herself obliquely through the patriarchal discourse as "other" is to assent to this structure. For a critic, male or female, to read this discourse as representative of the true nature of masculinity or femininity is to accept this structure. For a feminist critic to deconstruct this discourse is simultaneously to recognize her own historicity and to engage in the process of dislocation of the unconscious by which she begins to affirm her own reality.

NOTES

1. *A Midsummer Night's Dream, The Complete Signet Classic Shakespeare,* ed. Sylvan Barnet (New York: Harcourt Brace Jovanovich, 1963, 1972), p. 530. Quotations from Shakespeare in this essay refer to this edition.

2. Two critics have dealt specifically with the relation between sex and violence in this play. A. K. Nardo notes that "To the youths who rekindle the feud on a point of honor, sex, aggression, and violence are inextricably united." While Juliet undergoes an extraordinary process of development, Nardo argues, she is ultimately unable to survive in this hostile atmosphere and is finally "thrust to the wall by the phallic sword her society has exalted." "Romeo and Juliet Up Against the Wall," *Paunch,* 48–49 (1977), 127–31. Coppélia Kahn in a more extensive consideration of this subject relates the ethic of the feud, in which sex and violence are linked, to the patriarchal structure of the society, commenting on the extent to which the conclusion of the play, associating death with sexual consummation, is also contained within this structure. Fate is thus not only a result of powerful social forces, but also of the individual subjective responses to these forces. "Coming of Age in Verona," *Modern Language Studies,* 8 (1977–78), 5–22.

3. Theodore Lidz represents Hamlet as torn between the impulse to kill his mother for having betrayed his father and the desire to win her to a state of repentance and renewed chastity. My reading of Hamlet is very much indebted to his analysis in *Hamlet's Enemy: Madness and Myth in Hamlet* (New York: Basic Books, 1975).

4. Murray Schwartz discusses the difficulty of the hero's recognition of his relation to a nurturing woman in "Shakespeare through Contemporary Psychoanalysis," *Hebrew University Studies in Literature,* 5 (1977), 182–98. While Lear's dilemma, according to Schwartz, results from a "refusal to mourn the loss of maternal provision" (p. 192), Macbeth's difficulty may be seen as the result of an attempt to usurp maternal functions and to control the means of nurturance himself.

5. My discussion of the ways in which masculinity and femininity are perceived in this play is indebted to Cleanth Brooks's classic essay on *Macbeth,* "The Naked Babe and the Cloak of Manliness," in *The Well Wrought Urn* (1947; rpt. London: Dobson Books, 1968), pp. 17–39. For Brooks, it is Macbeth's war on children which reveals most clearly his own weakness and desperation. In Brooks's view,

the issue of manliness is related ultimately to the theme of humanity or lack of it, but he does not raise questions about masculine and feminine stereotypes.

6. I would assent to the following description by Gayatri Spivak of the task of deconstruction: "To locate the promising marginal text, to disclose the undecidable moment, to pry it loose, with the positive lever of the signifier, to reverse the resident hierarchy, only to displace it; to dismantle in order to reconstitute what is always already inscribed. Deconstruction in a nutshell." Jacques Derrida, *Of Grammatology,* translator's preface (Baltimore: Johns Hopkins University Press, 1976), p. lxxvii. While Spivak points out that there is no end to this process in that the work of deconstruction is itself subject to deconstruction, she also notes that "as she deconstructs, all protestations to the contrary, the critic necessarily assumes that she at least, and for the time being, means what she says," p. lxxvii. While it may not be strictly necessary to borrow this terminology for the reading I am proposing, it may be useful to observe that any large-scale reinterpretation, from a minority position, of a majority view of reality must appear at least in the eyes of some as a "deconstruction."

7. Here, the problem inherent in the use of the masculine pronoun to refer to both sexes emerges. Textually speaking, the construction often obscures a shift of consideration from the development of the infant, male or female, to the exclusive development of the male infant. This convention is related to the cultural assumption by which the male of the species is taken as a norm, of which the female then becomes a variant. To remove this convention would not merely introduce a stylistic awkwardness (for some people at least), it would also reveal a fundamental awkwardness in the structure of an author's argument. While the male pronoun often *is* used generically to indicate both men and women, its use frequently serves to exclude consideration of the female without calling attention to the process by which she has been removed from the discussion.

8. Although Freud approaches the subject of femininity from different angles in his three major discussions of it, there is no question that he links the process of feminine development indissolubly to the recognition on the part of the little girl that she is castrated. It would seem at least reasonable to argue, however, that the presence or absence of a penis is of far greater significance to the boy or man, who feels himself subject to the threat of its removal, than it could ever be to the girl or woman, for whom such a threat can have little anatomical meaning. I wonder too, why, in Freud's argument, a little girl

would be inspired to give up the manifestly satisfying activity of masturbation on the basis of the illusion of a loss—the assumption perhaps that she might have had more pleasure if she had once had a penis, of which she seems mysteriously to have been deprived? The problem which gives rise to these baroque speculations is, of course, Freud's assumption that there must be some reason why the little girl would withdraw her love from her mother in order to bestow it upon her father. Freud can imagine no other reason than the little girl's recognition of her own inferiority and thus "penis envy," and her resentment of her mother, equally deprived, for not having provided her with the desired organ. There can be no heterosexual love, in this account, without the theory of feminine castration. One can understand, from this vantage point, why Freud was reluctant to give it up. See "Some Psychical Consequences of the Anatomical Distinction between the Sexes" (1925), "Female Sexuality" (1931), and "Femininity" (1933), *Standard Edition*, trans. and ed. James Strachey (London: Hogarth Press, 1961, 1964), XIX, 241–60; XXI, 221–46; XXII, 112–35. For various critiques of Freud, see also Roy Shafer, "Problems in Freud's Psychology of Women," *Journal of the American Psychoanalytic Association*, 22 (1974), 459–85; *Women and Analysis*, ed. Jean Strouse (New York: Grossman, 1974); *Psychoanalysis and Women*, ed. Jean Baker Miller (Baltimore: Penguin Books, 1973).

9. One might wish to argue that social, psychic, and literary structures are so intimately interwoven that the relation between plot and culture is like that between Hamlet and his fate, between a text which is given and that which is generated, enacted, in part, chosen. With this in mind, one might begin to speak of "patriarchal plots," the complex set of figures by which Western culture has elaborated its relation to the structures by which it lives. The question then becomes the extent to which a powerful social movement warps, flexes, alters, reimagines these essential structures, how genres are born, how transformed.

10. James Hillman, *The Myth of Analysis: Three Essays in Archetypal Psychology* (Evanston: Northwestern University Press, 1972), pp. 215–98.

11. Thomas Kuhn, *The Structure of Scientific Revolutions* (Chicago: University of Chicago Press, 1966).

12. Denis de Rougemont, *Love in the Western World*, trans. Montgomery Belgion (New York: Harcourt Brace, 1940, 1956), p. 243. I have chosen the passages from de Rougemont because they are central to the elucidation of the courtly love tradition and because they

are so clearly, though unintentionally, biased. A more contemporary (and more complex) example of the same kind of bias might be found in the concluding chapters of Leo Bersani's *A Future for Astyanax: Character and Desire in Literature* (Boston: Little, Brown, 1976).

13. De Rougemont, *Love in the Western World*, p. 244.

14. Ortega y Gasset, *History as a System, and Other Essays Toward a Philosophy of History* (New York: Norton, 1941, 1961), pp. 165–233.

15. The following articles make a case for the relevance of Freud's personal history to the structure of his thought: Arthur Efron, "Freud's Self-Analysis and the Nature of Psychoanalytic Criticism," *The International Review of Psychoanalysis*, 4 (1977), 253–80; Jim Swan, "*Mater* and Nannie: Freud's Two Mothers and the Discovery of the Oedipus Complex," *American Imago*, 31 (1974), 1–64; Patrick Mahony, "Friendship and Its Discontents," paper presented to the Canadian Psychoanalytic Society, Montreal, May 19, 1977. Freud's instrument of self-analysis, from the point of view of these critics, becomes a double-edged sword, a manifestation of his genius for the articulation of the structural principles of his own psyche, as well as a measure of the necessary limitation of his method. Murray Schwartz elucidates this point further in "Shakespeare through Contemporary Psychoanalysis." Juliet Mitchell might be seen to treat this subject on a large scale in *Psychoanalysis and Feminism* (New York: Pantheon, 1974), when she argues that the Oedipus complex acts as a structural representation of the psychic organization of patriarchal society.

16. Dorothy Dinnerstein, *The Mermaid and the Minotaur: Sexual Arrangements and Human Malaise* (New York: Harper & Row, 1976).

17. Julia Kristeva, who seems to accept the Lacanian explanation of the process of the child's induction into the symbolic order in Western culture, presents the position of women within this construct as one of agonized conflict in the opening chapters of *About Chinese Women*, trans. Anita Barrows (New York: Urizen Books, 1977). Shoshona Felman states the problem of defining a feminist discourse within a masculinist ethic as follows: "If, in our culture, the woman is by definition associated with madness, her problem is how to break out of this (cultural) imposition of madness *without* taking up the critical and therapeutic positions of reason: how to avoid speaking both as *mad* and as *not mad*. The challenge facing the woman today is nothing less than to 're-invent' language, to *re-learn how to speak*:

to speak not only against, but outside of the specular phallocentric structure, to establish a discourse the status of which would no longer be defined by the phallacy of masculine meaning. An old saying would thereby be given new life: today more than ever, changing our minds—changing the mind—is a woman's prerogative." "Women and Madness: The Critical Phallacy," *Diacritics*, 5, No. 4 (1975), 2–10.

18. This statement derives from remarks made by Gayatri Spivak toward the end of a session at the 1977 MMLA convention in Chicago in which she spoke of "the womb as a tangible place of production," as the point of departure for a new discourse on femininity. She has suggested that since the work on which this comment is based is not yet in print, I refer to my memory of her statements. I wish to apologize in advance for any error of understanding on my part of her position.

MARVIN CARLSON

Othello in Vienna, 1991

Unserer Shakespeare ("our Shakespeare") is an expression especially understandable in Vienna, where the English dramatist is more often presented at the national theaters than any German-speaking author, and where the most acclaimed production in the 1991 repertoire was the Akademie Theater's *Othello*. The new translation by Erich Fried is on the whole sensitive and accurate in rendering the speeches of the major characters. It takes a number of liberties in cutting and rearranging the material but not more than might be expected in many stage versions. The cast is reduced to eleven—Othello, Iago, Desdemona, Emilia, Cassio, Brabantio, Roderigo, Bianca, Gratiano, Ludovico, and Montano—with the lines of most lesser characters cut or distributed to the latter three and with the Clown's lines given to Bianca. The most noticeable deletion is the scene of Brabantio's awakening by Iago, 1.1, a cut that allows all of the action before the departure for Cyprus to be played in a single location, for this production a Racinian "reception room" in Venice. This translation also gathers (as do many productions) all the bedchamber scenes from the fourth and fifth acts into a single final act.

This *Othello* was directed by George Tabori, better known as a playwright outside Austria and Germany but also one of the leading directors at the National Theater, both of his own and others' plays. Tabori made several

This review was originally published in *Shakespeare Quarterly* 44 (1993): 228–30, and is reprinted with the permission of the author and of *Shakespeare Quarterly*.

modifications of Fried's translation, most notably in the character of Bianca. By conflating this character with the Clown, Fried emphasizes her crudeness and physicality. Tabori took her in a completely different direction, cutting all of the scenes given her by Fried and making her instead a dark, forbidding figure, never speaking and never spoken to but often hovering on the edge of the action. She was dressed as an Arab woman in flowing black robe and head-covering, her face and hands a deathly white, her lips and eyes outlined in black.

Like the witches in *Macbeth,* this strange creature looked unlike the inhabitants of Earth and suggested some external dark power controlling the actions of the play. When the audience entered the theater, she was already visible, her back turned, leaning on the railing at the front of the forestage. As the house darkened, she shook an unseen mysterious rattle, a disturbing sound that was echoed elsewhere in the auditorium at the end of each act. From time to time throughout the evening, this menacing shadow could be glimpsed moving quietly in the peripheral darkness or even creeping about under the stage itself, as she did in one particularly chilling moment in the fourth act, when Desdemona seemed to catch a glimpse of her and then, looking more closely, found that she had disappeared. She did not actually participate in the action onstage until the second act, when she was seen as a servant in Cyprus, moving quietly about the stage, observed by none of the major characters but observing all.

The stage itself was a carefully controlled minimal space, a raked square with one corner pointed toward the audience. The two rear walls, with entrances at each side, were painted a dull orange from the floor to about eye level and black above the orange; for the final act they became completely black. In each of three sets, a central element defined this space. In Act 5 this element was, of course, the bed, itself a square, surrounded by gauze curtains. A light hanging over it illuminated the bed area from within, creating an island of light.

This set, with the geometrical simplicity of its forms, was almost timeless. The other two sets were much more clearly contemporary, reflecting the modern feeling of the translation. Although this translation makes no attempt to update specific lines or references, it is clearly designed for a modern-dress production, most strikingly in the way it presents the encounter with Cassio that Iago stages for Othello. In Fried's version Iago resorts to the more contemporary and foolproof device of playing the conversation for Othello from a pocket tape recorder. Othello reacted to this by savagely unwinding the tape, then crushing both it and the machine.

For the scene with the Duke and Senators of Venice, 1.3, Tabori transformed the reception-room set into a military strategy room with a dark, bunker-like feeling. The central element here was a map table situated under a green light. Gratiano appeared as a crisply suited bureaucrat, perhaps Venetian Minister of Defense; the others wore elegant white uniforms. Brabantio was richly but hastily dressed and unshaven. The dark, conspiratorial feeling of this set was sharply contrasted with the Cyprus set of Acts 2, 3, and 4, a Rick's-style bar strikingly evoked with minimal means—brilliant lighting, a few palm fronds hanging from the proscenium, a piano at center under a slowly turning ceiling fan, and plenty of iced drinks and tropical fruits, served by Emilia and the Arab servant.

The second act opened with the Third Gentleman's line "News, lads, our wars are done," here given to Montano; a celebratory party, with toasts, banners, and popular songs around the piano, began almost at once. Amid this frivolity the Arab woman, unnoticed by the others as usual, tossed a black veil onto a blade of the fan overhead, where it remained, slowly turning during the central portion of the play, a grim accent among the party decorations. Perhaps nowhere was this veil more effective than in the moment before the fight. Roderigo had been taunting Cassio by directing obscene noises at him with a party balloon. As the tension increased, they circled the piano. Suddenly Roderigo released the balloon, which shot past Cassio through the air. Everyone onstage realized that a fight was imminent, but all froze in expectation, and the only movement was the veil trailing from the fan as it turned.

Early in this scene the Arab woman offered another grim surprise. As the others gathered around the piano with funny hats and false noses, joking and singing, she came down-stage and turned her back to the audience, revealing as she did so that she wore a mask on the back of her head—a black, full-face mask, disturbingly similar to Othello him-self. This moment highlighted another unusual aspect of this production. The blackness of Gert Voss as Othello was con-stantly emphasized. He played the Moor as a physical outsider, especially in the opening act, when he seemed powerful but a bit awkward and gangly, given to an emo-tionalism clearly alien to his stiff, Anglo-Saxon fellow offi-cers. His makeup was negroid and quite heavy, so heavy that it tended to rub off on other characters, particularly of course on Iago and Desdemona, who came most often into contact with him.

Iago (Ignaz Kirchner) played up close to all his victims, clutching them, holding their arms and shoulders, whis-pering into their ears or rubbing against their cheeks. He was often close to Othello, especially during their violent en-counter in the third act. As Iago swore his oath and cradled the exhausted Othello in his arms, the white uniforms of both were equally rumpled and soiled, and streaks of Oth-ello's makeup covered Iago's face and hands, binding them visually as well as psychologically. Desdemona also was marked by contact with Othello. In Act 1, when she stepped back from their first embrace, her cheek was blackened from the contact, as if Brabantio's anxiety had been given physical reality and she, like Prince Hal in his own father's memorable metaphor, had received pitch-like darkening from an unworthy consort. At first the audience probably took this as an unfortunate accidental effect, but the actors emphasized it by laughing together as Othello used his hand-kerchief to wipe the blackness from her cheek (almost every character in this production was equipped with a hand-kerchief, and frequent use was made of them for a variety of purposes). Here and later the transfer of makeup remained in a liminal zone between theatrical illusion, stage device, and metaphor, never clearly confirmed as any one of these.

The choices of the Arab Bianca and of the black makeup pointed to a larger pattern of imagery in the production in which light and darkness continually struggled for mastery. When Othello gave himself over to revenge in the famous

"Farewell the tranquil mind" speech, he removed and tore
apart his white military jacket, laying it out like a corpse on
the stage and standing in black undergarments. Similarly, in
the final act he covered Desdemona's white dress with his
black jacket before approaching the bed, and once there, he
sat on the bed's edge, a black shadow outlined by the pool of
white light in which Desdemona slept.

The final scene, though abbreviated in Fried's translation,
was highly effective as played here. After Emilia's revela-
tion of Desdemona's innocence, Othello, sobbing out his
lines, ripped the fatal handkerchief into shreds and on the
line "If that thou be'st a devil, I cannot kill thee" thrust them
into Iago's face as if to smother him. There was a sudden
blackout, and the lights came up to reveal Iago and Othello
upstage center, handcuffed together and under arrest by
Cassio, the new commander of Cyprus. Only these three and
Emilia, at the far left, were onstage. Othello moved down to
confront Cassio, bringing Iago with him. When he cut his
own throat, he pulled Iago to the floor in his agonized
spasms; dragging him to the bed where Desdemona lay,
Othello then died across her body, while Iago, still shackled
to him, crouched at their side. Cassio rushed off, and the
Arab woman entered to stand over this tableau of death like
an avenging angel. From the darkness of the auditorium, the
mysterious rattle sounded for the last time.

In addition to the strength of its directorial vision, this
production offered powerful and rich individual performances. Gert Voss's Othello, a bit supercilious at first,
became deeply moving in his later emotional torment. Ignaz
Kirchner's Iago was from the outset an almost demonic
figure, working upon those about him with a vampire-like
intensity. Julia Stemberger as Desdemona came across as
totally charming and open, though a bit flirtatious, indeed
coy enough with Cassio and with others to give Iago ideas
and material for exploitation. Her relationship with the more
solid and down-to-earth Emilia (Elisabeth Orth) was engag-
ingly developed, and their scene in the last act, where they
drank champagne, smoked cigarettes, and exchanged romantic confidences like naughty schoolgirls, was one of the
delights of the production and a very effective pause in the
movement toward disaster.

At the end one wondered whether in Tabori's production the catastrophe was not over-justified. Kirchner's Iago was fully capable of spreading destruction about him, while the association from the beginning of Othello with darkness and defilement drew him symbolically into the creation of this catastrophe as well. And beyond them both hung the darkness that surrounded the stage, that heart of darkness with its primal sounds, embodied in the alien figure of the mysterious Arab woman, who presided over the play like a malignant fate from before the opening curtain until the final image.

Rather than defusing the production effort, however, these various manifestations of darkness for the most part powerfully reinforced each other, or at least they did so for this reviewer and apparently for the sell-out audiences that made this the most successful National Theater offering of the 1991 season.

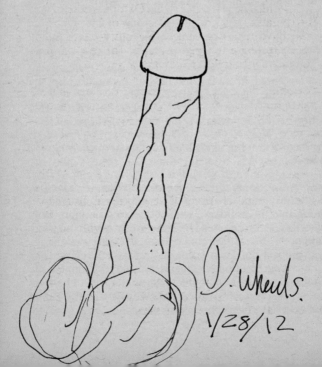

SYLVAN BARNET

Othello on Stage and Screen

The earliest mention of a performance of *Othello,* in an account of 1604, reports only that the play was acted before James I at Whitehall Palace. Next come two references to performances in 1610, one telling us that it was acted at the Globe in April, the other telling us that it was acted in September at Oxford. The reference to the Oxford production is especially valuable, since it provides one of the very few glimpses we have of early seventeenth-century acting and of an audience's response to a performance. The relevant passage, in Latin, may be translated thus:

> In their tragedies they acted with appropriate decorum; in these they caused tears not only by their speaking, but also by their action. Indeed Desdemona, although greatly successful throughout, moved us especially when at last, lying on her bed, killed by her husband, she implored the pity of the spectators in her death with her face alone.

This may not seem like much, but it is more than we have for all but a few of Shakespeare's other plays, and it is especially valuable as a reminder that the Renaissance boy actors—a boy played Desdemona—were highly skilled performers.

There are only a few additional references to performances in the first half of the seventeenth century, but a very large number of rather general references to the play (as opposed to specific performances) allows us to conclude that the play must have been popular on the stage. From 1642 to

1660 the theaters were closed by act of Parliament, but when the theaters reopened in 1660, *Othello* was staged almost immediately. Samuel Pepys saw it in 1660:

> To the Cockpit to see *The Moor of Venice,* which was well done. [Nathaniel] Burt acted the Moor: by the same token, a very pretty lady that sat by me called out, to see Desdemona smothered.

He saw it again in 1669, this time with less pleasure:

> To the King's playhouse, and there in an upper box . . . did see *The Moor of Venice:* but ill acted in most parts; [Michael] Mohun which did a little surprise me not acting Iago's part by much so well as [Walter] Clun used to do . . . nor, indeed, Burt doing the Moor's so well as I once thought he did.

During this period, the great interpreter of the title role was Thomas Betterton, who performed it from 1684 to 1709. Although he was the leading Othello of the period and was much praised, the only informative contemporary account of his performance in the role tells us little more than that his

> aspect was serious, venerable, and majestic. . . . His voice was low and grumbling, though he could time it by an artful climax, which enforced attention. . . . He kept this passion under, and showed it most.

Betterton's successor as Othello was James Quin, who played the part from 1722 to 1751. Wearing a white wig and the white uniform (including white gloves) of a British officer, he was said to have presented an impressive appearance, but his acting was characterized as statuesque, even stiff, lacking in tenderness, pathos, fire, and any suggestion of inner pain. Quin was eclipsed in 1745 by David Garrick, whose Othello was quite different: the complaint now was that this Othello lacked dignity. The accusation was not merely a glance at Garrick's relatively short stature (he sought to compensate for his height by adding a turban to the costume of an officer in the British army), or even at his bold restoration of the fainting episode (4.1.45), which had been cut by his predecessors. Rather, it was directed at Garrick's violent gestures, which suggested to one critic that Othello seemed afflicted with St. Vitus dance. Garrick defended his interpretation by arguing that Shakespeare

> had shown us white men jealous in other pieces, but that their jeal-
> ousy had limits, and was not so terrible. . . . [In] Othello he had
> wished to paint that passion in all its violence, and that is why he
> chose an African in whose being circulated fire instead of blood,
> and whose true or imaginary character could excuse all boldness
> of expression and all exaggerations of passion.

Garrick's rival, Quin, was not convinced. Of Garrick's Othello, Quin said: "Othello! . . . psha! no such thing. There was a little black boy . . . fretting and fuming about the stage; but I saw no Othello."

A reader can scarcely overlook the racism in these remarks, and something should be said about attitudes toward Moors. There is no doubt that most Elizabethans regarded Moors as vengeful—largely because they were not Christians. That Moors were black—the color of the devil— was thought to be a visible sign of their capacity for endless evil. (In fact, Shakespeare specifies that Othello is a Christian, and this is only one of several ways in which Othello departs from the stereotype.) Othello's physical blackness, by the way, seems not to have been doubted until the early nineteenth century. Certainly Quin and Garrick played him in blackface, and presumably so did their predecessor Betterton. And there is no doubt that on the Elizabethan stage Othello was very black. The only contemporary illus- tration of a scene from Shakespeare shows another of Shake- speare's Moors, Aaron in *Titus Andronicus,* as having an inky complexion. But in the early nineteenth century one finds expressions of distinct discomfort at the thought that Othello is black rather than, say, bronzed, or (to use an even loftier metaphor) golden. Even the best critics were not exempt from the racist thinking of their times. Thus, in 1808 Charles Lamb, picking up Desdemona's assertion that she judged Othello by his mind rather than by his color, argued that although we can share her view when we read the play, we cannot do so when we see a black Othello on the stage:

She sees Othello's color in his mind. But upon the stage, when the imagination is no longer the ruling faculty, but we are left to our poor unassisted senses, I appeal to every one that has seen Othello played, whether he did not, on the contrary, sink Othello's mind in his color; whether he did not find something extremely revolting in the courtship and wedded caresses of Othello and Desdemona, and whether the actual sight of the thing did not over-weigh all that beautiful compromise which we make in reading. . . .

At about the time that Lamb offered his comment on Othello, Lamb's friend Coleridge made some notes to the effect that Shakespeare could not possibly have thought of Othello as a black:

Can we suppose [Shakespeare] so utterly ignorant as to make a barbarous *negro* plead royal birth? Were negroes then known but as slaves; on the contrary, were not the Moors the warriors? . . . No doubt Desdemona saw Othello's visage in his mind; yet, as we are constituted, and most surely as an English audience was disposed in the beginning of the seventeenth century, it would be something monstrous to conceive this beautiful Venetian girl falling in love with a veritable negro. It would argue a disproportionateness, a want of balance in Desdemona, which Shakespeare does not appear to have in the least contemplated.

Given Coleridge's certainty that Othello could not possibly have been black, it is well to reiterate that the Elizabethans thought of Moors as black. True, there are a few references in Elizabethan literature to "tawny" Moors, but there is no evidence that the Elizabethans distinguished between tawny and black Moors, and in any case, if they did, various passages in *Othello* indicate that the protagonist is surely a black Moor. Admittedly, most of the references to Othello's Negroid features are made by persons hostile to him— Roderigo calls him "the thick-lips" (1.1.63), for instance, and Iago speaks of him as "an old black ram" (1.1.85)—but Othello himself says that his name "is now begrimed and black / As mine own face" (3.3.384–5). Of course "black" is sometimes used in the sense of brunette, but there really cannot be any doubt that Othello is black in the most obvious modern sense, and to call him tawny or golden or bronzed, or to conceive of him as something of an Arab chieftain, is to go against the text of the play.

When Spranger Barry, the actor who displaced Garrick as Othello in the middle of the eighteenth century (he was said to have not only the passion of Garrick but also the majesty that in Quin was merely stiffness), the question of color seems not to have come up, nor did it come up when the role in effect belonged to John Philip Kemble, the chief Othello at the turn of the eighteenth century (he played his first Othello in 1785, his last in 1805). Kemble, tall and stately, acted in what can be called a classic rather than romantic manner, a style suited more to, say, Brutus than to Othello. His interpretation of the role was criticized for its superabundance of dignity and for its lack of variety and fire, but not for its blackness. But when Edmund Kean played the role in 1814 he is said to have used a light brown makeup in place of the usual burnt cork. Oddly, there is some uncertainty about this—most critics of the period did not comment on the novelty—but putting aside the question of who made the change, and exactly when, about this time the color changed. By 1827 Leman Thomas Rede's *The Road to the Stage* (a book on makeup) could report that "A tawny tinge is now the color used for the gallant Moor." Here it is evident that the makeup no longer uses burnt cork. Most of the Othellos of the rest of the century were tawny, their bronze skin suggesting that they were sons of the desert, but Henry Irving's Othello of 1881 was conspicuously dark (darker than his "bronze" Othello of 1876), and, as we shall see, in the twentieth century dark Othellos have been dominant, especially in our own generation, when American blacks have often played the part.

Putting aside the point that Kean's Othello was lighter than usual, it was exceptional for its power and its pathos. If Kemble is the paradigm of classical acting, Kean—passionate, even spasmodic—is the paradigm of romantic acting. Coleridge wrote: "Seeing [Kean] act was like reading Shakespeare by flashes of lightning." Another great romantic writer, William Hazlitt, at first found Kean too passionate. In the following passage Hazlitt complains that the fault in the performance is not in the color of Kean's face, or in Kean's relatively short stature:

Othello was tall, but that is nothing; he was black, but that is nothing. But he was not fierce, and that is everything. It is only in the last agony of human suffering that he gives way to his rage and despair. . . . Mr. Kean is in general all passion, all energy, all relentless will. . . . He is to often in the highest key of passion, too uniformly on the verge of extravagance, too constantly on the rack.

Kean later moderated the passion, perhaps under Hazlitt's influence, but, curiously, Hazlitt regretted the change, remarking: "There is but one perfect way of playing Othello, and that was the way . . . he used to play it." Equally compelling is the tribute to Kean offered by the American actor Junius Brutus Booth, who in England in 1817–18 played Iago to Kean's Othello. Booth said that "Kean's Othello smothered Desdemona and my Iago too." Kean's triumph in the role was undoubted, but in 1825, two weeks after he had been proved guilty of adultery, public opinion turned against him, denouncing the hypocrisy of an adulterer who dared to play the outraged husband lamenting his wife's infidelity. Still, he continued in the role, playing Othello almost to the day of his death. His last performance was in this role, in 1833, when he collapsed on the stage and died a few weeks later.

Other nineteenth-century actors have made their mark in the role—for instance William Macready (he sometimes played Iago against Kean's Othello) and Samuel Phelps—but here there is space to mention only four, Ira Aldridge, Edwin Booth, Tommaso Salvini, and Henry Irving. Aldridge, a black, was born in New York in 1807. As a very young man he determined to be an actor, but seeing no possibility of a career as an actor in America, he went to London in 1824 and never returned to the United States. At least one black actor, James Hewlett, had already played Othello in America, but that was with the all-black African Company, and Aldridge's ambition was to be accepted as an actor, not as a black actor, an ambition impossible to fulfill in the United States, where there were no interracial companies. He performed throughout the British Isles and also on the Continent, playing not only Othello but also (with white makeup) such roles as Richard III, Shylock, Hamlet, Macbeth, and Lear.

In America, Edwin Booth (son of Junius Brutus Booth) acted Othello almost annually from 1826 to 1871. From time to time he changed his performance, sometimes working in the violent style associated with Tommaso Salvini, hurling his Iago to the ground, but sometimes he played with restraint—occasionally he even omitted striking Desdemona at IV.i.240—and he was especially praised for his tender passion. Most critics, however, preferred his Iago, which seemed genial, sincere, and terrifyingly evil; he was widely regarded as the greatest Iago of the later nineteenth century. (Among the performers with whom he alternated the roles of Othello and Iago were Henry Irving and James O'Neill, Eugene O'Neill's father; and he played Iago to Salvini's Othello.) Here is his advice on how to play Iago:

> Don't *act* the villain, don't *look* it or *speak* it (by scowling and growling, I mean), but *think* it all the time. Be genial, sometimes jovial, always gentlemanly. Quick in motion as in thought; lithe and sinuous as a snake. A certain bluffness (which my temperament does not afford) should be added to preserve the military flavor of the character; in this particular I fail utterly, my Iago lacks the soldierly quality.

Henry Irving played Othello only in 1876 and 1881. Although he had already achieved success in the roles of Hamlet, Macbeth, and Lear, his Othello did not find equal favor. It was not especially violent, but it was said to lack dignity (apparently there was much lifting up of hands and shuffling of feet), and after the attempt in 1881 Irving decided to drop the role. Still, some things about the 1881 performance should be mentioned. The makeup was very black, the costume exotic (a white jeweled turban, an amber robe), and the killing of Desdemona very solemn—until Desdemona tried to escape, at which point he flung her on the bed. The play ended with Othello's suicide, the curtain descending as he fell at Gratiano's feet. Iago (played by Booth) stood by, smiling malignantly.

By common consent the greatest Othello of the later nineteenth century was Tommaso Salvini, who acted in Italian—

even when in England or the United States, with the rest of
the company speaking English. Some Victorians regarded
Salvini as too savage, too volcanic, too terrifying to arouse
pity—he seized Iago by the throat and hurled him to the
floor, and put his foot on Iago's neck, and of course he did
not hesitate to strike Desdemona—but most audiences were
deeply moved as well as terrified by his performance. We
are told that especially in the first three acts, where some of
the love play seemed almost to be high comedy, his Othello
was "delightful" and "delicate." Still, the overall effect was
that of enormous energy, though not of mere barbarism.
Henry James was among Salvini's greatest admirers:

> It is impossible to imagine anything more living, more tragic,
> more suggestive of a tortured soul and of generous, beneficent
> strength changed to a purpose of destruction. With its tremendous
> force, it is magnificently quiet, and from beginning to end has not
> a touch of rant or crudity.

Actors of note who played Othello or Iago in the early
twentieth century include Johnston Forbes-Robertson,
Oscar Asche, and Beerbohm Tree, but none of these was
widely regarded as great. Indeed, the standard opinion is
that the twentieth century did not have a great Othello until
Paul Robeson, an African American, played the role in
1943. But Robeson was not primarily an actor. As a college
student at Rutgers he distinguished himself not in theatrics
but in athletics (all-American end in football in 1918, and
letters in several varsity sports) and in scholarship (Phi
Beta Kappa). He next prepared for a career in the law,
taking a law degree at Columbia University, but while at
Columbia in 1921 he performed in his first amateur production. He soon began to appear in some professional productions, including *Showboat,* where his singing of "Ol'
Man River" led to a career as a concert singer, especially of
spirituals and work songs, though he returned to the stage
to play Othello in 1930 in England, in 1942 in Cambridge,
Boston, and Princeton, in 1943 in New York, and in 1959
at Stratford-upon-Avon. Observers agree that the 1959 performance was poor; Robeson had been weakened by an
attack of bronchitis, his political beliefs had been shaken

(earlier he had praised Stalin, but now the crimes of the Stalin era were evident), and, perhaps worst of all, the director's presence was too strongly felt, for instance in a distracting fog that supposedly was the result of the storm at Cyprus. Many scenes were so dark that spectators could not see the actors' faces, and there seems no reason to doubt the accuracy of those reviewers who accused the director of obliterating the principal actors.

Robeson's first Othello—indeed, his first performance in a play by Shakespeare, in 1930—was much more enthusiastically received. The London *Morning Post* said: "There has been no Othello on our stage for forty years to compare with his dignity, simplicity, and true passion." But not all of the reviewers were entirely pleased. James Agate, the leading theater critic of the period, said that Robeson lacked the majesty that Shakespeare insists on early in the play, for instance in such lines as

> I fetch my life and being
> From men of royal siege,   (1.2.20–21)

and

> Were it my cue to fight, I should have known it
> Without a prompter,   (82–83)

and

> Keep up your bright swords, for the dew will
> rust them.   (58)

The majesty displayed in such passages, Agate said, tells us how Othello must behave when he puts down Cassio's drunken brawl, but according to Agate, Robeson (despite his height—six feet, three inches) lacked this majesty. Thus, when Robeson's Othello said "Silence that dreadful bell! It frights the isle / From her propriety" (2.3.174–75), he showed personal annoyance rather than the "passion for decorum" (Agate's words) that the line reveals. Agate found Robeson best in the third and fourth acts, where he captured the jealousy of the part, but weak (lacking in dignity) in the last act, where he failed to perform the murder with a solemn sense of sacrifice.

Despite the reservations of Agate and others, there was some talk of bringing the production to the United States, but nothing came of it, doubtless because of uncertainty about how American audiences (and perhaps performers?) would respond to a company that mixed whites and blacks. In 1938 Margaret Webster again raised the topic, but she was discouraged by the Americans with whom she talked. It was acceptable for a black actor—a real black man, not a white man in blackface—to kiss a white girl in England, but not in the United States. Fortunately, however, Webster later persuaded the Theatre Guild to invite Robeson to do *Othello* in the United States in 1942, if not on Broadway at least as summer stock, with José Ferrer as Iago and Uta Hagen as Desdemona. The production was enthusiastically received, but Robeson's concert commitments prevented it from going to New York until the fall of 1943. When it did open in New York, the reviews were highly favorable, but some of them contained reservations about Robeson's ability to speak blank verse and to catch the grandeur of the role. In any case, the production was an enormous success, running for 296 continuous performances. The previous record for a New York *Othello* had been 57.

Robeson inevitably was asked to discuss his conception of the role; equally inevitably, he said different things at different times, and perhaps sometimes said what reporters wanted to hear—or perhaps the reporters heard only what they wanted to hear. Sometimes he was reported as saying that the matter of color is secondary, but on other occasions he is reported as saying: "The problem [of *Othello*] is the problem of my own people. It is a tragedy of racial conflict, a tragedy of honor, rather than of jealousy."

Until Robeson, black actors in the United States were in effect limited to performing in all-black companies. With Robeson, a black actor played Othello with an otherwise white company. His appearance as Othello in 1943 was an important anticipation of the gains black actors were to make in later decades. Earle Hyman, Moses Gunn, Paul Winfield, William Marshall, and James Earl Jones are among the black actors who have played impressive Othellos in mixed-race companies. More important, however, as the careers of these actors show, a black may now also play a role other than Othello, as Ira Aldridge did a hundred and fifty years ago, though he had to cross the Atlantic to do it.

Before looking at Laurence Olivier's Othello in 1964, mention should be made of Olivier's Iago in a production of 1937, directed by Tyrone Guthrie at the Old Vic. Olivier and Guthrie talked to Ernest Jones, friend of Sigmund Freud, and came away with the idea that Iago's hatred for Othello was in fact based on a subconscious love for Othello. That Iago protests "I hate the Moor" means nothing, for he is unaware of his true emotions. Ralph Richardson was Othello in this production, but Guthrie and Olivier decided not to shock him (remember, this was 1937) by any such unconventional idea, and so, the story goes, Richardson could never quite understand what Olivier was making out of the role. (What Olivier apparently made out of it was something like this: Iago is manic because he cannot face his true feelings.) The critics, like Richardson and the general public, were in the dark, and the production was poorly reviewed. Guthrie himself later called the production "a ghastly, boring hash," and Olivier has said that he no longer subscribes to Jones's interpretation.

In 1964 Olivier played Othello, with Frank Finlay as Iago, and Maggie Smith as Desdemona, in a production directed by John Dexter. (This production was later filmed, and most of what is true of the stage production is true also of the film.) Far from suggesting that Othello was some sort of desert chief, Olivier emphasized the Negroid aspects, or at least the white man's stock ideas of Negroid aspects. Thus, Othello's skin was very dark, his lips were red and sensuous, and his lilting voice had something of a West Indian accent. He rolled his eyes a good deal, and he walked (barefooted and adorned with ankle bracelets) with a sensuous sway. More important (worse, some viewers felt), was the idea behind this Othello, which was indebted to some thoughts by T. S. Eliot and F. R. Leavis. For Eliot (in an essay called "Shakespeare and the Stoicism of Seneca," first published in 1927) and for Leavis (in an essay first published in a journal in 1937 but more readily available, in reprinted form, in Leavis's *The Common Pursuit*), Othello is not so much a heroic figure—the noble Moor who gains our sympathy despite the terrible deed he performs—as a fatuous simpleton, a man given to egotistical self-dramatizing. The playbill included some passages from Leavis's essay, which the director in effect summarized when he told the cast that

> Othello is a pompous, word-spinning, arrogant black general. . . . The important thing is not to accept him at his own valuation. . . . He isn't just a righteous man who's been wronged. He's a man too proud to think he could ever be capable of anything as base as jealousy. When he learns he *can* be jealous, his character changes. The knowledge destroys him, and he goes beserk.

Thus, Olivier delivered "Farewell the tranquil mind" (3.3.345)—a speech customarily delivered reflectively—in a frenzy. It's probably fair to say that the gist of the idea underlying this production is fairly odd: Othello is a barbarian with a thin veneer of civilization. Thus, the early speeches were delivered with easy confidence because Othello had no understanding of how simple and how volatile he really was. The change from civilized man to barbarian was marked by Othello tearing off a crucifix he wore, an effective enough bit of business but one at odds with two aspects of the end of Shakespeare's play: Othello (who just before he kills Desdemona is careful to urge her to make her peace with God; "I would not kill thy soul" (5.2.32) murders Desdemona partly because he believes she has been false to the highest ideals. Second, when he comes to understand the horror of his action he executes justice upon himself. Still, although much in the conception could be faulted, it was widely agreed that Olivier's acting was a triumph—a triumph won, among other things, at the expense of an unprepossessing Iago and a negligible Desdemona.

The film with Olivier (1965), directed by Stuart Burge, was made in a sound studio, using sets that were essentially those of the stage production—even for scenes set out-of-doors—but it was not simply a filmed version of what a spectator sitting in the third row center would have seen. For instance, because close-ups are used for all of Iago's soliloquies, Iago becomes considerably more prominent in the film than he was on the stage.

Olivier said that the backgrounds in the film were minimal because he was concerned with "offering as little visual distraction as possible from the intentions of Shakespeare—or our performance of them." For a film of the opposite sort, a film that does not hesitate to introduce impressive visual effects not specified in the text, one should look at Orson Welles's *Othello,* a black and white film begun in 1951 and completed and released in 1955, with Welles in the title role. The film was shot on location, chiefly in Morocco and Venice, but what especially strikes a viewer is not that the camera gives us a strong sense of the real world, but that the camera leads us into a strange, shadowy world of unfamiliar and puzzling appearance. The film begins with Welles reading a passage from Shakespeare's source while we see a shot of the face of the dead Othello. The camera rises above the bier, which is carried by pallbearers, and we then see Desdemona's body, also being borne to the grave. We see the two funeral processions converge, and then we see Iago, in chains, thrust into a cage and hoisted above the crowd. From above—Iago's viewpoint—we look down on the bodies of Othello and Desdemona. All of this is presented before we see the credits for the film. The film ends with a dissolve from the dying Othello to a shot of the funeral procession and then to shots of the fortress at Cyprus, the cage, and Venetian buildings and ships. Between this highly cinematic beginning and ending, other liberties are taken with the text. The murder of Roderigo, for instance, is set in a steamy bathhouse. Welles had intended to shoot the scene in a street, but because he had run out of money and didn't have costumes, he set it in a steam bath, where a few towels were all the clothing that was needed. In short, Welles's *Othello* is not for the Shakespeare purist (too much is cut and too much is added), but it is imaginative and it often works. Admirers will want to see also *Filming "Othello,"* a film memoir (1978) in which Welles and others discuss the work.

The BBC television version of *Othello,* directed by Jonathan Miller and released in 1981, is, like Olivier's film, somewhat in the Eliot-Leavis tradition. In the introduction to the printed text of the BBC version, Miller says that the play does not set forth "the spectacle of a person of grandeur falling." Rather,

> what's interesting is that it's not the fall of the great but the disintegration of the ordinary, of the representative character. It's the very ordinariness of Othello that makes the story intolerable.

Miller is insistent, too, that the play is not about race. "I do not see the play as being about color but as being about jealousy—which is something we are all vulnerable to." In line with this emphasis on the ordinary, Othello (Anthony Hopkins) is relatively unheroic, though he is scarcely as commonplace as Miller suggests, since he is full of energy and rage. More successful is Iago (Bob Hoskins), a bullet-headed hood who delights in Othello's anguish. The sets, in order to reduce any sense of heroism or romance, are emphatically domestic; no effort was made to take advantage of the camera's ability to record expansive space. Interestingly, however, the domestic images on the screen are by no means ordinary; notably beautiful, they often remind us of Vermeer.

During the course of this survey it has been easy to notice racist implications in the remarks of certain actors and critics. And it was racism, of course, that kept blacks from acting in *Othello* (and in other plays) along with whites. One point that has not been raised till now is this: Does it matter if a black plays Othello? When Robeson played the part, some theatergoers found that the play made more sense than ever before, partly because Robeson (whatever his limitations as an actor) was a black. Others found that it was distracting for a black to play the part; it brought into the world of *Othello* irrelevant issues of twentieth-century America. Jonathan Miller, holding the second position, puts it thus:

> When a black actor does the part, it offsets the play, puts it out of balance. It makes it a play about blackness, which it is not. . . . The trouble is, the play was hijacked for political purposes.

Many things can be said against this view, for instance that when the white actor Olivier played Othello he expended so much energy impersonating a black that a spectator was far more conscious of the performer's blackness than one is of, say, James Earl Jones's. In any case, Miller has not said the last word on this topic, which will continue to be debated.

Bibliographic Note: For a modern edition of *Othello* prefaced with a long stage history, and equipped with abundant footnotes telling how various actors delivered particular lines, see Julie Hankey, *Othello* (1987), a volume in a series entitled Plays in Performance.

For a survey of *Othello* on the stage, see Marvin Rosenberg, *The Masks of "Othello"* (1961); for a brief study of five recent productions (including Robeson in 1943, Olivier in 1964, and the BBC television version of 1981), see Martin L. Wine, *"Othello": Text and Performance* (1984). Errol Hill's *Shakespeare in Sable* (1984), a history of black actors of Shakespeare, contains much information about *Othello*. Other items especially relevant to the productions discussed above include: Arthur Colby Sprague, *Shakespearian Players and Performances* (1953), for Kean's Othello and Edwin Booth's Iago; Daniel J. Watermeier, "Edwin Booth's Iago," *Theatre History Studies* 6 (1986): 32–55; Kenneth Tynan, ed., *"Othello" by William Shakespeare: The National Theatre Production* (1966), on Olivier; *The BBC TV Shakespeare: "Othello"* (1981), on the version directed by Jonathan Miller. On Robeson, see Susan Spector, "Margaret Webster's *Othello*," *Theatre History Studies* 6 (1986): 93–108. For film versions, see Jack J. Jorgens, *Shakespeare on Film* (1977), and, for Welles's film only, see Micheal MacLiammoir, *Put Money in Thy Purse* (1952).

For a review of a recent Austrian production, see the essay by Marvin Carlson, printed above, pages 211–16.

Suggested References

The number of possible references is vast and grows alarmingly. (The *Shakespeare Quarterly* devotes one issue each year to a list of the previous year's work, and *Shakespeare Survey*—an annual publication—includes a substantial review of biographical, critical, and textual studies, as well as a survey of performances.) The vast bibliography is best approached through James Harner, *The World Shakespeare Bibliography on CD-Rom: 1900–Present*. The first release, in 1996, included more than 12,000 annotated items from 1990–93, plus references to several thousand book reviews, productions, films, and audio recordings. The plan is to update the publication annually, moving forward one year and backward three years. Thus, the second issue (1997), with 24,700 entries, and another 35,000 or so references to reviews, newspaper pieces, and so on, covered 1987–94.

Though no works are indispensable, those listed below have been found especially helpful. The arrangement is as follows:

1. Shakespeare's Times
2. Shakespeare's Life
3. Shakespeare's Theater
4. Shakespeare on Stage and Screen
5. Miscellaneous Reference Works
6. Shakespeare's Plays: General Studies
7. The Comedies
8. The Romances
9. The Tragedies
10. The Histories
11. *Othello*

The titles in the first five sections are accompanied by brief explanatory annotations.

1. Shakespeare's Times

Andrews, John F., ed. *William Shakespeare: His World, His Work, His Influence,* 3 vols. (1985). Sixty articles, dealing not only with such subjects as "The State," "The Church," "Law," "Science, Magic, and Folklore," but also with the plays and poems themselves and Shakespeare's influence (e.g., translations, films, reputation)

Byrne, Muriel St. Clare. *Elizabethan Life in Town and Country* (8th ed., 1970). Chapters on manners, beliefs, education, etc., with illustrations.

Dollimore, John, and Alan Sinfield, eds. *Political Shakespeare: New Essays in Cultural Materialism* (1985). Essays on such topics as the subordination of women and colonialism, presented in connection with some of Shakespeare's plays.

Greenblatt, Stephen. *Representing the English Renaissance* (1988). New Historicist essays, especially on connections between political and aesthetic matters, statecraft and stagecraft.

Joseph, B. L. *Shakespeare's Eden: the Commonwealth of England 1558–1629* (1971). An account of the social, political, economic, and cultural life of England.

Kernan, Alvin. *Shakespeare, the King's Playwright: Theater in the Stuart Court 1603–1613* (1995). The social setting and the politics of the court of James I, in relation to *Hamlet, Measure for Measure, Macbeth, King Lear, Antony and Cleopatra, Coriolanus,* and *The Tempest.*

Montrose, Louis. *The Purpose of Playing: Shakespeare and the Cultural Politics of the Elizabethan Theatre* (1996). A poststructuralist view, discussing the professional theater "within the ideological and material frameworks of Elizabethan culture and society," with an extended analysis of *A Midsummer Night's Dream.*

Mullaney, Steven. *The Place of the Stage: License, Play, and Power in Renaissance England* (1988). New Historicist analysis, arguing that popular drama became a cultural institution "only by . . . taking up a place on the margins of society."

Schoenbaum, S. *Shakespeare: The Globe and the World*

(1979). A readable, abundantly illustrated introductory book on the world of the Elizabethans.

Shakespeare's England, 2 vols. (1916). A large collection of scholarly essays on a wide variety of topics, e.g., astrology, costume, gardening, horsemanship, with special attention to Shakespeare's references to these topics.

2. Shakespeare's Life

Andrews, John F., ed. *William Shakespeare: His World, His Work, His Influence,* 3 vols. (1985). See the description above.

Bentley, Gerald E. *Shakespeare: A Biographical Handbook* (1961). The facts about Shakespeare, with virtually no conjecture intermingled.

Chambers, E. K. *William Shakespeare: A Study of Facts and Problems,* 2 vols. (1930). The fullest collection of data.

Fraser, Russell. *Young Shakespeare* (1988). A highly readable account that simultaneously considers Shakespeare's life and Shakespeare's art.

———. *Shakespeare: The Later Years* (1992).

Schoenbaum, S. *Shakespeare's Lives* (1970). A review of the evidence and an examination of many biographies, including those of Baconians and other heretics.

———. *William Shakespeare: A Compact Documentary Life* (1977). An abbreviated version, in a smaller format, of the next title. The compact version reproduces some fifty documents in reduced form. A readable presentation of all that the documents tell us about Shakespeare.

———. *William Shakespeare: A Documentary Life* (1975). A large-format book setting forth the biography with facsimiles of more than two hundred documents, and with transcriptions and commentaries.

3. Shakespeare's Theater

Astington, John H., ed. *The Development of Shakespeare's Theater* (1992). Eight specialized essays on theatrical companies, playing spaces, and performance.

Beckerman, Bernard. *Shakespeare at the Globe, 1599–1609* (1962). On the playhouse and on Elizabethan dramaturgy, acting, and staging.

Bentley, Gerald E. *The Profession of Dramatist in Shakespeare's Time* (1971). An account of the dramatist's status in the Elizabethan period.

―――. *The Profession of Player in Shakespeare's Time, 1590–1642* (1984). An account of the status of members of London companies (sharers, hired men, apprentices, managers) and a discussion of conditions when they toured.

Berry, Herbert. *Shakespeare's Playhouses* (1987). Usefully emphasizes how little we know about the construction of Elizabethan theaters.

Brown, John Russell. *Shakespeare's Plays in Performance* (1966). A speculative and practical analysis relevant to all of the plays, but with emphasis on *The Merchant of Venice, Richard II, Hamlet, Romeo and Juliet,* and *Twelfth Night.*

―――. *William Shakespeare: Writing for Performance* (1996). A discussion aimed at helping readers to develop theatrically conscious habits of reading.

Chambers, E. K. *The Elizabethan Stage,* 4 vols. (1945). A major reference work on theaters, theatrical companies, and staging at court.

Cook, Ann Jennalie. *The Privileged Playgoers of Shakespeare's London, 1576–1642* (1981). Sees Shakespeare's audience as wealthier, more middle-class, and more intellectual than Harbage (below) does.

Dessen, Alan C. *Elizabethan Drama and the Viewer's Eye* (1977). On how certain scenes may have looked to spectators in an Elizabethan theater.

Gurr, Andrew. *Playgoing in Shakespeare's London* (1987). Something of a middle ground between Cook (above) and Harbage (below).

―――. *The Shakespearean Stage, 1579–1642* (2nd ed., 1980). On the acting companies, the actors, the playhouses, the stages, and the audiences.

Harbage, Alfred. *Shakespeare's Audience* (1941). A study of the size and nature of the theatrical public, emphasizing the representativeness of its working class and middle-class audience.

Hodges, C. Walter. *The Globe Restored* (1968). A conjectural restoration, with lucid drawings.

Hosley, Richard. "The Playhouses," in *The Revels History of Drama in English*, vol. 3, general editors Clifford Leech and T. W. Craik (1975). An essay of a hundred pages on the physical aspects of the playhouses.

Howard, Jane E. "Crossdressing, the Theatre, and Gender Struggle in Early Modern England," *Shakespeare Quarterly* 39 (1988): 418–40. Judicious comments on the effects of boys playing female roles.

Orrell, John. *The Human Stage: English Theatre Design, 1567–1640* (1988). Argues that the public, private, and court playhouses are less indebted to popular structures (e.g., innyards and bear-baiting pits) than to banqueting halls and to Renaissance conceptions of Roman amphitheaters.

Slater, Ann Pasternak. *Shakespeare the Director* (1982). An analysis of theatrical effects (e.g., kissing, kneeling) in stage directions and dialogue.

Styan, J. L. *Shakespeare's Stagecraft* (1967). An introduction to Shakespeare's visual and aural stagecraft, with chapters on such topics as acting conventions, stage groupings, and speech.

Thompson, Peter. *Shakespeare's Professional Career* (1992). An examination of patronage and related theatrical conditions.

———. *Shakespeare's Theatre* (1983). A discussion of how plays were staged in Shakespeare's time.

4. Shakespeare on Stage and Screen

Bate, Jonathan, and Russell Jackson, eds. *Shakespeare: An Illustrated Stage History* (1996). Highly readable essays on stage productions from the Renaissance to the present.

Berry, Ralph. *Changing Styles in Shakespeare* (1981). Discusses productions of six plays (*Coriolanus, Hamlet, Henry V, Measure for Measure, The Tempest,* and *Twelfth Night*) on the English stage, chiefly 1950–1980.

————. *On Directing Shakespeare: Interviews with Contemporary Directors* (1989). An enlarged edition of a book first published in 1977, this version includes the seven interviews from the early 1970s and adds five interviews conducted in 1988.

Brockbank, Philip, ed. *Players of Shakespeare: Essays in Shakespearean Performance* (1985). Comments by twelve actors, reporting their experiences with roles. See also the entry for Russell Jackson (below).

Bulman, J. C., and H. R. Coursen, eds. *Shakespeare on Television* (1988). An anthology of general and theoretical essays, essays on individual productions, and shorter reviews, with a bibliography and a videography listing cassettes that may be rented.

Coursen, H. P. *Watching Shakespeare on Television* (1993). Analyses not only of TV versions but also of films and videotapes of stage presentations that are shown on television.

Davies, Anthony, and Stanley Wells, eds. *Shakespeare and the Moving Image: The Plays on Film and Television* (1994). General essays (e.g., on the comedies) as well as essays devoted entirely to *Hamlet*, *King Lear*, and *Macbeth*.

Dawson, Anthony B. *Watching Shakespeare: A Playgoer's Guide* (1988). About half of the plays are discussed, chiefly in terms of decisions that actors and directors make in putting the works onto the stage.

Dessen, Alan. *Elizabethan Stage Conventions and Modern Interpretations* (1984). On interpreting conventions such as the representation of light and darkness and stage violence (duels, battles).

Donaldson, Peter. *Shakespearean Films/Shakespearean Directors* (1990). Postmodernist analyses, drawing on Freudianism, Feminism, Deconstruction, and Queer Theory.

Jackson, Russell, and Robert Smallwood, eds. *Players of Shakespeare 2: Further Essays in Shakespearean Performance by Players with the Royal Shakespeare Company* (1988). Fourteen actors discuss their roles in productions between 1982 and 1987.

————. *Players of Shakespeare 3: Further Essays in Shake-*

spearean Performance by Players with the Royal Shakespeare Company (1993). Comments by thirteen performers.

Jorgens, Jack. *Shakespeare on Film* (1977). Fairly detailed studies of eighteen films, preceded by an introductory chapter addressing such issues as music, and whether to "open" the play by including scenes of landscape.

Kennedy, Dennis. *Looking at Shakespeare: A Visual History of Twentieth-Century Performance* (1993). Lucid descriptions (with 170 photographs) of European, British, and American performances.

Leiter, Samuel L. *Shakespeare Around the Globe: A Guide to Notable Postwar Revivals* (1986). For each play there are about two pages of introductory comments, then discussions (about five hundred words per production) of ten or so productions, and finally bibliographic references.

McMurty, Jo. *Shakespeare Films in the Classroom* (1994). Useful evaluations of the chief films most likely to be shown in undergraduate courses.

Rothwell, Kenneth, and Annabelle Henkin Melzer. *Shakespeare on Screen: An International Filmography and Videography* (1990). A reference guide to several hundred films and videos produced between 1899 and 1989, including spinoffs such as musicals and dance versions.

Sprague, Arthur Colby. *Shakespeare and the Actors* (1944). Detailed discussions of stage business (gestures, etc.) over the years.

Willis, Susan. *The BBC Shakespeare Plays: Making the Televised Canon* (1991). A history of the series, with interviews and production diaries for some plays.

5. Miscellaneous Reference Works

Abbott, E. A. *A Shakespearean Grammar* (new edition, 1877). An examination of differences between Elizabethan and modern grammar.

Allen, Michael J. B., and Kenneth Muir, eds. *Shakespeare's Plays in Quarto* (1981). One volume containing facsimiles of the plays issued in small format before they were collected in the First Folio of 1623.

Bevington, David. *Shakespeare* (1978). A short guide to hundreds of important writings on the subject.

Blake, Norman. *Shakespeare's Language: An Introduction* (1983). On vocabulary, parts of speech, and word order.

Bullough, Geoffrey. *Narrative and Dramatic Sources of Shakespeare*, 8 vols. (1957–75). A collection of many of the books Shakespeare drew on, with judicious comments.

Campbell, Oscar James, and Edward G. Quinn, eds. *The Reader's Encyclopedia of Shakespeare* (1966). Old, but still the most useful single reference work on Shakespeare.

Cercignani, Fausto. *Shakespeare's Works and Elizabethan Pronunciation* (1981). Considered the best work on the topic, but remains controversial.

Dent, R. W. *Shakespeare's Proverbial Language: An Index* (1981). An index of proverbs, with an introduction concerning a form Shakespeare frequently drew on.

Greg, W. W. *The Shakespeare First Folio* (1955). A detailed yet readable history of the first collection (1623) of Shakespeare's plays.

Harner, James. *The World Shakespeare Bibliography.* See headnote to Suggested References.

Hosley, Richard. *Shakespeare's Holinshed* (1968). Valuable presentation of one of Shakespeare's major sources.

Kökeritz, Helge. *Shakespeare's Names* (1959). A guide to pronouncing some 1,800 names appearing in Shakespeare.

———. *Shakespeare's Pronunciation* (1953). Contains much information about puns and rhymes, but see Cercignani (above).

Muir, Kenneth. *The Sources of Shakespeare's Plays* (1978). An account of Shakespeare's use of his reading. It covers all the plays, in chronological order.

Miriam Joseph, Sister. *Shakespeare's Use of the Arts of Language* (1947). A study of Shakespeare's use of rhetorical devices, reprinted in part as *Rhetoric in Shakespeare's Time* (1962).

The Norton Facsimile: The First Folio of Shakespeare's Plays (1968). A handsome and accurate facsimile of the first collection (1623) of Shakespeare's plays, with a valuable introduction by Charlton Hinman.

Onions, C. T. *A Shakespeare Glossary*, rev. and enlarged by

R. D. Eagleson (1986). Definitions of words (or senses of words) now obsolete.

Partridge, Eric. *Shakespeare's Bawdy*, rev. ed. (1955). Relatively brief dictionary of bawdy words; useful, but see Williams, below.

Shakespeare Quarterly. See headnote to Suggested References.

Shakespeare Survey. See headnote to Suggested References.

Spevack, Marvin. *The Harvard Concordance to Shakespeare* (1973). An index to Shakespeare's words.

Vickers, Brian. *Appropriating Shakespeare: Contemporary Critical Quarrels* (1993). A survey—chiefly hostile—of recent schools of criticism.

Wells, Stanley, ed. *Shakespeare: A Bibliographical Guide* (new edition, 1990). Nineteen chapters (some devoted to single plays, others devoted to groups of related plays) on recent scholarship on the life and all of the works.

Williams, Gordon. *A Dictionary of Sexual Language and Imagery in Shakespearean and Stuart Literature*, 3 vols. (1994). Extended discussions of words and passages; much fuller than Partridge, cited above.

6. Shakespeare's Plays: General Studies

Bamber, Linda. *Comic Women, Tragic Men: A Study of Gender and Genre in Shakespeare* (1982).

Barnet, Sylvan. *A Short Guide to Shakespeare* (1974).

Callaghan, Dympna, Lorraine Helms, and Jyotsna Singh. *The Weyward Sisters: Shakespeare and Feminist Politics* (1994).

Clemen, Wolfgang H. *The Development of Shakespeare's Imagery* (1951).

Cook, Ann Jennalie. *Making a Match: Courtship in Shakespeare and His Society* (1991).

Dollimore, Jonathan, and Alan Sinfield. *Political Shakespeare: New Essays in Cultural Materialism* (1985).

Dusinberre, Juliet. *Shakespeare and the Nature of Women* (1975).

Granville-Barker, Harley. *Prefaces to Shakespeare*, 2 vols. (1946–47; volume 1 contains essays on *Hamlet, King*

Lear, Merchant of Venice, Antony and Cleopatra, and *Cymbeline*; volume 2 contains essays on *Othello, Coriolanus, Julius Caesar, Romeo and Juliet, Love's Labor's Lost*).

——. *More Prefaces to Shakespeare* (1974; essays on *Twelfth Night, A Midsummer Night's Dream, The Winter's Tale, Macbeth*).

Harbage, Alfred. *William Shakespeare: A Reader's Guide* (1963).

Howard, Jean E. *Shakespeare's Art of Orchestration: Stage Technique and Audience Response* (1984).

Jones, Emrys. *Scenic Form in Shakespeare* (1971).

Lenz, Carolyn Ruth Swift, Gayle Greene, and Carol Thomas Neely, eds. *The Woman's Part: Feminist Criticism of Shakespeare* (1980).

Novy, Marianne. *Love's Argument: Gender Relations in Shakespeare* (1984).

Rose, Mark. *Shakespearean Design* (1972).

Scragg, Leah. *Discovering Shakespeare's Meaning* (1994).

——. *Shakespeare's "Mouldy Tales": Recurrent Plot Motifs in Shakespearean Drama* (1992).

Traub, Valerie. *Desire and Anxiety: Circulations of Sexuality in Shakespearean Drama* (1992).

Traversi, D. A. *An Approach to Shakespeare,* 2 vols. (3rd rev. ed, 1968–69).

Vickers, Brian. *The Artistry of Shakespeare's Prose* (1968).

Wells, Stanley. *Shakespeare: A Dramatic Life* (1994).

Wright, George T. *Shakespeare's Metrical Art* (1988).

7. The Comedies

Barber, C. L. *Shakespeare's Festive Comedy* (1959; discusses *Love's Labor's Lost, A Midsummer Night's Dream, The Merchant of Venice, As You Like It, Twelfth Night*).

Barton, Anne. *The Names of Comedy* (1990).

Berry, Ralph. *Shakespeare's Comedy: Explorations in Form* (1972).

Bradbury, Malcolm, and David Palmer, eds. *Shakespearean Comedy* (1972).

Bryant, J. A., Jr. *Shakespeare and the Uses of Comedy* (1986).

Carroll, William. *The Metamorphoses of Shakespearean Comedy* (1985).

Champion, Larry S. *The Evolution of Shakespeare's Comedy* (1970).

Evans, Bertrand. *Shakespeare's Comedies* (1960).

Frye, Northrop. *Shakespearean Comedy and Romance* (1965).

Leggatt, Alexander. *Shakespeare's Comedy of Love* (1974).

Miola, Robert S. *Shakespeare and Classical Comedy: The Influence of Plautus and Terence* (1994).

Nevo, Ruth. *Comic Transformations in Shakespeare* (1980).

Ornstein, Robert. *Shakespeare's Comedies: From Roman Farce to Romantic Mystery* (1986).

Richman, David. *Laughter, Pain, and Wonder: Shakespeare's Comedies and the Audience in the Theater* (1990).

Salingar, Leo. *Shakespeare and the Traditions of Comedy* (1974).

Slights, Camille Wells. *Shakespeare's Comic Commonwealths* (1993).

Waller, Gary, ed. *Shakespeare's Comedies* (1991).

Westlund, Joseph. *Shakespeare's Reparative Comedies: A Psychoanalytic View of the Middle Plays* (1984).

Williamson, Marilyn. *The Patriarchy of Shakespeare's Comedies* (1986).

8. The Romances (*Pericles, Cymbeline, The Winter's Tale, The Tempest, The Two Noble Kinsmen*)

Adams, Robert M. *Shakespeare: The Four Romances* (1989).

Felperin, Howard. *Shakespearean Romance* (1972).

Frye, Northrop. *A Natural Perspective: The Development of Shakespearean Comedy and Romance* (1965).

Mowat, Barbara. *The Dramaturgy of Shakespeare's Romances* (1976).

Warren, Roger. *Staging Shakespeare's Late Plays* (1990).

Young, David. *The Heart's Forest: A Study of Shakespeare's Pastoral Plays* (1972).

9. The Tragedies

Bradley, A. C. *Shakespearean Tragedy* (1904).

Brooke, Nicholas. *Shakespeare's Early Tragedies* (1968).

Champion, Larry. *Shakespeare's Tragic Perspective* (1976).

Drakakis, John, ed. *Shakespearean Tragedy* (1992).

Evans, Bertrand. *Shakespeare's Tragic Practice* (1979).

Everett, Barbara. *Young Hamlet: Essays on Shakespeare's Tragedies* (1989).

Foakes, R. A. *Hamlet versus Lear: Cultural Politics and Shakespeare's Art* (1993).

Frye, Northrop. *Fools of Time: Studies in Shakespearean Tragedy* (1967).

Harbage, Alfred, ed. *Shakespeare: The Tragedies* (1964).

Mack, Maynard. *Everybody's Shakespeare: Reflections Chiefly on the Tragedies* (1993).

McAlindon, T. *Shakespeare's Tragic Cosmos* (1991).

Miola, Robert S. *Shakespeare and Classical Tragedy: The Influence of Seneca* (1992).

———. *Shakespeare's Rome* (1983).

Nevo, Ruth. *Tragic Form in Shakespeare* (1972).

Rackin, Phyllis. *Shakespeare's Tragedies* (1978).

Rose, Mark, ed. *Shakespeare's Early Tragedies: A Collection of Critical Essays* (1995).

Rosen, William. *Shakespeare and the Craft of Tragedy* (1960).

Snyder, Susan. *The Comic Matrix of Shakespeare's Tragedies* (1979).

Wofford, Susanne. *Shakespeare's Late Tragedies: A Collection of Critical Essays* (1996).

Young, David. *The Action to the Word: Structure and Style in Shakespearean Tragedy* (1990).

———. *Shakespeare's Middle Tragedies: A Collection of Critical Essays* (1993).

10. The Histories

Blanpied, John W. *Time and the Artist in Shakespeare's English Histories* (1983).

Campbell, Lily B. *Shakespeare's "Histories": Mirrors of Elizabethan Policy* (1947).

Champion, Larry S. *Perspective in Shakespeare's English Histories* (1980).

Hodgdon, Barbara. *The End Crowns All: Closure and Contradiction in Shakespeare's History* (1991).

Holderness, Graham. *Shakespeare Recycled: The Making of Historical Drama* (1992).

———, ed. *Shakespeare's History Plays: "Richard II" to "Henry V"* (1992).

Leggatt, Alexander. *Shakespeare's Political Drama: The History Plays and the Roman Plays* (1988).

Ornstein, Robert. *A Kingdom for a Stage: The Achievement of Shakespeare's History Plays* (1972).

Rackin, Phyllis. *Stages of History: Shakespeare's English Chronicles* (1990).

Saccio, Peter. *Shakespeare's English Kings: History, Chronicle, and Drama* (1977).

Tillyard, E. M. W. *Shakespeare's History Plays* (1944).

Velz, John W., ed. *Shakespeare's English Histories: A Quest for Form and Genre* (1996).

11. *Othello*

In addition to the items listed in Section 9, The Tragedies, and the items concerning stage history listed on page 231, consult the following:

Barthelemy, Anthony Gerard, ed. *Critical Essays on Shakespeare's* Othello (1994).

Calderwood, James L. *The Properties of* Othello (1989).

Colie, Rosalie. *Shakespeare's Living Art* (1974).

Goldman, Michael. *Acting and Action in Shakespearean Tragedy* (1985).

Granville-Barker, Harley. *Prefaces to Shakespeare*, vol. 2. (1947).

Greenblatt, Stephen. *Renaissance Self-Fashioning* (1983).

Heilman, Robert B. *Magic in the Web, Action & Language in* Othello (1956).

Honigmann, E. A. J. *Shakespeare: Seven Tragedies* (1976).

————. *The Texts of* Othello *and Shakespearean Revision* (1996).

Knight, G. Wilson. *The Wheel of Fire*, 5th rev. ed. (1957).

McPherson, David. *Shakespeare, Jonson, and the Myth of Venice* (1990).

Neill, Michael. "Unproper Beds: Race, Adultery, and the Hideous in *Othello*," *Shakespeare Quarterly* 40 (1989): 383–412.

Vaughan, Virginia Mason. Othello: *A Contextual History* (1994).